———————

November 1, 1990

To Sally,

Daring
TO BE
Yourself

Continue to
dare to be yourself.
I loved meeting
you today.
Affectionately,

Alexandra
Stoddard

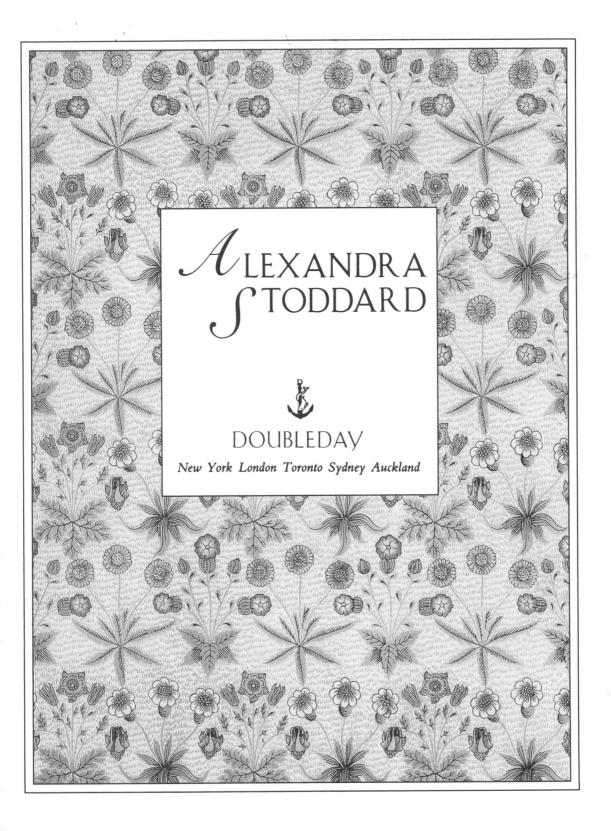

ALEXANDRA STODDARD

DOUBLEDAY

New York London Toronto Sydney Auckland

DARING
TO BE
YOURSELF

PUBLISHED BY DOUBLEDAY

a division of Bantam Doubleday Dell
Publishing Group, Inc.
666 Fifth Avenue, New York, New York 10103

DOUBLEDAY and the portrayal of an anchor
with a dolphin are trademarks of Doubleday,
a division of Bantam Doubleday Dell
Publishing Group, Inc.

BOOK DESIGN BY MARYSARAH QUINN

Library of Congress Cataloging-in-Publication Data
Stoddard, Alexandra.
Daring to be yourself / Alexandra Stoddard. —1st ed.
p.   cm.
1. Interior decoration—Psychological aspects. 2. Aesthetics.
I. Title.
NK2113.S83   1990
646.7—dc20   90–31435
                                                     CIP

ISBN 0-385-24779-6
November 1990
FIRST EDITION

To
NANCY EVANS
A friend of
rare instincts
who dares beautifully.

CONTENTS

Prologue xiii

ONE   Your Treasure Hunt for Personal Style   1

Why You Need Personal Style . . . Recording Your
Journey . . . What Is Personal Style? . . . Personal Style vs. "In
Style" . . . Finding Your Own Style . . . Simplicity . . .
Appropriateness . . . Beauty . . . Creativity . . . Fantasy
First . . . Learning to Trust Your Instincts . . . Where Are You
Right Now? . . . Taking Stock . . . Role Models . . . Being
Aware of Your Senses . . . Growing Through Your Mistakes . . .
Seven Vital Personal Style Points to Remember . . .

TWO   Your Personal Style at Home and Entertaining   53

Your Personality Dictates Your Style at Home . . . Selecting

Your Personal Style of Home . . . Knocking Down Walls . . .
Do Your Homework . . . Association . . . How to Edit . . .
How Do You Like to Decorate? . . . Start Now Where You
Are . . . Privacy . . . Light . . . Knowing What You Like . . .
Does Your Home Smile? . . . Overnight Guests . . . Being
Party-Ready . . . Why Entertain? . . . How to Throw an Ideal
Party . . . Invitations . . . Make an Inventory List . . . What to
Wear . . . Flowers . . . Setting the Table . . . Quiet Time . . .
Getting Dressed . . . You Be the First Guest . . . The First to
Arrive . . . Introducing Friends . . . Be Yourself . . .
Conversation . . . Parties with Style . . . Special Kinds of
Parties . . . The Party Isn't Over . . .

THREE   Your Personal Style of Appearance   125

Finding Suitable Clothes for Your Lifestyle . . . Your Dream
Style of Appearance . . . Projecting the Image of Who You
Want to Be . . . Everything You Wear Sends Signals . . .
Gaining Clues from People You Admire . . . What to Look
For . . . How to Build Your Dream Wardrobe . . . Ten Tips to
Finding Your Personal Style of Dress . . . Dressing Up Rather
Than Down . . . Your Appearance Is You . . . Ingredients of a
Well-rounded Wardrobe . . . Housing Your Clothes . . . Using
a Personal Shopper . . . Finding a Seamstress . . . Your Clothes
Garden . . .

FOUR   Your Personal Style of Work and
Communicating   173

Realistic Expectations About Your Work . . . Questions Reveal
Clues . . . Bringing Yourself to the Workplace . . .
Mr. Keating . . . People Who Love Their Work . . . Do You
Love Your Work? . . . Finding Work You Love . . . Your Style
of Self-worth . . . Preparing for Your Career . . .
Professionalism . . . The Atmosphere Where You Work . . .
Setting Up Your System . . . Working with Others . . .
Switching Gears . . . You're the Boss . . . How to Avoid

Burnout . . . How to Move On . . . Self-confidence—an
Important Style Factor . . . Becoming an Entrepreneur . . .
Your Business Style . . . Communicating with Confidence . . .
One on One . . . Groups . . . Speech . . . Public Speaking . . .
Telephone Manner . . . Communicating on Paper . . . Opening
Up Your Senses . . .

FIVE: Your Personal Style of Leisure and Travel   233

Relaxation and Your Health—Privacy . . . Sports . . .
Interests . . . High Arts . . . Health Spa . . . Working in Your
Leisure Time . . . Leisure Alone . . . Leisure Shared . . .
Personal Awareness . . . Fitting Leisure into a Busy Day . . .
Exercising Your Mind . . . Balancing Leisure Throughout Your
Life . . . Make a Travel List . . . Your Options—Keep a Travel
Folder . . . Travel Books . . . Planning Your Trip . . . Your
Budget . . . Anticipation . . . What's the Climate? . . .
Itinerary . . . Transportation . . . Traveling Alone or with
Another? . . . Traveling with Others . . . Traveling on
Business . . . Keep a Travel Journal . . . Travel Light . . . What
to Bring with You . . . Packing . . . What to Bring Home . . .
Coming Home . . .

SIX   Your Personal Style of Gifts and Giving   285

What Special Gifts Do You Have to Offer
Others? . . . Presents . . . Nonmaterial Gifts . . . What's
Appropriate? . . . Doing Favors . . . Giving a Present Without
an Occasion . . . The Gift of Yourself . . . Giving to the
World—Sharing Your Talent . . . Philanthropy . . . Loving
Others . . . Expressing Love . . .

My business is not to remake myself,
But make the absolute best of what God made.

ROBERT BROWNING

PROLOGUE

One of the great rewards of being an interior designer is gaining a close glimpse into people's lives and thereby learning about personal style. Through my design work and with help from others who exude great personal style, I've trained myself to be an observer. Wherever I am, I adore watching strangers and wondering about what is on their minds and what is most passionate in their hearts. I've slowly discovered that all of us reveal significant clues about our personalities—about how we see ourselves, how we see the world around us and how we want to be seen by others. I now understand that every aspect of our personality adds up to a wholeness that represents our character, values, affections and sense of beauty.

As a young design student blind to the scope of possibilities, I studied rules. I learned techniques, observed conventions, sought out standards. I learned facts about house styles and fashion styles throughout history. As students, we were taught how to draw by

"TO THINE OWN SELF BE TRUE"
—*William Shakespeare*

copying. We were told about taste and proper scale and proportion and were shown fine examples of quality and refinement. We were to learn how to put things together harmoniously and in a tasteful manner.

How little I understood about style. I first became aware that there was such a thing as personal style about six years after I graduated from design school when I became exposed to the fine and tasteful houses of clients all over America. I began to sense what was at the heart of style. Many of the homes were beautiful, though stiff, and revealed more about the style of Louis XV and Louis XVI or Hepplewhite, Chippendale and Sheraton than they did about the owners. Interior design and decoration seemed to be outer-directed, an exercise in ornamenting a house rather than a process of focusing on the personalities of those who lived there. To decorate in English Colonial or Baroque seemed artificial because some of the owners had never been to Europe. By the same token, few revealed any childhood associations or memories in the room interiors. Something didn't ring true and made me feel uncomfortable. I felt cheated by the lack of individuality, vitality, color and real life in many of the most beautiful and expensive houses. I wondered, where do these people really live? What are they really passionate about? Who are these people?

Gradually it occurred to me to take a closer look at the owners of the houses. If a woman discovers her own style she will automatically find creative outlets through which to express herself—in her home, her clothes, travel and in the way she entertains. When we find a sense of calm at our center, we can reach out to express ourselves honestly. True personal style is the outward manifestation of the inner spirit.

When I began to discover the life and enthusiasm of the people I met, I found that in most cases people who express their own style reveal an independent, lively, exciting, original self. People who are afraid and reticent or just unaware tend to avoid self-expression and hide behind traditional period styles or fashion trends, which makes for dullness. Everyone is hungry to be tasteful, but when no personality is expressed, being tasteful can be sterile and dreary.

THERE ARE NO BEGINNINGS OR ENDINGS, ONLY MOVEMENT.

Personal style and self-confidence go hand in hand. As you discover your own style, your authentic self increases. You approach the world in a happier and more effective manner. It is possible to start out by making the smallest changes—1 percent, 2 percent—and suddenly without difficulty you are able to make big decisions.

We all secretly want to have a personal style—a way of handling the mechanics of home, clothes, entertaining, working that is truly our own. We always feel more comfortable when we have made these discoveries. We begin to identify certain things in positive, life-enhancing ways. When we allow everything to come together in harmony, we become content because we are being true to ourselves.

Having all the varied parts of our personality flow together eliminates the feeling of being scattered, and we become less awkward, gain assurance and begin to see pleasing results. Self-confidence is a by-product. We reveal the essence of our style, like breathing, around the clock. When we are feeling good about ourselves, our pleasure and also our self-esteem and sense of adequacy increase.

BE YOURSELF.

What is your unique point of view? How do you want your home to look and feel? What is your attitude about how you want to dress? What are the factors that help you decide where to go for a weekend retreat? Since everything you feel and do becomes an outlet for self-expression, concentrate on putting yourself in the center of where you want to be. Joseph Campbell said that the center of the universe is where you are.

Begin by pleasing yourself. Absorb style by paying attention. You can learn how to put exciting finishing touches on everything you do if you are willing to try things out. Think of the experiments all creative artists undertake. Until something pleases you, it is not right for you. Express your preferences in satisfying ways; you will discover great joy in the active process of creating and becoming.

In this book, I want to think out loud with you and ask questions that will help you discover pleasures and surprises in all areas of life. When you find your style at home, you can move on to clothing or to your way of spending leisure time or your special way of giving. It doesn't matter where you begin. I want you to feel the delight of becoming fully aware of your *self* so that you can enthusiastically explore the possibilities in store for you. Finding your personal style is a rich journey of discovery, wonder, adventure and excitement.

ONE

Your TREASURE HUNT FOR PERSONAL STYLE

WHY YOU NEED PERSONAL STYLE

oday we have such an overload of information that we feel confused and frustrated by the wide range of choices available. Television and the print media bombard us, causing "information anxiety." Glossy picture magazines make real life seem gray in comparison to their make-believe land where skinny models and expensive merchandise show us how we're supposed to dress, decorate and entertain. We feel inadequate as people marketing materialism press on us. Buy and be happy. Bigger is better. Newest and latest is best. Trade in, trade up. Excess becomes a need. We lose trust in salespeople. Worse, we lose confidence in ourselves and in our ability to make pleasing, sensible choices.

All this emphasis on money and acquisition can increase our sense of insecurity and lower our self-esteem unless we focus on

"WILL TO BE THAT SELF WHICH ONE TRULY IS."
—*Søren Kierkegaard*

what our needs and desires dictate. We must take hold of life, grasp it with both hands.

When I was a young apprentice decorator earning a little over a hundred dollars a week, living in an inexpensive rent-controlled apartment on East Sixty-fifth Street between Madison and Fifth avenues in New York City, I had a small dinner party for a few of the senior decorators and some of my colleagues from the office. After the party was over and my guests were in the elevator, my assistant commented to our bosses on how attractive my apartment was when someone said, "Yes, but Sandie has nothing of quality."

I remember how much it hurt when I learned of this offhand remark; now, twenty-five years later, I am finally able to shrug it off.

The older decorator who made the remark is typical of many people who think of quality as high-priced items rather than charm, flair and warmth. To equate quality with money is foolish. My apartment was light, cheerful, full of color and warmth. I had indoor window boxes brimming with red geraniums, and books, music, a warm fire, a general feeling of love and hospitality that had more charm than most rooms filled with "quality" possessions. If we try to keep up with the way our parents or bosses live or with our neighbors or relatives, we will never find contentment. Yet others always are quick to judge us and want to influence us no matter how little they know about us. The answer is to become inner-directed. While we will always care what other people think, we have to find out what really speaks to us even if others won't fully understand.

WHAT DO YOU
YEARN FOR?

Much of what I do as a residential interior decorator is detective work. Over the last twenty-seven years, I've helped thousands of clients develop their own style. I ask them questions that will give me clues to translate their wishes and dreams into tangible, workable, meaningful rooms that enhance and express their lives. "How personal do you want your home to be?" "How do you want to feel in your rooms?" "How are you affected by light?" "Do you want your rooms to stimulate or soothe you?" "What are your favorite colors?" "Are there any colors you loathe?" "What activities do you want to perform in your rooms?" "Are the rooms used in the morning? Midday? Afternoon? Evenings?" "How often do you have friends over?" "How do you like to entertain?" "When you are alone in the evening, where do you like to sit?" "How often do you watch television?" "Are you musical?" "Do you like to live in a formal manner or are you more casual?" "How do you dress when alone at home?" "Are you a careful planner or do you act spontaneously?" "Do you enjoy rearranging furniture and objects?" "How neat are you?" "Are you a collector?" "Is it hard to give things away?"

When a client asks me what I think about a decorating matter I inquire, "How does it make you feel?" I interview each family member privately. I take notes and try to come up with plans that will work well for each person and for the family as a whole. My clients seem so appreciative—almost surprised—when I help them get what *they* want. This book is aimed to give you what *you* want. Instead of becoming anxious and confused by your options, you can embrace the world's vast possibilities, identifying what speaks to your most real self and editing out the rest. This book is about becoming yourself, being as pure and honest as possible, both inside and out, so that your style truly becomes you in all areas. We are shaped and fashioned by what we have, observed Goethe. When we identify what we love we can more easily find our personal style.

RECORDING YOUR JOURNEY

Because this book is one of self-discovery, I encourage you to record your progress. And to do it in your own style! If you want to keep a master style notebook, you could make it a 9 × 12-inch loose-leaf and insert tabs to separate each different style category. Or you might keep separate style file folders, labeled according to subject (one on home, one on clothes, and others on each of the chapters of this book); these folders could be filed together under the general heading "Style." Many people also keep a style journal, in which they jot down notes about their reactions to current tastes, styles, fads and fashions. If you like to doodle, sketch, cut out pictures or keep notes, you might enjoy starting a style journal. If you decide it would be fun to begin one, art supply stores have inexpensive black bound sketchbooks in a variety of sizes. On the other hand, maybe you're more attracted to the visual stimulation of pictures. When you see something that appeals to you in a magazine you can cut it out and either clip or paste it into a scrapbook or toss it into a box.

Twenty-five years ago I began to compile decorating scrapbooks: separate ones on gardens, living rooms, bedrooms, baths and kitchens. What fun to see the styles change over the years! Now I keep hatboxes and colorful boxes brimming with pretty clippings as well as interesting articles I've saved. Before I throw out a magazine, I cut out articles I want to save and pictures I want to keep for reference. When I need time alone to collect my thoughts, I separate the articles and file them according to subject matter. The pretty pictures I keep in nests of boxes near my bed so I can look at them when I'm in need of fresh inspiration. Most of my clients keep a decorating file with pictures and information that will be useful to them on a specific project.

However you operate best is *your* style. If you want to keep a record of your discoveries, you will have a great deal of fun and you will also see how one new idea can help you open up other aspects of yourself that may be underdeveloped or as yet undiscovered. If you like tailored clothes, for example, chances are you will be more attracted to simple lines in decorating. Everything is connected; we can discover the links. When you think about why you don't like something it can draw you closer to what delights you.

FOCUS ON YOUR ACHIEVEMENTS, NOT YOUR EFFORTS.

WHAT IS PERSONAL STYLE?

As you develop your personal style you will become increasingly motivated by what you like and what makes you happy, and you will have less need to seek the approval of others. True style is

already within you and can be expressed. Find your self by recognizing what gives *you* pleasure, what makes *you* feel good,
what makes *you* feel comfortable, what brings *you* delight. Your
inner light is revealed. The act of separating yourself from what
is phony, pretentious or trendy opens wide doors to reveal the
real you.

Just as a pilot finds his altitude in order to fly, or as we adjust
the dial on a radio to tune in to our favorite music station, when
you have personal style you are fully in tune with yourself. Think
about how you'd ideally like to express your feelings in several
different ways. You know where you are. There may be areas of
your life in which you are stuck and others where you are gliding.
When you understand what you want to do, you will experience
an increased flow of natural energy. This feeds you and gives you
the drive to go on. You soar in your own orbit once you move
in the direction of self-discovery. You find out most about your
essence by taking action.

Anytime you do something that doesn't feel right, trust your
instincts and try it another way until you find *your* way. For
example, if circumstances call for a dinner party but you don't
have the proper crystal, silver, china or help for it to be formal,
it may be best to offer a more casual atmosphere in which you
create small tables where each one is set differently and has its
own charm and you serve an attractive buffet. Or if you inherited
a large Victorian house when your mother died and find you don't
enjoy living in it because it feels too grand, you can sell the house
and buy a more modest one. Often the kind of furniture you
are naturally drawn to helps you to see the kind of lifestyle and
home that will bring the most pleasure. If you love Shaker furniture, for example, a New England farmhouse may be your ideal
style.

The same theory applies to acquiring a table or a hat. If you
own a table that you feel is too dark, it can be stripped and
bleached, turning mahogany into the color of maple. If a new hat
is ornamented with flowers and after wearing it once you discover
it makes you feel silly, replace the flowers with a wonderful striped
scarf or ribbon. In other words, don't accept everything as you

see it but evaluate how you feel about it so that it will give you personal satisfaction.

I tell my clients not to be purists with furniture styles when they decorate. I want them to make choices based on their hearts. This requires taking action. If you buy an old house and the dark beams in the bedroom feel gloomy, paint them white. If a carved gilt mirror seems heavy, it too can be painted.

Personal style is spontaneous, involving some whimsy. Nothing is set in stone. You can always be ready to add your own touches and make adjustments—try this and that until you find what feels right. If you stay up too late one night to be convivial and are wiped out the next day, you discover that late nights are not your style. If you are rushing around too fast, spreading yourself too thin, consciously make an effort to rediscover your own pace. If you don't weigh yourself regularly and put on pounds and you catch sight of yourself in the closet mirror, you can begin a daily regimen of diet and exercise so that you will return to your ideal weight.

Most of us were raised to conform to other people's standards and not to be conspicuous. Yet when we conform we can feel uncomfortable. We have to learn to become more comfortable with change in order to find our own style. As adults we are responsible for our own style of living. We can never eliminate all the conflicting messages from others about what we should or should not do. Yet when we find our true selves we feel empowered, and no one else's opinions mean as much. Feeling comfortable with change, identifying what we want and going after it satisfies our souls.

When something *feels* right for you, it usually *is* right for you at the time. Use everything you see around you as a springboard. For example, if you see a friend twist a scarf in an interesting way, experiment and add that to your own look. People of great personal style show us how much fun life can be, and the message they bring is one of vitality, hope and inspiration. Once you begin to make meaningful connections and feel the exhilaration of self-expression, your energy and enthusiasm will increase.

DO YOU HAVE AN IMPULSE TO DO SOMETHING RIGHT NOW?

You will find, much to your delight, how different you are from your family, friends, spouse and coworkers. Embrace these differences. You love working late at the office Monday evenings because you're rested from the weekend. Others might not feel the same way; it doesn't matter. After summering with the in-laws in Maine, you've discovered you need more privacy with your immediate family. So you quietly look for a cozy house to rent in the country where you and your spouse can enjoy your weekends with your children.

Why dread taking vacations where others expect you to become a golfer? Maybe you'd rather stay at home, or go to a city where you can learn something. *You* arrange your leisure time. Look forward to your Saturday morning ritual of going to the farmers' market where you select the colorful bounties of the earth. Be true to your own real pleasures. Experiment so that you'll find what's right for you. Think of this process of finding your own style as a blossoming. As you pursue all the different aspects of life, putting things together with your own signature, you will feel energy from identifying so many satisfactions. You will be learning and absorbing new ideas for the rest of your life.

Personal style, like love or anything of great human passion and interest, can never be successfully delegated.

If the spirit moves you to see a friend who is ill, go. If it isn't a good time for you, it is best to wait and go when it is. Trust your feelings. Your friend obviously needs cheering up, but when you do something out of duty or guilt, it usually backfires. When we make personal choices based on self-knowledge and self-love, not on guilt or self-consciousness, we feel more contentment.

Your moods can teach you more about yourself. Even bad moods can be constructive if you are willing to make changes. Bad moods are signals that something is wrong. Become more aware of why it is you feel happy or sad, tired or rested. I complained to my friend Kate once that I was overwhelmed, and she laughed and said, "Alexandra, you are just whelmed." Are you whelmed right now? If you are, question the authenticity of your choices. What makes you feel content? A sunny, crisp day? Or a

DO YOU PREFER THE MOUNTAINS OR THE SEA?

WHAT LITTLE THING CAN YOU DO RIGHT AWAY?

morning off, freedom away from the grip of others? A good book, a delicious meal, a lecture, dancing, or wine and thoughtful, meaningful conversation? A simple good night's sleep?

Become more opinionated about the details of your daily life at home. Be fussy about the scent of your potpourri or room spray because, depending on your selection, you can conjure up memories of being in a rose garden, a peach orchard or a pine forest. Scent can call up long-forgotten memories. Don't fall back on your grandmother's lavender scent unless you inherited her love of lavender or you want to think of her when you walk into a scented room. Baked apples, cinnamon and cloves in your kitchen may remind you of autumn. Best of all, try lilac and lily-of-the-valley at the end of May to remind you of your childhood, or gardenia to remind you of your first prom.

PERSONAL STYLE VS. "IN STYLE"

Personal style has little to do with trends and fashion, although it is interesting to see what's new and to check whether anything is right for you. Enjoy new fashion ideas as you build your own style. You are the best barometer. Continue to build from your strengths, never losing sight of who you are, what your fantasies are and what's real for you. You may have an old blue Shetland sweater that will never go out of style. In fact it may be more meaningful to you because it is twenty years old and has become a part of you.

If hemlines go way up and you are tall and you follow the fashion trend, your dresses and skirts could look like lampshades. Once you discover the ideal hem length based on your anatomy and not on what everyone else is wearing, stick with it for your lifetime. Women of great personal style keep their hems consistent within two inches over decades of fashion ups and downs. Men find out what length and width trousers are suitable to their body type and never have to be concerned whether bell bottoms are in or out because they choose the cut that is most flattering.

ADD A COLORFUL HANDKERCHIEF TO A SUIT.

I enjoy seeing trends come and go and be revived. If we use pictures to help us find our style, magazines can be extremely useful but we can't feel frustrated every time we see new directions. Magazines are supported by advertisers who want us to consume their products. Look at the advertisers and you'll see the editorial slant of the magazine. The new trend toward "advertorials" is unrefreshing.

When decorating editors declare the English country look is dead, I feel sorry for all those people who were sold a look that has faded from being the "in" style and now feel they must change. I've had the same chintz in the living room for a dozen years and it pleases me every day. I read about chintz being "out" and I read about all these new "looks" and I smile. All the newest and the latest trends need is time to become old-hat. The best advice I can give clients is to urge them to gather things they love as they go along and that way they will love them no matter what happens around them. By responding personally to each decision we make so that we make a commitment that expresses, "This is me," our style will never go out of style.

FINDING YOUR OWN STYLE

Now that we've established the differece between personal style and popular taste—what others say you should like—I'll discuss the key that opens the way for us to accomplish our goals. During the years I've studied design, there have been three basic elements that have helped me. These three distinct ideas are simplicity, appropriateness and beauty, and they seem to encompass all the characteristics of those who have great personal taste and style. Think of these as a triangle made up of straight lines that rise from a wide base at specified angles to an apex.

On a clean sheet of paper, draw a triangle and on the lower left-hand side write *Simplicity*. On the lower right-hand side write *Appropriateness,* and at the apex write *Beauty*.

WHAT ARE *YOUR* COLORS?

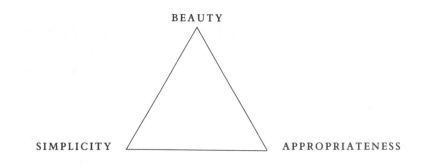

This is an image to keep in mind as you read this book. Throughout, I will indicate how this triangle will be there for you in the style decisions you make. Let's look at each vital point in the triangle. Begin with simplicity, the first to anchor your sense of personal style.

SIMPLICITY IS A
TRIUMPH OVER
CONFUSION.

SIMPLICITY

It takes courage to be simple. Think of a blue-and-white spatter-ware pitcher brimming with hot-pink peonies or a centerpiece of a few sprigs of fuchsia azalea for the dining room table. Think of being served a few big ripe red strawberries with stems still intact or having one perfect pear for dessert. Think of a brilliantly white church, or of old wide, bare floorboards dappled by the sun. Think of a robin's egg, a geranium, white eyelet curtains catching a mild breeze from an open window. Think of a white wicker rocking chair with a blue-and-pink chintz cushion on the porch of a New England house, or the curves of an adobe house in Santa Fe. Think of crisply ironed white linen bedsheets, a cloudless blue sky, a window box brimming with indigo and yellow pansies, a basket of sour green apples, a pine farm table, a running brook, a stone wall, an evening reading a good book, a day off, a walk in a meadow.

"THE WAY TO DO IS
TO BE."
                    Lao-tzu

Begin with the simplest forms first. Simplicity is classic. Serve pure French vanilla ice cream for dessert and taste the vanilla beans. Gloppy sauce takes away from the true flavor. Serve fresh, steamed asparagus with lemon. Artichokes the same. There is no need for fattening dips and sauces. Fresh steamed corn on the cob is nutty and sweet and needs no butter to bring out the flavor.

How refreshing it is to see a man in white pants or a woman in a solid yellow dress. I can still remember the impact of the Ascot scene of the play *My Fair Lady,* which was a study in the basics of black and white. Eliminating the other colors intensified the drama.

Recently I was helping a client with her living room, and I noted that all four corners were crowded with clutter—chairs, folding tables, odd and rather useless things. When I inquired why we couldn't leave the corners free "to breathe," my client laughed. "I thought they had to be filled. I now see how ugly and junked-up they looked."

My favorite example of the maxim "Style is what you leave out, not what you add" occurred when I was asked to help clients in Birmingham, Alabama, with their house. One of the first decisions was how to treat the huge Palladian window in the living room which dominated the double-height vaulted ceiling of this graciously proportioned room. Surrounding this grand window were terraces and gardens. I smiled and suggested we do nothing to the window. At night the lights in the trees would extend the view outside, and by day the sun dappled inside to make this room alive with natural beauty. We painted the ceiling soft sky blue to create even more drama. My clients had assumed I would come up with some dramatic window treatment with tassels and tie-backs, using yards and yards of expensive fabric. But when we have beautiful architecture we want to show that off, not cover it up—just as, on a beautiful face with ideal bone structure, the hair can be pulled back off the face to expose the real beauty.

Simplicity is the key to true sophistication. The Japanese have taught us about rhythmic negative space and restraint. A rock garden, with carefully raked pebbles, becomes a spiritual place of meditation. The Shakers believed it was a gift to be simple and

HOW MUCH CLUTTER
MAKES YOU FEEL
COMFORTABLE?

the only embellishments they made to their pure, honest forms was the use of color, which for them had a practical application, as each color had a meaning.

Look for the essence and go straight to the core; avoid pretension and ostentation. When something is simple it looks effortless and easy; it is confident, exudes warmth and has an integrity and an honesty, an authenticity, that feels good. You know that three fresh lemons on a pretty pottery plate delight the eye. This feast costs you little because these three lemons may be squeezed into lemonade in a day or two, and yet they are as pretty a sight and more satisfying to your spirit than a fancy piece of porcelain statuary that gathers dust and screams, "Don't touch me, I'm fragile and *very* expensive."

When you stay simple you show your appreciation of what natural gifts you've been freely given. For example, clean windows allow you to wonder at the changing character of the sky without having a depressing, dingy film separate you from the true beauty and intensity of the light. Think of your windows as doors to light and nature—not as opportunities to come up with an expensive window treatment that blocks out the energy of natural light. When you think about simplicity, you will be happy to expose large borders of bare wooden floors, waxed and polished so that they come alive for you like the trees from which they originated. Always look at the natural resources you have—the innate character of things—and not how to embellish and turn things into something they are not.

Think of the image of an artichoke where you peel off the leaves until you get to the heart. You will always be able to figure things out when you seek the bone truth about yourself and your situation. If you feel under financial pressure, ask yourself what expense you can eliminate so you feel more comfortable. You can entertain your friends informally and inexpensively when you simplify. When we sincerely want to see our friends, we can prepare fresh ingredients served invitingly. Whenever we are outer-directed, we complicate our lives. If this isn't the year to cook Thanksgiving dinner, accept an invitation to go to friends'. By

HOW AFFECTED ARE
YOU BY LIGHT?

having the courage to be simple, you shed layers of meaningless complications. In an urge to impress others, one can develop a phony accent, a fancy manner and an affected formality that turn people off. We all see through artificiality.

Root your personal style in the rich soil of wholesomeness. Serving a roast chicken and a fresh salad at a dinner party is disarmingly simple. What could be nicer than a succulent, moist, roasted chicken?

The fashion designer Hubert Givenchy uses one floral print on everything in his bedrooms—curtains, walls, furniture. His aunt and his mother did this as he grew up and it pleased him, so he carries on the same notion, using new fresh flower patterns and sheets of his own design.

YOU KNOW WHEN IT'S RIGHT.

As much as I admire the lavish multiflower bouquets at my favorite restaurant, La Grenouille, in New York—arrangements created first by Charles Masson, the founder, and now by his son, Charles Jr.—I am often struck by the simplicity of some of the bouquets. Recently, while enjoying a lovely lunch at the restaurant, I saw a vase brimming with sunflowers. The impact of one flower in profusion intensifies the experience, awakens the senses and conjures up powerful memory associations.

Focus clearly on what impact you want to make. Distill your options until the ideal solution presents itself. Gather everything together, see what your choices are, then edit. Everything you choose should hit the mark for you. When you think about your style of living, keep things simple and uncomplicated. When you do, you will have more time, more money, less frustration and more fun. Be strict. Guard what you value. Pare things down so you can take away nothing without losing beauty, and you will achieve the essence of simplicity and style.

YOU AND ONLY YOU DECIDE.

Always keep simplicity in mind. If you're tense and tired, cut back. If you feel strapped for money, cut back. If you want to write well, write simply and clearly. When you travel, concentrate on principal points of interest. When you need to lose a few pounds, take away the sauces, not the meal. When decoarating, work on the bones of the architecture, and the decorations will come more easily. Appreciate the pure and simple. Picking six different kinds of lettuce to make a salad can be overdoing it. Pick one and let style have a chance to emerge.

APPROPRIATENESS

The second link in the triangle is appropriateness, placed horizontally on a straight line to the right of simplicity. With these together, equally strong, you are now on terra firma, and your style will have deep roots that will weather most storms. Aristotle understood that good style "must be appropriate." But how do we know when something is appropriate? We have to do what a client of mine does. He passes all his decisions through the "tummy test": What do you feel deep down? When something is appropriate it taps into your heart and is consistent with the rest of your personal style.

A friend began to discover her personal style through a bitter lesson in appropriateness. This woman is large and has a heavy frame. All during her girlhood her mother gave her tiny, miniature things, including delicate, small jewelry. Sensing an awkwardness, it was difficult for Maria to grasp the problem fully. But a friend understood her far better than her mother had. She helped Maria choose furniture that fit her and the bold, handsome scale was appropriate. When Maria told her casually how uncomfortable she was wearing jewelry, her friend said, "It isn't jewelry that makes you feel uncomfortable, it is the inappropriate scale. You need big things around you. You must wear big jewelry. Mothers, bless them, are often wrong." She helped Maria select some bold pieces, and it transformed Maria's personal style.

A young, struggling professional saved his money so that he could buy his wife some earrings for their third anniversary. He went to the diamond market and chose some tiny diamond earrings. His selection was based on his pocketbook. When he gave them to his wife, who is a willowy five feet, eight and a half inches tall, she put on these wee earrings and they were unnoticeable. It was a disappointing moment for them both. After some pain, they returned them and a plain pair of simple gold earclips replaced the diamonds.

Ease, grace and confidence build as you begin to define appropriateness—not what others think and feel is right for you, but what is your unique honesty. You can't inherit appropriateness like a hand-me-down coat. Take an active role in determining what is appropriate for you in all situations. If a father tries to turn his feminine, blue-eyed daughter into a tomboy, it could cause tension because she might feel he wished he'd had a son. Why play ball if you'd rather play house?

Appropriateness should govern all of your life decisions. You give money, for example, according to your financial ability and concerns. There is no need to pretend to have more money than you do or to give out of guilt or social standing. Appropriateness is the best check-and-balance aid available to you. Decision-making is relatively easy when everything has to be appropriate.

Right now you live by a particular set of circumstances that govern your life. There are certain guidelines and standards and you act accordingly. But before making any decisions, ask the honest question—is this appropriate? How much should you pay for an object? Should you express your affections physically? Should you work harder or take more time off? Should you buy an expensive car? What would motivate you to buy such a fancy piece of equipment? Status? Pleasure? Is it appropriate to be rude to your boss? To take advantage of your spouse? To spend more than you have? To stretch yourself thin? Smack a child? Read trash? Watch television more frequently than you spend time with your spouse and children? Or, watch more television than you read?

Acting appropriately shows consideration for the feelings of others. Should you have another helping of salad? If you need more roughage in your diet and you are not full, the answer could be yes. Should you have another cigarette is another question. Ask yourself. Once you pass the test of appropriateness, you are free to make up your own mind. When we behave appropriately we don't have to waste a minute wondering what others may be

"TIME FOR A LITTLE SOMETHING."
A. A. Milne

thinking. We know our own truth. There will be lots of times when you aren't ready to face certain truths, and that is normal, but whenever you are ready, pull in your reins and steady yourself by getting in touch with your feelings.

Judge what is suitable for each occasion. Envision the circumstances. I have a client who has excellent taste but claims she only knows what she likes when she sees something tangible. "I can't envision anything in my mind. I have to see something before I know how I react." The problem with this is that once she sees something it can be too late! Teach yourself, through practice, to visualize the reality of a future event. Imagine, plan ahead, picture things, so that ultimately you will have a richer imagination.

Keep reminding yourself that it is always appropriate to be yourself. By definition, when you find your personal style you are making a commitment to a particular lifestyle. Use your style as your guide and strength, not as a restriction. Be open and flexible. Weigh each circumstance independently. If you hate cocktail parties and, as a rule, avoid them but find yourself going to one for whatever reason, make it your style to have a good time. The international designer Andrée Putman does this. She might not like a situation in theory, but in reality she has the ability to turn it into something positive and fun.

Learn about style by feeling what is appropriate. Most of us agree it is inappropriate to wear pearls at a beach cookout. Who wants her pearls to break over the sand while she is running on the beach under a full moon? However, we can't rule out pearls at a beach picnic. I know several regal women who could carry it off in great style. If a woman feels like wearing a low-cut dress to a cocktail party, she might feel fine even though many people come to cocktail parties directly from work.

Why is it that some people seem always to know how to conduct themselves while others are insecure? How is it that some people break away from tradition and do things that are accepted as proper and correct, while others appear out of control? Certain people, I've found, are blessed with an abundance of common sense. Others have to struggle to learn to be sensible, and they do so awkwardly. Common sense is considered one of the three basic

ALLOW OTHERS TO
KNOW YOU.

WHEN THE URGE
HITS—ACT.

ingredients of intelligence, the other two being creativity and knowledge. They are all connected. You can increase your intuitive experience by observation. Register everything. Observe both the situation and your own reaction to each event.

Next to using our common sense, we must learn to become more practical. The real world requires functional, useful solutions to ever increasing problems. If something works, why change it? Years ago I told my mentor, the great interior designer Eleanor McMillen Brown, that I was the only New York decorator I knew who didn't own or rent a house outside the city. I rationalized why this seemed best for our particular lifestyle. "We don't have that kind of money and we really love New York on weekends. We enjoy going to museums, galleries and auctions. And, we love to travel." Eleanor, who rarely interrupts, excused herself. "But, Sandie, if it works for you and you're happy, how could you even think of changing a good thing? Stick with what works." Sound, abiding advice.

Your style has to have ease in order to last. So many of my clients are trying to find a more appropriate style of living so that they can celebrate life with family and friends more easily. If you discover something is no longer working well for you, make an effort to enact some changes. For example, if you find your large house has become a burden to you and is lonely now that the children are grown, accept this as reality. Nothing lasts forever. You may prefer to move to a smaller, more manageable place so that you will have money, time and mobility to travel.

When you are happy, you are living appropriately. Remember Helen Keller's wise words: "Your success and happiness lie in you. . . . Resolve to keep happy, and your joy and you shall form an invincible host against difficulties." Are you doing certain things out of duty, habit or need that are no longer appropriate? Work things out so that your life suits you, because when it does style emerges.

TAKE RISKS.

BEAUTY

Once you've thought about the significance of simplicity and appropriateness as tools to help you find your personal style, you are free to elevate those two elements. Join them together at the apex of your triangle. Beauty dwells on a high spiritual note of harmony. Here, focus on beauty—the inner beauty reflected as outward grace. Understand that everything is connected. The added harmony of beauty makes the difference. The beauty that is around us and within us is the password to truth and happiness. There is no higher calling or finer art form than to live a beautiful life. When you think a beautiful thought it shows on your face and in your acts. When you say a kind word to a loved one it spreads grace.

My parents were given a treasured present almost fifty years ago—a Merriam-Webster's Unabridged New International Dictionary. As a small child I remember this great book open on a mahogany pedestal stand in our study. There was a reflector light illuminating the pages. My parents and friends enjoyed bantering back and forth about words, their roots and meanings. The gift of fortune has passed this book on to me and I have it placed on a slant-top barrister's standing desk outside my office. Recently I looked up the word *beauty:* "That perfection in the sensuous order, and, by extension, in the spiritual order, which excites admiration or delight for itself rather than for its uses." Like a butterfly, a rainbow, a daisy, a ship at sail, a sunset, a child painted by Mary Cassatt. The particular grace that beauty conveys adds resonance and meaning to the experience of living.

Hunt for new ways to see and create beauty, as in a private moment with a child. Be kind to yourself, to others and everything around you. Beauty becomes an attitude and a way of life.

My mother was strict and insisted on order. She believed there was no possibility of beauty amidst chaos. I observed the pleasure my mother derived from having a pristine garage. Everything had a storage place and was gleaming, ready for use when needed. Even the lawn mower was wiped clean after each mowing. The

"BEAUTY IS AN EXPRESSION OF THAT RAPTURE OF BEING ALIVE."
—*Bill Moyers*

STAY OPEN.

garage floor was regularly painted hunter green and was wet-mopped each week. Looking back on the three houses where my memories of childhood are rooted, I can't think of an area in any house that was messy. When we moved from a large, rambling old onion farm in Westport, Connecticut, to a small saltbox with dormer windows, some of my happiest hours were spent organizing things in the attic. Mother had a huge steamer trunk for each child and our names were spray-painted on the lid. She gathered all the paraphernalia of our childhood so we would have these souvenirs long after camp, school, prom, graduation and horse-show memories faded.

I absorbed from these rituals of preservation, conservation and maintenance a respect for the most humble household necessity. When well cared for, these tools could be of service to enhance beauty, so they were kept in order and respected.

An attitude of reverence permeated every crack and corner of my mother's house. We learned how to put our personal stamp on things, no matter what we were doing at home, by showing respect and care. Mother loved to restore and mend, to bring things back to mint condition. She created beauty and she encouraged this in her children.

She sculpted and painted and we did too. I learned from my mother and later from my godmother, Mitzi Christian, a lady of enormous personal style and grace, that everything at home can be made more beautiful with some thought, a little care and extra attention. Mitzi lived on a farm in Framingham, Massachusetts, when I was young and I remember how beautiful her stable was. Mother and Mitzi taught me that once you see, you appreciate and then you become inspired.

Both Mother and Mitzi took me to museums and exposed me to style and beauty. I remember as a young child experiencing their happiness at the sight of fine American furniture, porcelain and paintings as well as their pleasure in observing museum gardens, friends' gardens and, of course, their own. Mother and Mitzi enjoyed cooking and creating a festive atmosphere for the families to share in while they were gathered at Mitzi's antique tavern table for laughter and delicious food and the beauty of being together.

WHO IS YOUR
FAVORITE ARTIST?

Beauty always delights the senses and the spirit. A pretty face has a physical loveliness and charms our senses. An attractively served, delicious dinner stimulates our appetite for all the positive blessings in life and lifts our spirits. The Impressionist painters have such a place in my heart because they have forced me to learn how to see the changing light which colors everything and lets me feel more deeply. They didn't literally paint what they saw, they painted an impression of their senses. They painted what they felt. When you look at a room full of their pictures, you discover you are in a beautiful world. These artists were in accord with nature and so full of awe, they used light and color to glorify the radiance of what surrounded their spirit. Each Impressionist artist found his or her own style, and collectively they represented a commitment to natural beauty that will last as long as we have light to appreciate their passion. When we think of simplicity, appropriateness and beauty as a means of finding our personal style, we will want to find creative outlets in all we do.

CREATIVITY

If the world had been created for us alone, we wouldn't have to lift a finger to express ourselves. Creativity is utterly natural in us and doesn't have to be manufactured. Each of us is empowered with a creative spirit.

Vitality is the secret to all pleasure and meaning. Dwell on your interpretation of what is simple, appropriate and beautiful—in people, in literature, in your surroundings. Some people are innately more in tune with their spirit and sense of self than others. At an early age Shirley Temple and Judy Garland knew they enjoyed acting. Fred Astaire loved to dance. When you accept your talent as your gift and listen to your conscience, you will feel the contentment and fun that are only possible through imagination and creativity.

What is your form of play? What you think, say, and do; *how* you do things, what you *don't* do, who you love—all are clues

TURN THINGS UPSIDE DOWN.

that add up to your inner light and truth. Thoreau told us, "Let nothing come between you and the light." When you make a deliberate and confident statement about these personal choices, you will be beaming signals to the world. Everyone you admire has made this commitment. Creativity is an essential ingredient to a beautiful life. Most people have the capacity to increase their creativity. To people like Marysarah, work is play. Give up trying to conform to inherited notions about how to live. Guard your own integrity. You will be most creative and alive when you believe in and love what you're doing.

How can you tap into the playfulness and freshness of your childhood? Friends just had a baby and they are going to take up piano lessons with their daughter as soon as Samantha's fingers are big enough. Bring yourself back to your favorite childhood memories through association. Read Proust to help teach you how. Take time to remember positive images from your past. The gift of youthful innocence—when you often played with abandon and lost all sense of time and place—can be recaptured. If you have a child you can grab, go run in the rain. Or, you become the child and go for a walk in the rain alone. Sing, Gene Kelly style. On a sunny day, tumble down the lawn, do somersaults in the water, read a book by a stream, have a nap under a tree. Lick a double-scoop coffee ice cream cone. Take off your watch.

Be a sponge and absorb each moment. Turn things upside down. Take things apart and put them together in your own way. Use a flowered hatbox to store your tray of slides. Use a basket to hold your stationery. Use a silk scarf to cover a sofa pillow. A mustard crock can become a container for wooden spoons. A pretty pillbox can hold paper clips. Use ordinary objects in unusual ways. Look at the back of a painting resting on an easel. Cover the back with marbleized paper. If you place it in front of a mirror you will see one of your finishing touches. Turn things around. Group things together. Explore new territory until you find secret delights.

Make something beautiful with your hands: wrap a pretty package using a scrap of leftover chintz; decorate the dining room table for a party; paste a favorite colorful fabric on boxes; paint

THERE ARE NO RULES, THERE IS ONLY EXPERIMENTATION.

flower decorations on your note cards. Stencil your bedroom floor with flowers and leaves. Hand-paint some flowers on plain white dinner plates. Have fun defining and honing your sense of personal pleasures.

Be certain to add a little "ta-da!" to the next thing to do. When you greet someone, have a little exchange. When you call your love, give him a compliment. When you write a letter, tell a sweet story. Press a flower between the folds. Try hard to express something personal. Dream up a new dish for dinner. Mix sweet and sour in your cooking and try marinating lamb chops in soy sauce, ginger and honey. Another time try a leg of lamb smothered in a paste of espresso coffee, mustard and garlic with Spanish olives— roast it to a crisp in the pan. If you are a watercolor artist, play with oils or acrylics. Sketch in a different medium. Try charcoal.

Stretch your creative talents by adding vitality to everything you do and you will continually increase your options. Tap into the fresh inspiration all around you. Use the universe as your canvas. Learn how to pluck out the best and most fun ideas you observe; absorb the good and the useful. You never know where you're going to get your next inspiration. A walk on the beach could be the basis of a beautiful photograph or a seascape painting, a collection of seashells or a poem. A friend started a perfume company and found she could scent rooms by perfuming sand— an inspiration from a walk on a deserted beach in Bermuda. Believe in your imagination and your ability to transform your world. Mold clay, rub stone, sand wood, plant seeds, knead dough, dabble with felt-tip pens and put the finishing touches to all you encounter. Analyze everything honestly and then respond by putting your own creative sensibilities to use. If the inside of a drawer is dark, line it with a chintz wrapping paper glued in place with rubber cement. Laura Ashley sells pretty books of a variety of wrapping papers. Each drawer could be a different, colorful pattern. Or use flower-scented drawer liners. When we feel a void, we can fill it with our own expression of beauty. If we see something ugly, we can turn it into an opportunity to create something pleasant.

WE FULFILL OUR POTENTIAL IN LITTLE DETAILS.

FANTASY FIRST

The ability to imagine is a distinctively human capacity. We wouldn't have novels without fantasy. We wouldn't have *Cinderella, Alice in Wonderland* or *The Tale of Peter Rabbit* if it weren't for minds that can make up a story. (When Beatrix Potter drew people she never achieved the same feelings as she did when drawing the tiny pets she loved so dearly.) Fantasy opens us up to whimsy and reverie. We observe more keenly what we love.

Fantasies can tell you what your needs and desires are, and by turning your fantasy into reality you will be meeting your own needs. Fantasize. Say "yes" to creating a lot more fun and satisfaction in your daily life. Jot down your fantasies in your style journal. Record big and sweet dreams. The late interior designer Dorothy Draper gave a lecture that electrified me when I was in art school: "Don't design scared. Dream." As designers we have been trained to envision something that doesn't exist. Jot down today's fantasies in your journal: an archaeological dig in Cairo, a house in the country, a baby, a week alone observing grizzly bears in the mountains of Colorado, a new red purse, strong legs.

Whatever your fantasy, it has every possibility of turning into reality. How can you ever get what you want until you identify what it is you want? It's far easier for us to read our own minds than for someone else to do so. For sixteen years a successful account executive followed an artist's work and put one of his paintings on her fantasy list. When Margaret became a partner at her firm and came into a windfall, she knew this particular painting was meant to live with her forever. Luck was on her side; it is now hanging over the mantel in her living room as a warm companion and as a tangible symbol of her wishes.

As well as becoming aware of your daily fantasies, think about this new dramatic decade. What fantasies do you have that will bring you to the twenty-first century—sensibly, sensuously and with personal style?

LEARNING TO TRUST YOUR INSTINCTS

I've grown to believe that dishonesty about feelings usually arises from concern with image. Striving to impress others is based on a sense of low self-worth. Style must always feel natural. Adopt your personal style from elements that you instinctively understand. Personal style is a consistency of one person's point of view. Your natural way of expression will always be original because no one else could ever mimic your actions exactly.

One of the most vital, visionary, effective and intuitive businesswomen I know bases all her decisions on an instinctive, gut response. When she feels something is right, it is right. "My mother taught me to trust my first thoughts and never look back." This support and wise advice has led the way to Nancy's brilliant career. She visualizes things in her mind and has complete confidence in her judgment. She lets marketing people do tests and surveys to prove her point and to make them feel confident she is right. Decisions flow through her like a clear brook of refreshing water, instinct washes away any confusion or doubt. Nancy is wise, intelligent and informed. But so are lots of people. Her gift is her sensitive artistic side which she nourishes by being in tune with her intuition.

When something pleases you, save it. Before you throw away an envelope, study the stamp, the handwriting, the watermarks on the rag paper. Does the lining color in the envelope speak to you? The embossing? The hand-painted border where the corners have definition? What can you do to put your discoveries to use? I have a friend who peels off all pretty stamps from envelopes she receives and leaves them in a porcelain dish on her writing table for inspiration. If you've been undecided on what color silk dress to buy, red or blue, and the blue lining of an envelope jumps out at you, yes, you want an amazingly intense blue dress. Or maybe you can look at a purple hyacinth plant the way Sandy Duncan did and know that is the color you want your lacquer coffee table to be.

Every stimulus becomes an opportunity to find fresh ways to

BE FAITHFUL.

"SMALL IS BEAUTIFUL."
Professor E. F. Schumacher

express your personal vision. Once things begin to click, find connections that link one area of your life to another, and feel the rewards of unexpected energy. The world is your resource. Study the most obvious everyday things. Where there is little color, study the texture and form, light and shadow. Tree trunks, branches, bark—pebbles, rocks, stone walls. Don't take anything for granted. Question the size, shape, texture, material and use of everything.

Look at the color and smoothness of the stationery you select. Smell it. Being drawn to a particular kind of paper can inspire you to put the paper to creative use, as an artist's colorful pigments are put on canvas. If an artist chooses a rough canvas, it affects the painting. The paper becomes you in much the same way as a suit fits. Long after you send a letter, someone may save it, reread it, admire the paper and sense your style. You can pick blue with a white border or white with a blue border. The writing paper you choose represents you, as does everything else. Trust your instincts. Pay attention to the tools you buy, your equipment; choose them with the same care as the ingredients you select for cooking.

WHERE ARE YOU RIGHT NOW?

Where are you, this minute, as you read this book? I often write in bed. Before I was ever published, I used to trudge to a musty library in order to write. I felt more intellectual surrounded by serious paneling and bookcases filled with books written by famous authors. I assumed this was the spirit I needed in order to write well. I love libraries and go to them often, but no longer do I go to libraries to write. I prefer my bed! It's cozy, comfortable, private, pretty and secure. I have good light, I'm near a window, I have my favorite books at hand and I feel a privacy and intimacy here that I want to express in my writing.

I also love desks, as did the first woman decorator in America, Elsie de Wolfe (Lady Charles Mendl). She insisted on having a lady's desk in every room, including entrance halls and dressing rooms. I am desk-oriented and have turned counters in the kitchen and bathroom into standing desks. The ironing board is a great height for an impromptu standing desk. But I have a special fondness for turning my side of our bed into a lap desk. I've covered a clipboard with a favorite fabric so I can lean my writing pad against something firm. I feel like a kindred spirit to Winston Churchill and Edith Wharton who also adored writing in bed.

What I've learned about myself is that I love to write! So, I'll turn wherever I am into an ideal place to write. When I was putting the finishing touches on my first book, *Style for Living,* I developed pneumonia and had to go to Lenox Hill Hospital. My family doctor had listened to my chest, taken an X ray and my temperature, and sent me straight from his office to the third floor of the hospital around the corner. I was weak and didn't feel I could tell the doctor I was under deadline with Doubleday so it was an extremely inconvenient time for me to be incarcerated in a hospital! But there I was, stuck in bed, incapable of going off to a paneled, book-lined room in a library. I made the best of a losing proposition by finishing my book in my hospital bed. There is a sense of practicality to personal style; you find ways to manage.

My personal style is to write longhand on a pad of smooth, unlined white paper attached to a colorful clipboard. I write with a fountain pen, using a rainbow of different ink colors depending on my mood. I collect pens the way a golfer collects clubs or an artist gathers brushes. I now have a "space pen" that defies gravity. If necessary, I can write while flat on my back! I have no desire to drag a typewriter or word processor around with me nor do I want to limit myself to having to go only where I can take them. My personal style of writing makes me free and spontaneous. I write where I am.

Every writer eventually finds a particular style of equipment that is most comfortable. Next, we each develop our own writing style—how to put words on paper or on a screen. The writer Dominick Dunne told me that he loves to use his word processor, and Tom Wolfe lets his gather dust. Tom is used to his typewriter from his journalism days. Neil Simon uses a typewriter and also

IS THERE SOMETHING YOU WANT TO BEGIN COLLECTING?

writes longhand while sitting in a comfortable upholstered chair. Mary Jane Pool, author, design consultant, and former editor in chief of *House & Garden* (now *HG*) can't think without her twenty-year-old red Olivetti typewriter. Whatever works, works! Be grateful when you've found your style. I smile at well-meaning people who want me to use a word processor. I listen attentively and continue to put pen and ink to paper guided by my conscience and a sense of pleasure.

Perhaps you are also in bed. Or you might be in a car waiting for a friend or a child, or for your love to get off a train or a plane. Is it your pattern to carry a book with you when you know you might be kept waiting? A mother of five wrote me that she left my book, *Living Beautifully Together,* in her car because her only free time was while waiting for children when she did car pool. When you can put time to use instead of being wasteful it is less stressful to be delayed. When I was a child I had a favorite fragrant magnolia tree in our front yard where I went to read in the spring. I enjoyed snuggling against the trunk for support and feeling cozy yet quietly alone. Where is your favorite spot for reading? Or is it your personal style to read wherever you are?

What is beautiful to you right now? Express your delights and blessings to yourself. If you are in a friend's driveway in your car waiting to pick up a child, you may be listening to a tape of Frank Sinatra singing "I Only Have Eyes for You." Does that put a smile on your face? What kind of music soothes you? Being kept waiting is not necessarily your choosing. But you can read, listen to music, make a list, do a sketch or simply look up at the sky. Count how many colors of blue you can see. Are there any clouds? Birds? How warm is it? How does the air smell? What sounds do you hear? How do you feel?

Maybe you're sitting in your living room in a comfortable reading chair next to a bouquet of anemones. They have such style and life. The colors are something the fashion designer Christian Lacroix might dream up. How outrageous can a bouquet's color combination be—flame red, white, lilac, rich purple and fuchsia with black fuzzy centers? Each blossom has pinwheel petals; the stems bend in dignity. Do the colors of the anemones subtly blend

HOW DO YOU USE
YOUR FREE TIME?

into the color scheme of your living room or do they boldly contrast? What are your favorite flower scents? Keep sorting through your preferences. Name some favorite flowers. What colors do you like best if the flower has a variety of colors? If you keep a style journal, number each flower in order, beginning with your favorite, based on your feelings right now. If you need inspiration, look in some colorful garden books. My husband Peter's favorite flower is freesia—he loves a mixture of yellows, lavender and white. He also enjoys delphinium and white lilies, sweet peas, peonies and pansies.

Next, put a star in front of the flower that carries the most sentiment. I star lily of the valley which in flower lore signifies "return of happiness." I carried a nosegay of this delicate, romantic, nostalgic, ephemeral little white flower on our wedding day. A few weeks ago I was given as a present two little terracotta pots planted with lily of the valley. I put them in our bedroom on the window ledge next to the bed so that I could study the delicacy of the little white bells and go to sleep smelling the purity and sweet goodness of their aroma. What flower have you starred? Remind yourself why. Now, think of your favorite seasonal delights that open up fresh fond memories of your childhood. If you have already listed some, put the month next to the name. For example, crocus—March. Your dates will vary depending on the climate. Daffodils—May. Remembering the iris in June might also refresh your memory of picking iris for your high school graduation party.

If you were to go out and buy a flowering plant to bring home, assuming you could get anything you wanted, what would you select? What would bring you the greatest pleasure right now? Add some plant preferences to your flower list. Never mind that you don't have a green thumb, dream of your desires; the plant you pick will be in bloom. Would it be an orange tree bursting with little oranges? Or a gardenia plant filled with dozens of fragrant white blossoms? If you had both, the air would be scented with the combination of mandarin oranges and gardenia.

Why do you like a certain flowering plant more than another?

GO BACK TO BASICS.

What are the qualities that attract you most? Is it a combination of the color and shape of the blossom, leaves and fragrance? Or are you sentimental about a gardenia plant because it reminds you of going to your first prom? Does the time of year have anything to do with your personal preference? Has your taste in flowers and flowering plants changed over the years? Have your color preferences shifted? Do you prefer African violets to geraniums? Do you like narcissus more than tulips? Would you rather have some amaryllis in bloom, or azalea? What color azalea would you choose? Do you prefer forsythia over quince? Focus on your preference. Does dogwood conjure up memories of early May when the pink and white dogwood created natural arches across the hill? My friend Sally has a flaming raspberry azalea plant on her desk which goes beautifully with her Pierre Deux patterned desk accessories. I am reminded of walking through the azalea gardens at Winterthur in Wilmington, Delaware, in May, whenever I go to her office.

DO YOU ENJOY ARRANGING FRESH FLOWERS?

Possibly you prefer strong-scented plants for your home. Hyacinths, narcissus and gardenias smell delicious. So, at night, when you can't appreciate their pretty form and delicate color, you can have sweet dreams simply by putting a scented bouquet or plant next to your bed. Of all our senses, smell is the one that within seconds can take us back to an August afternoon on Cape Cod twenty years ago when we were seeing and smelling a rose garden.

Your style notebook in which you list all your current preferences in flowers and plants (including some trees) can tell you a great deal about your own style. Rate the flowers and plants from one to ten. Flowers are pretty to look at, sensuous to smell, arrange and tend, and they're delicate. Nothing manufactured exceeds their beauty. Flowers make us feel good because they are living and are metaphors for our own fragility. Robert Herrick wrote: "Gather ye rosebuds while ye may / Old Time is still a-flying / And this same flower that smiles today / Tomorrow will be dying."

Look now at your favorite-flower list in terms of color. Do these colors translate into other areas in your life? Are these the colors you like to wear and to use in your decorating? If you focus on your favorite flowers you can transport these feelings to the selection of a blouse, a quilt, towels or a chintz.

Look at all the flowers and flowering plants on your list. What is feasible for you to pick from the garden or field and what can you buy from the market or a florist? Base your decision on what's available, what you can afford, and what will bring you the greatest pleasure. If you select a bunch of daisies, let's start there. Once you remove many of the leaves, the white flowers have more punch. Go into your cupboard and look at your vases and pitchers. Choose one you like. Experiment. Try several. The stems of daisies aren't attractive so you may select a white glass vase designed by the Finnish architect Aalto. Or, you may be drawn to a Metropolitan Museum reproduction of an American blue grass pitcher given to you by a dear friend. For the price of a few dollars, you have something of real beauty and style that will last about ten days. Wild flowers you pick in a field, gathered in abundance, can be put into a white pottery cylinder vase and will have the same impact.

Or possibly you want to splurge on one perfect Sonia pink rose. Instead of leaving the stem long, cut it so it is eight inches tall and put it in a clear crystal bud vase, or polish your sterling silver bud vase and feel the glow of the reflections. When you place this vase on your writing desk it could hold magical powers to inspire you. Think of Fantan-Latour's still-life paintings. One lovely rose can conjure up hundreds of beautiful images. Perhaps you want something more elaborate than a single flower. If you can afford to buy two dozen white lilies, cut the center pollen out of each bloom so it won't stain and put them in a gleaming silver pitcher. The profusion of white will last several weeks and will perfume a whole room.

THINK OF
EVERYTHING YOU DO
AS AN OPPORTUNITY
TO EXPRESS
YOURSELF.

If you buy an inexpensive narcissus plant that has a plastic pot, transfer it into a terra-cotta or a decorated porcelain cachepot, depending on your mood and where you want to put it. When the stems begin to droop, tie them together in a bow with pretty, colorful grosgrain ribbon. Whichever flower or plant you choose, do something to stamp it with your signature.

You've noted your favorite flowers in your style notebook. When you're in the mood take a few minutes to jot down your preferences in styles of furniture, architecture, fashion, cooking, and your favorite artists, writers, actors and composers. Leave space to add to your lists as you become aware of new discoveries.

TAKING STOCK

What is it that gives you a real lift? Is it the beauty of your view or do you appreciate the interior landscape of your living room? Perhaps you have all your upholstered chairs on swivels. Billy Baldwin encouraged his clients to make everything comfortable. Sipping a cool drink with a friend while discussing literature in a well-stocked, attractive library will give most people a lift.

When you have a few spare moments, what do you do? Do you read, garden, listen to music, go hiking, paint or putter? What revitalizes you? Do you write, sculpt, knit or play tennis? What are your luxuries? What makes you feel good? I have a friend who went out to buy a lamp and found her heart wasn't in the purchase. The timing wasn't right. Instead, she bought some music tapes with the money and felt happy. Brenda told me she danced in her bedroom to a Cat Stevens tape that Saturday night. Someday she'll buy the much-needed lamp, but her real pleasure was in having some new music to liven up her life.

If your office or house is disorganized, you have to take time out to straighten things up. Don't worry about all the reasons the house got ahead of you. Once you attack it, you'll feel better instantly. Maybe your style is to go to a movie first and then come back and face the disarray. The late Bishop Fulton Sheen preached, "First the famine, then the feast." Maybe you should work for a few hours, take a break and then go back to finish the task.

After the house is in order, you can try new ideas, from a new shade of lipstick to a new dish to reading a new writer. Explore all options open to you. Point yourself in the right direction by being informed. Read catalogues. Read directions and instructions

"AN OUTWARD AND VISIBLE SIGN OF AN INWARD AND SPIRITUAL GRACE."
— *The Book of Common Prayer*

and how-to advice. Communicate clearly. I remember going out looking for Louis XV furniture for a couple's bedroom (Ted had said he wanted Louis XV), and afterward Linda and I took Ted around to show him our finds. He wasn't pleased. He had confused the Louis XV style, with its curves, with the Louis XVI style, which has straight lines. We were showing him one and he preferred the other. Bad communciation all around. Do your homework.

Do you prefer going camping in the mountains of Colorado, or would you rather lie on a beach on a deserted island in the Caribbean? Do you want to be alone or see others? Do you enjoy cities? Which ones are your favorites? San Francisco, New Orleans, Seattle, Paris? What do you want to get out of travel and what are you seeking in your leisure time?

As you develop your personal style you eliminate negative stress, so that suddenly things seem clearer and brighter. You may decide to take up painting again, or tennis. You may join a new church or learn a new form of meditation. Review all your old interests because it is possible you may go to museums and art galleries on a regular basis again. Spend Saturdays gallery-hopping. Take a course in Chinese cooking. A couple did this together and over several months they both lost more than fifteen pounds and now they share in the cooking. Take a cruise in the Greek islands. You may rediscover your love of Greek architecture. Write a series of articles for your local newspaper. Learn about quilts or silver. There's always time for what's exciting to you. Caroline Rose Hunt of the wealthy Texas Hunt family has distinguished herself for creating beautiful hotels—the Remington in Houston, the lovely Bel-Air Hotel in Beverly Hills, and in Dallas the Mansion on Turtle Creek and the Hotel Crescent Court, where she has an antique shop, Lady Primrose's Shopping English Countryside. She happily refers to her shop as her living room.

"In my childhood I went antiquing with my mother—once to England—and we went to New England and New Orleans several times. One of the things I find so fascinating is that when you are antiquing you are always learning. Your curiosity teaches you as you go on this wonderful adventure, expecting to find the golden egg at a bargain price. I have five children and thirteen grandchildren so I can't say I have more time now. However, I started the shop because I decided to do the things I enjoy doing most. I'm not an acquisitive person as people go. I now live in a very small apartment. The fun is enjoying these beautiful antiques. I don't like clutter. Each New Year's Eve I make a resolution to be better organized. If you're not organized, you have no tranquillity. I want to stay tranquil punctuated by stimulation."

Her shop and her buying trips to the English countryside give her this precious balance.

Keep exploring what *you* like to do. This treasure hunt to find your personal style is a private exploration. When you're free to do what you love to do, in your own style, you won't fatigue. When you do things you really don't enjoy, however, or are kept from doing what you want to do—whether it's painting, composing, writing or bird-watching—you become exhausted. Protect your time. What are the present patterns in your life that frustrate you? Have a plan—organize things so that you will have more time to do what interests you.

Let those close to you know what you're trying to accomplish and when you'll be unavailable. When you are fulfilling domestic obligations, make them fun. For example, when you have to prepare dinner, you're in charge. Set a stage. Make it wonderful. Have shoestring noodles and pesto sauce if that pleases you. You hold the power to create something delicious and memorable. What you do is often far less important than your style and attitude.

Look around and pay close attention to your surroundings—your clothes, your cooking, your work habits. Observe how much you've grown. You don't learn everything over a long weekend but as you make improvements and as your eye becomes wiser, more educated, you'll see major changes.

When you look around you, it is possible to discover you have outgrown many things in your immediate surroundings. Times arrive when we are more receptive to change and growth. One client went around her bedroom pointing to the furniture they

HOW DO YOU RATE
YOUR ENERGY LEVEL?

MAKE YOUR OWN
CHOICES AND LEARN
FROM THE
CONSEQUENCES.

had bought when her husband was in medical school. Laughing, Nana said, "That was over forty years ago." When we find we no longer hold a sentimental attachment to a piece of furniture that is less than representative of our ideal style, far better to take it away and see empty space. Seize these rare moments of revelation. Sometimes when I lecture, showing attractive pictures of clients' houses and apartments, people come up to me afterward, perhaps half joking, saying they want to light a match to their house. One of the reasons they came to the lecture is because of their love for their home. Many want to use every opportunity to refresh their personal vision.

HOW ORGANIZED ARE YOU?

You may wake up one morning and while you're doing something quite ordinary—taking a shower or walking the dog—you'll look around and see clearly what you want. You can never go back to where you were, because it no longer fits your vision. Most of us find that some of our style choices we thought were great at one time are no longer satisfying to us. Don't live with things you don't appreciate; pass them on to someone who will. As your quest for defining and honing your style continues, your visual taste will improve. In order for you to grow in personal style, weeding out and editing some of the things you used to feel sentimental about is essential.

We don't live our lives year to year or month to month. We live moment to moment, like the waves that tumble to shore. Samuel Johnson pointed out that the present passes so quickly that we can hardly think at all except in terms of the past or the future. We are aware that blissful moments—when we feel at one with the universe—are fleeting. Our moods shift like the weather. Take advantage of the fullness of your time by concentrating on the present. If you find you are stuck at an airport in Chicago—the flight to Denver is delayed because of a blizzard—make it your style to remain calm and composed, and go about your business grateful that you are safe. Do some reading; write letters. Do some work that you are carrying in your briefcase. Think of the delay as a gift of time.

All of us experience struggles as we try to make sense out of existence. We express ourselves unevenly as we grow. Alexander Liberman, in a discussion of Paul Cézanne in his book *The Artist in His Studio,* said, "The stimulus of creation seems to be favorable to the human system; perhaps boredom and lack of activity kill faster than the difficulties of creative living." Self-expression or self-realization is a fundamental human need. I've interviewed hundreds of artists, writers and photographers and generally they are happiest when they are in the flow of their creative work. Ralph Waldo Emerson agreed: "Nothing great was ever achieved without enthusiasm." One of the benefits of creative activity is the vitality and intensity of the focus which causes an awakening of the senses and alters your mood. You feel part of the universe and feel empowered to improve the world. This exhilaration makes you feel needed and gives your life real meaning. Creativity is electricity and people feel it when they are with you.

Find the best outlet for your talents and energies. Everyone who is courageous enough to express a unique vision feels tension. That is the gift and the curse of having an independent mind. Professor Anthony Storr tells us in his well-documented book *Solitude: A Return to the Self* that imagination has given man flexibility but in doing so has robbed him of contentment. Samuel Johnson believed that our hunger for imagination preys incessantly on us, and those who already have all that they can enjoy must enlarge their desires.

You can live peacefully with this creative tension once you accept it as a blessing and a personal treasure.

"I LOVE THOSE WHO YEARN FOR THE IMPOSSIBLE."
—*Goethe*

LET YOUR STYLE SPEAK FOR YOU.

ROLE MODELS

All of us have favorite role models, people we look up to as examples. We can feel the exhilaration and pleasure other human beings have when they define their essence. Some of my role models are:

KATHARINE HEPBURN

Miss Hepburn has classic pluck with depth and strength of character. She challenges herself, is disciplined and believes in herself. Miss Hepburn was brought up never to complain. She is courageous. Her style is authentic. She maintains her privacy and yet projects her consistent taste and style through her exceptionally successful acting career. Her manner, the way she dresses, her love of tennis and gardening are hers alone. "Katie" has spunk.

A few years ago she wrote, "I only do things I'm passionate about." She keeps things simple. She knows what she wants and what she doesn't want. She is free. Katharine Hepburn can't bear the thought of being bored or of boring others. She detests talking about herself. She is one of my heroines because she is so real. What a blessing that she is such a talented actress so that we can know her vicariously. I find her physical appearance attractive because she allows us to see into her character. The turtleneck T-shirts help hide her generous torso. Her hands are gnarled with arthritis yet she has learned to show off her hands beautifully. Katharine Hepburn wears no masks; she exudes personal style.

CLAUDE MONET

My favorite Impressionist painter of the living light of the outdoors, colorist Monet was also a passionate gardener. Monet said once, "I'm good for nothing except painting and gardening." He attributed his success as a painter to his lifelong love of gardening because the hues fulfilled his thirst for visual sensations. Ever since I was a little girl, when I saw my first Monet painting at the Boston Fine Arts Museum, I have been captivated by his vision. His satisfaction from painting and from improving his garden at his last house at Giverny is touching. Monet represents something of great significance because he tirelessly pursued exactly what he most loved, and as a result he was extremely prolific as an artist. He also spent thousands of hours making a dream reality with flowers, lily ponds and winding garden paths. Monet understood

clearly how to focus his life; he also loved good food and friendship, and his beloved garden at Giverny gave him spiritual grace
as he lost his eyesight toward the end of his long, creative life.
One complains less about loss when one has lived fully.

BE AT EASE.

COCO CHANEL

Since I first became aware of fashion I have identified with Chanel's
tailored smartness. When I began my own design career in New
York, I wanted to create a classic Chanel look for myself. One of
my friends nicknamed me Coco because I am such a Chanel admirer. Chanel had chic, confidence and direction. She knew how
to make women feminine and, at the same time, potent. A Chanel-
styled suit can go from early morning until late at night and be
stunning. My older sister Barbara was a fashion assistant to Eu-
genia Sheppard at the *New York Herald Tribune* in the early sixties,
and once she had me model some Chanel suits and coats. I'd never
felt so elegant, graceful or pretty. Chanel's style helped me define
my own. I identify with her clothes, image and strong design
statement. I think of my own look as tailored, smart and crisp,
and Chanel has guided me in my understanding of how I want to
feel and appear to others. Karl Lagerfeld identified what set Chanel
apart from others: "the ability to wear her own clothes, to set an
example through her own personal style."

IN ORDER TO BE
ORIGINAL, YOU MUST
BE DIFFERENT.

BEING AWARE OF YOUR SENSES

Be alert to how your senses affect you. What you see and hear,
what you touch, your sense of smell and taste are your very own.

You educate your eye by looking at beauty, line and proportion. You learn about literature by reading the classics. You learn
about music by listening to great composers. Often, because you
sing or play an instrument, you will listen with more recognition
to the quality, tone and pitch of sounds. Smell has always been
important to humankind for hunting and gathering and it still

TRUTH IS
EXPERIENCED
INDIVIDUALLY.

plays a role in our daily lives. The scent of the shampoo you use should appeal to your olfactory sense because messages travel to the area of the brain that deals with emotions and memories. I wash my hair with shampoo that smells of watermelons and reminds me of carefree summer days, eating huge juicy watermelon wedges on the grass with my sister and brothers. Lemon scent refreshes. Jasmine makes you drowsy. Peppermint stimulates. Lavender soothes. Fragrance affects our sleep and how much tension we feel.

I first wore Chanel No. 5 when I was sixteen years old and going to a prom. While I wear other perfumes now, I still have a warm spot for the fresh innocence of Chanel No. 5 and wear it intermittently. Do you wear one scent as a signature or do you vary your perfumes according to your mood, where you're going, the weather and the season?

DO YOU WEAR ONE COLOGNE OR DIFFERENT SCENTS?

Think about the textures in your life. What kind of fabric do you want for your desk chair? You may want to select a soft fabric (a cotton chintz or a velvet) for a slipcover because you enjoy sitting at your desk dressed in your nightgown and most other fabrics would scratch you and cause irritation. Throw pillows on a sofa, for example, can be of a sensuous fabric because we tend to play with and hug pillows. When you touch something, become aware of how it feels. The ridges of a pencil, for example, may drive you crazy as you write. The feel of a sisal rug to your sensitive bare feet could turn you off. The feel of your hairbrush or toothbrush, the temperature of marble, the softness of your bed sheets and nightclothes are important. Feel things, register and react.

Touch things and shut your eyes. Eliminate all mean textures. When you cook, wash your hands well with a favorite soap, dry them and then enjoy using your fingers to prepare food. Register good textures like Jell-O, Junket and whipped cream by feeling them with your hands, not just your forefinger. What results is a fresh awareness of your reaction to textures. Hold a glass in your hand before you consider buying it and run your fingers around the rim. Touch everything that appeals to you and make sure the textures around you are inviting. Think of the example of a bar of soap. When you enjoy the texture, the feel, combined with the size, shape, color and scent, then once the soap is in your hands you are pleased.

GROWING THROUGH YOUR MISTAKES

All creativity is based on trial and error. Take chances. Extend yourself. Dare. No experience is wasted if you grow through it, learn and come out wiser.

Tomorrow morning upon waking, lie in bed a few extra minutes and turn over a new leaf. Begin anew with the philosophy that your wholeness is contained inside your body. Create the image of yourself as whole.

W. S. Gilbert noted that "you can't get high aesthetic tastes, like trousers, ready made. . . ." You absorb taste and refine it over your lifetime. Taste has to do with selection and when you combine it with your personal style you acquire your own, not popular, taste. Start where you are right now: react subjectively to everything. Don't concern yourself with anything but your instinctive reaction—in art, clothes, decoration, flowers, wines, travel, food, literature, you be the *only* judge. Be true and your taste will be your own. I went through some awful phases—fake Spanish Colonial, awkward wrought-iron objects, harsh colors. But I loved my first apartment! Your taste is acquired by trial and error and naturally will change in time. Experiment. Keep an open mind. Your style emerges from sorting through everything and eliminating what isn't you.

There is far too much ugliness and pretension around us. A professor in design school taught his students that they would have to edit out roughly 90 percent of everything that is available—in furniture, textiles, clothes, books, colors—and then choose carefully, selecting sparingly from the remaining 10 percent. You too can gather your likes from approximately 10 percent of everything you are exposed to and then use that selection as your well to draw from. You will outgrow some of your current tastes in years to come, but record honestly where you are now and you will slowly, steadily grow in your level of appreciation and in nuance. When you weed out the negative 90 percent of all the input around you, the personally pleasurable 10 percent emerges and this gives you a clearer picture of your style.

Possibly you bought your dream house and took on more than you could comfortably afford. You'll have to cut way back until you get on your feet again. Before you invested in this house you may have spent your money in a variety of other ways and now you are merely rearranging how you spend what you have. If the house is deeply meaningful to you then this shift shouldn't be a burden. One young couple saved their change in order to afford paint to turn depressing, dull-colored rooms into fresh, cheerful ones. Enjoy a few sparsely furnished rooms. The Japanese believe "space to breathe" is important psychologically. You probably bought the house because you desperately needed more space both emotionally and physically. Enjoy the pure space and slowly build from there. How many of us have the luxury of a personally colored, empty room?

SEVEN VITAL PERSONAL STYLE POINTS TO REMEMBER

1) Seize Your Writing Tools

Write some notes to yourself. What are the materials you use? Did you select a spiral notebook, loose-leaf paper or a pad? Is the paper lined or plain? What color is the paper? Did you select a pen or a pencil? If a pen, what style? What color? How wide is the nib? What color is the ink? Or do you enjoy using colored marking pencils or felt-tip pens? Or a typewriter or word processor? I know a woman who always uses red ink. This is not an affectation, it is her style. My mother always used green ink. She even used green typewriter ribbon. What is your preference? I use different colors depending on my mood and the season. In December I use green and red ink. When I'm in the Caribbean I use turquoise. I enjoy hot rose pink, black, blue and purple ink for letter and journal writing. My journal notebooks and manuscripts are a mixture of many different colors. What is your personal style of communicating words on paper?

2) Personalizing Family Traditions

I know of a mother and daughter who grew to be so much alike they acquired the same mannerisms, looked and dressed alike and decorated in the same style and colors. Eventually it occurred to this attractive daughter, now in her early forties, that it was time to branch out and create a life of her own. It was difficult at first and she was insecure. Cora was especially resistant because she loved the way her parents decorated and their style of life was pleasant. Why change?

I've advised hundreds of people whose parents I've also helped decorate before them. This gravitational pull to follow the known, comfortable path is common. Influences of colors, textures and furniture designs can be passed on from one generation to the next like recipes or a love of literature. Furniture is often inherited. But whenever you try to re-create a look, it fails because it's not original. Examine how closely you adhere to the styles and customs you were exposed to while growing up so you can be sure the ones you live with now are right for you. If your mother made a big family Sunday dinner every week, you may, out of habit, feel you must, too. Yet there are sensible shortcuts to meal preparation for busy working women.

Your style may include many elements from your family, but it should be your own.

3) Take Clues from Others

If the world is your research center, observe the style and taste of people with whom you identify. Once you can define the elements that compose their style, pick up on specific details and see which ones work for you. Note what is attractive and charming in others so you can dream up ways to incorporate these ideas into your own style. I was using the powder room of a friend and looked down into her flower-painted wicker wastebasket. There was a white lace doily. When I inquired where she got the idea she smiled. "A European hotel." Many of the simple yet inspiring things you see can be adapted to work in some way in your own life.

Seek only images that are aesthetic and pleasing to your eye. Use a new idea. You may like the way someone ties a sash around her waist or how someone else has decorated a wide-brimmed straw hat with ribbons. Or you may go to a friend's house and in the bathroom there are pretty porcelain dishes filled with miniature perfume bottles and tiny boxes of guest soaps. These simple ideas can be picked up and brought home to be used in your own way.

Remember that all "things" are man-made. Seek objects that have originality. I have a large white wooden swan sitting on a blue granite ledge in front of a window in my office. This regal swan with a graceful neck was made in Maine as a decoy in 1890. I am attracted to this piece of folk art because it is one of a kind. The swan reminds me of our trips to the Bel-Air Hotel in Beverly Hills where swans swim in ponds, enhancing the spirit of the lovely gardens that surround this special hotel. Think of a woodcarver sitting at his bench shaping this beautiful object and how much pleasure he must have had as he became lost in the wonderful mystery of creativity.

Notice people and things that please you and look for continuity. If you love being with a happy couple, observe how they treat each other and notice their manners. Chances are they are accommodating to each other's individual personality. If you feel exhilarated after a weekend in New England, you may discover that you love white clapboard houses. Once a client who was originally from Connecticut and who now lives in Texas whitewashed his natural brick house exclaiming, "I'm only happy living in white houses." Another client told me that he detests claw-and-ball feet on tables or chairs but loves the graceful curves of French provincial furniture. His apartment reflects these happy curves because he identifies with this relaxed, easy style of furniture.

If you unexpectedly come across something that excites you and if you can afford it and feel it fits into your lifestyle, buy it.

Don't analyze why something speaks to you—whether it is a painting, a chandelier, a piece of antique jewelry, a tablecloth, a Windsor chair or a lavender dress. It is meant to be yours. Act. Clients of mine saw a table in the window of an antique shop on Madison Avenue on their way back to the Carlyle Hotel after dinner. Before leaving for the airport the next morning they went into the shop, bought the table and had it shipped to their home in California.

4) Secret Fantasies

We have dreams of what we'd like to look like, how we'd like to live, how our dream house should look. My daughters Alexandra and Brooke played "Prince and Princess" when they were little. They'd play house, dressing up in my evening dresses: they'd parade around in high heels and pile on lots of necklaces and makeup. It was all so glamorous. Our childhood fantasies are so grand! Adult fantasies often are too. How do you keep your dreams alive? So much good has come from artists having dreams, visualizing something unreal and then creating it in original works of art. A photographer, Alex Gotfryd, had a recurring dream of a shadowy woman in Venice. Finally he went to Venice to photograph his dream, and he created a splendid picture book of Venice.

You don't have to be an artist or a photographer in order to dream. I became a writer because of a dream. When I was pregnant with Alexandra I awoke one morning having dreamed I'd written a book. So, I did! We have the ability to make our fantasies happen.

5) Break Away

Think of all the differences in your lifestyle from that of the family you left behind. You'll immediately see that you have already taken your independent steps. Perhaps you live in a small apartment in the city rather than in a house in the country. Maybe you are a working mother. Or you are successful and earn a good salary as a co-breadwinner. You wear your hair long. Think of Mary Cassatt and Berthe Morisot and how they had to forge their own way in a nineteenth-century male-dominated French society.

> "THE ART OF BEING WISE IS THE ART OF KNOWING WHAT TO OVERLOOK."
> —*William James*

Think about the great writers whose parents begged them not to write but to get "normal" jobs. Think of the consequences if these style blazers hadn't followed their own dreams. Once you see the light, you don't have to look for outside encouragement because you know what your needs are and how you intend to express them.

6) Rate Your Fun Factor

How many different things in your life give you pleasure? If we enjoy the simple details of ordinary daily events like eating, sleeping, bathing and working, then 95 percent of our lives will be enriched.

Make a wish list. Write down ten practical things you'd like to do right now that would give you pleasure. Do you want to play golf? Do some drawing? What can you do today to give yourself gratification, enjoyment and delight? Go to see a Goya or Rembrandt exhibition? Go to a flower show? A lecture? Take a walk in the woods alone? Walk on a beach? Bake a carrot cake while listening to Bach? What can you do to indulge your senses? Tenderly caress your child and brush her hair? Drive to a park and listen to the birds and smell the grass? Make your favorite meal for dinner—shrimp brochette with onions, tomatoes and peppers you've marinated in wine and herbs? Have some Pinot Grigio wine? Sing your favorite hymn while cooking? Take time to walk around your house on an appreciation tour, feasting your eye on all your favorite paintings and family photographs?

Perhaps you want to purchase some potted scarlet geraniums for your indoor window boxes. Possibly you are longing to splurge and go to an expensive restaurant with a friend and have an unhurried visit in a sensuous atmosphere while enjoying good food together. Maybe you want to go to a bookstore and browse, eventually treating yourself to an expensive art book you've been longing to own, read, look through and savor. You can go home, make some tea and indulge your senses with the great painters. Or you may want to take a dance or exercise class. When you

GO!

have paid for a series of classes you can go whenever you have time or are in the mood.

If you feel the urge, you can reorganize your entire closet so that your seasonal clothes are separated and everything remaining in your closet suits and fits you and is properly ironed and ready to wear. Quick gratification! Perhaps you want to go to a linen shop and purchase a new set of pastel-flowered sheets at their white sale, transforming the look and feel of your whole bedroom. There is nothing prettier than a fresh, crisp bed dressed up with pretty sheets, a coverlet or quilt and lots of pillows in ironed, embroidered white pillowcases, suggesting romance, elegance and grace.

It could be that you want to restyle your hair by cutting it short, which could bring you more confidence. Order some pink love roses (out of the blue!) from White Flower Farm in Litchfield, Connecticut, and dream about planting your own rose garden. Ask your love to give you a sensual backrub leading to love. Or be exotic and order in some sushi from a local Japanese restaurant. Play a video of *The African Queen* starring Katharine Hepburn and Humphrey Bogart. When I recently asked my daughter Alexandra what she most wanted to do I was surprised to learn she wanted to "go to Sassoon and buy some of their salon shampoo. I crave the smell. It smells like almonds." It's fun to do simple, satisfying things that please us and remind us how lucky we are.

Next, make a dream list. Write down ten impractical things that would be fun and make you happy. Take off today for a deserted tropical island and write a novel! Leave your job to pursue your painting full-time. Go to Paris, shopping at luxurious boutiques and antique shops mornings and afternoons, stopping only for a scrumptious lunch in the courtyard at the Plaza Athénée under the geranium-flowered umbrellas. Go on a theater spree. Get tickets for the top five Broadway plays and go to one each evening followed by after-theater dinners at the Four Seasons, the romantic La Grenouille, Aureole and Lutèce. Go to a spa in Switzerland, lose twenty pounds and leave your stress behind you. Move to a larger house with Palladian architecture. Hire a full-time housekeeper. Have a peach orchard in your backyard. Win

"OUR FIRST PROBLEM IS NOT TO LEARN, BUT TO UNLEARN, TO CLEAR OUT SOME OF THE OLD ASSUMPTIONS."
—*Gloria Steinem*

WHO'S STOPPING YOU?

a Pulitzer Prize. Write a successful screenplay. Become a bishop. A publisher. A diplomat. Win a golf tournament. Sail in the Bermuda races. Fall in love. Co-star in a movie with Meryl Streep. Have another baby.

Rate the measure of your contentment, creativity and fun in your life from one to ten. I've posed this question to hundreds of people of all ages and backgrounds, and the average rating is five to six. A jaunty man in his eighty-second year loves every second of his life. "The older I become the luckier I get," claims Bill Hutton. He recently got a double eagle (two golf shots to the cup)—he couldn't find the ball on the green until he looked in the cup! He finds it fun to challenge himself, read, write and travel. He exclaims with a smile, "I rate the fun factor in my life 'ten.' I live at ten every day. I have everything I want." Notice he has everything he wants; he doesn't have everything.

In your notebook jot down your score and the date. When you concentrate on where you are, you can then aim toward where you want to be. Bill Hutton has found his personal style. Some of us will have "ten" days and moments, but few of us stay at ten all the time.

The essential secret is the way you picture your life. You must believe that your life is important both to you and to the world. You deserve every pleasure, every happiness. What do you see? My friend Charles Masson—an artist, a restaurateur and a writer—told Peter and me not long ago how much fun he's having writing his first book. "When you create, you are positive. When you don't create, you become frustrated. When you are frustrated you become mean."

7) "Do It Now"

Create something that will bring you pleasure. Plan a patch for a vegetable garden. Go to some pretty place. Refresh your spirit. Take action. Do something now to increase your contentment. Have a picnic at the beach. Giggle. Whistle. Be silly. Go dancing. What you do to amuse yourself defines your personal style. Arrange your life so you have a warm atmosphere at home. Bring together an attractive color combination to wear to your next meeting. Write a love letter. Call a friend. Life is energy, light and fire. Do something *now,* and what you choose to do will enhance your personal style.

GRACE NOTES

❧ Read several books during the same time period. One book will feed the next.

❧ Keep a small clipboard with a pad of paper attached to it in the car, in the bathroom, next to your bed and on the kitchen counter. Every time an idea comes to you, write it down. You can buy inexpensive plastic clipboards in bright colors, and if you want to cover them in fabric it's easy. Sew two pieces of fabric together on three sides and use a pretty ribbon on the top for a drawstring. This way you can easily remove the fabric for cleaning.

❧ Preparing a good meal can be as creative as composing a song or painting a picture; the criterion is whether it gives you pleasure. Are you passionate about what you're doing?

❧ When you look at something and you don't really like it, take the chance and try something else. Never say, "Maybe I'll get used to it."

❧ True passion can never be faked. When you're on a roll, you're in the flow. When things aren't right, make little changes until you feel yourself at the center of things, instead of feeling uncomfortable as an outsider.

❧ Be a caretaker only to the things that give you pleasure. Learn to edit yourself.

❧ We live our lives in chapters. Phases come and pass and we evolve, changed from where we were. Figuratively, we have to prepare an empty room for our newer self. This continual sorting out of the outward symbols of our inner self is cleansing to our soul. Weed out the clutter so there is room to grow.

❧ Try things out. Experiment. Break from your routine. When you do things the same way at the same time every day your senses become dulled. The more sensitive we become, the more unexpected surprises will come our way.

❧ Work with what you have—yourself. You can't look at a friend's legs and desire them; you have to work with your legs. For better or for worse say to yourself, "I am who I am" and be comfortable.

❧ People will always question what you do. If you believe in what you're doing and you're excited about it, be content and don't expect admiration. If praise comes as a by-product, that can be enjoyable too.

❧ Observe, absorb, inwardly digest and then decide, "Is this me?"

❧ Think of yourself as an original work of art.

❧ "All things are sweetened by risk." There is a thrill to adventure and your style depends on a daring spirit. Live by the motto "Nothing ventured, nothing gained."

❧ When you think back on your childhood, did you play with stuffed animals? Did you love their soft, cuddly feel? Or, did you prefer to have dolls to dress and undress? Did you climb trees, or enjoy sitting on tall rocks? Looking back and remembering gives us interesting clues because we carry through doing things we enjoy. When I was little I arranged and rearranged furniture and played in the garden.

❧ Try something new every day. This is a wonderful way to assure yourself that you'll continue learning. Wear a blouse that didn't come with a suit, use napkins different from the ones that match the tablecloth. Use different plates. Experiment with a new color ink with your stationery. Arrange vegetables in a basket rather than fruit or flowers for your centerpiece. Float some flower petals in a fishbowl of water. Float short, fat candles in the bowl with the petals rather than using candelabra. Make it a game.

❧ Walk barefoot in the elements—sand, wet grass, pebbles. The more sensitive the soles of your feet, the better. You want to feel the delight of the cool, the warm and the tickle.

❧ Go out and play in the rain. Be grateful you don't have an umbrella. Let your hair get drenched, as though you were swimming. Feel the exhilarating splash of water's vitality.

❧ Take all the objects off a tabletop. Do the same with another tabletop; now switch objects so you can see everything freshly.

❧ A handshake reveals your sense of yourself. Make it your style to shake hands with confidence—firmly, with your whole hand, looking pleasantly into the other person's eyes. In America this is a neglected ritual we could all improve.

YOUR GRACE NOTES

TWO

Your PERSONAL STYLE AT HOME AND ENTERTAINING

YOUR PERSONALITY DICTATES YOUR STYLE
AT HOME

hen a writer from *House & Garden (HG)* called me to inquire about the design style of one of my clients I told him about the client's vibrant personality, her amazing energy, her love of life, her intellect, her passion for color and love of pretty things. The writer listened patiently and then pressed on for some copy—he wanted to know about my client's design philosophy. I explained that my client chooses colors, furniture, fabrics and objects that she and her husband love; her attitudes about her life guide all her design decisions. When an interior designer begins to understand a person, it becomes possible to translate their spirit into their physical environment.

When I begin a decorating job, I ask lots of questions, and with a family I interview my clients separately. In addition to learning about the use the rooms will be put to, I do a lot of

THE INNER AND
OUTER ASPECTS OF
YOUR LIFE SHOULD
BE IN HARMONY.

detective work about their interests and how they like to spend their leisure time. I inquire about the way they want to feel, what mood they're after, what colors they want to incorporate. I get clues from what I see and what I don't see. I ask if I can look around. Often my clients describe what they like and don't like, what works and what doesn't. (Sometimes their actual rooms suggest otherwise.) My questions and their answers lead to finding solutions that bring great delight.

Room by room I inquire: how much time do you want to spend in here? A room can only express a personality if it is used. Do you use your living room in the daytime? Is it a place for family and close friends when you are not entertaining? Do you want to read in your living room? Do you want bookcases? How much closed storage do you need? Do you want to do any projects in the room—say, sew or work on scrapbook albums or have a writing desk? The question of formality always comes up. How formal do you want the room to be? What is more important to you, formality or comfort?

Do you want to have plants and fresh flowers? Do you like to garden? How often do you entertain? On an average, how many people do you have as guests in your home at once? How many people do you want to seat? Do you ever want to have a friend sleep in this room? Are there times you'll need to rearrange the furniture for committee meetings or large receptions? Do you rearrange the furniture seasonally? Where do you put the Christmas tree?

Is your fireplace wood-burning? How often do you use it? Do you want the room to feel a bit spare or do you want it to be filled with objects and personal memorabilia? Do you intend to have framed family photographs on display? Do you enjoy arranging flowers?

How do you want the lighting to feel? How much pattern do you like? Do you like clearly defined patterns or more impressionistic designs? How big a scale should the fabric patterns be? Is there any kind of material you loathe? Do you like silk, wool and cottons more than synthetics? Do you prefer more tailored

WHERE DO YOU LIKE TO SIT TO READ?

STYLE IS THE OUTWARD EXPRESSION OF YOUR INNER SELF.

details to ruffles and frills? How strong should the colors be? Are there any colors you do not like?

What wood tones do you enjoy most? Mahogany, fruitwood, rosewood, oak, teak, walnut or pine? Do you like inlaid wood or do you prefer carving? Do you like decorated painted furniture—like pieces from Scandinavia or Pennsylvania Dutch?

What kind of lines do you like, straight or curved? What are your favorite furniture styles? Do you prefer antiques to reproductions? Do you think of yourself as being comfortable with simple lines? How much luxury makes you comfortable?

Do you consider yourself a collector? Would you ever buy a piece of furniture because you fell in love with it and then make a place for it in your home? Or do you like to have a master plan and follow it to the letter? How much time do you intend to put into this project? Do you enjoy the process of decorating or are you only interested in the final result?

How important is art to you? Who are some of your favorite artists? If you could hang your favorite painting in your living room from anywhere in the world (pretend it is a magical gift), describe the painting. If you could have one magical object what would it be?

How important is the comfort of your upholstered furniture? Do you worry when family and friends put their feet up on your furniture? How do you want to treat your windows? How much privacy do you need? What is a working budget for the room? Do you want to establish a master plan and spend the expenses over a period of, say, three to five years? Or do you want to decide on everything, estimate and order things and pay as soon as required?

I love interviewing children of all ages. I ask them if they'll show me where their secret place is, because all children live in a fantasy world. A secret place is usually a cozy spot in the bedroom where a child feels safe from the world. Some questions include: What are your favorite colors? Where do you love to paint? When you read, show me where you like to go and how you like to sit or lie down. Where do you like to do your homework? Do you

WHAT MADE YOU
SMILE TODAY?

have enough light? Where do you store your toys? Do you have enough storage space? How do you like to entertain your friends? How often do you have friends over? Are you allowed to eat in your room? How many friends do you like to have spend the night at one time? Where do they sleep? Do you consider yourself neat? Would you rather pick up your own room so you know where everything is or do you like someone else to help you? How much time do you spend alone in your room? Do you shut the door? Do you listen to music? Do you like a dark room for sleeping or do you like a little light?

Do you like your clothes? How often do you get dressed up? Show me your favorite outfit. What is the softest fabric you have in your closet?

Is your bed comfortable? How many stuffed animals do you have? Which is the softest, most cuddly animal? What are their names?

What do you want to do when you grow up? What is your favorite game?

Usually I sit on the floor with a child so I don't appear like a giant. I prefer being alone although the curiosity of many parents gets in the way of complete privacy. Children are so responsive to their serious interview (I take notes!), they become quite animated. One adorable five-year-old boy announced to me he wanted to be a decorator when he grows up "because I like measuring furniture and you don't have to work too hard because you always talk to people."

Because each client's situation and style are different, the way you and clients answer these questions, room by room, determines the direction your decorating will take and the way your rooms will grow. Just as sanding and preparation are 95 percent of a good paint job, these questions reveal clues to how dreams can be turned into reality.

I remember flying to Chicago to work on a house in a nearby suburb. There was a heavy snowstorm and when I arrived at the house there was a fire crackling in the library, where I was given a few minutes to sit and absorb the atmosphere before I was told to "get to work; time is money." I smiled, got up from the warmth

DO YOU ENJOY
WEARING HATS?

and comfort of the room and thought, "I *am* working." Decorators don't have to be on a stepladder measuring a window in order to be useful to a client.

Walk through your own rooms, one at a time. Ask yourself revealing questions. Think aloud. Do you feel a room is too quiet, verging on dullness? Is one room strong, does it shout? Is a room too crowded or too empty? A woman from Buffalo did this exercise in her living room and admitted to me that her room reflected her husband and three sons and was far too masculine for her taste. Sarah decided to move the portrait of her grown, married sons that hung over the sofa and put it in their paneled study, replacing it with a sunny flower-strewn landscape painting that I helped her find. For the sofa she selected a yellow-background chintz with big bouquets of flowers that puts a smile on her face.

As you put your towels away in the linen closet, question whether the colors are in your current color palette. Simply by being more aware of what delights you, you can make little changes to bring more of these happy associations to your rooms.

Often when you think out loud you identify reasons for why things are the way they are and you see how many of these situations are no longer current. This observation can help you appreciate what you really love.

DON'T ACCEPT EVERYTHING AS YOU SEE IT.

When I am in a client's home, in a specific room, and I ask which are the treasures and which the least loved objects, I hear happy stories of a table found in the window of an antique shop and I hear about the mistake or the compromise that eventually has to be replaced. "It was never right," I hear with a feeling of regret. Pretend I'm in a room in your home and tell me the same personal stories I'd hear if I were able to be there!

If you were to tell me that you want to turn a room into a library-dining room, how would you want that to be accomplished? What style? French provincial? Or a room with a garden feeling? Once you identify that you want to move in a certain direction, you are free to pick up ideas on how to accomplish your goals. Be specific about the mood, theme and use of each room. I have clients who admitted feeling intimidated decorating their paneled library. They aren't avid readers, preferring sports and games—so we turned the room into a game room. The theme was the outdoors, with a bird-patterned chintz and lots of hunting prints. The bookcases had miniature horses and birds interspersed among the books. I learned that the woman had been a champion horseback rider in her youth so this room held special meaning for her.

Solutions become more obvious once you create a dialogue among what you envision, what you have to work with and how much you're willing to change.

One of the favorite questions I ask when I'm in a client's home is, "Do you have a special treasure you want me to see?" I'm always surprised by the answer. One client from San Francisco showed me a picture of her three-year-old and five-year-old daughters and said with a smile, "This is the treasure of our house." I met the children within minutes when they came home from playing at a neighbor's house. I could easily understand why: Samantha and Christina are angelic.

Most often, however, I am shown objects, art and furniture, and the treasures have fascinating stories. I see trophies, medals, framed degrees. I was in the small library of a woman who gives a huge amount of money to the opera each year and she showed me sketches of different operas framed as wall decorations. One of my biggest surprises was when a client looked at me and said, "My view, my music system and my friends." One woman pointed to her garden.

Every client I've ever interviewed confirmed my personal belief that no one can be comfortable living in a style, no matter how authentic and correct, that is not intimate, symbolic and original. Elsie de Wolfe said in her popular watershed book *House in Good Taste,* published in 1915, that there could be no two living rooms exactly alike in scheme "if they were lived in." We all want to bring to our rooms what we know and understand. One of the definitions of the word "home" is "an environment that offers security and happiness." Another is "a valued place regarded as a refuge . . . comfortable and relaxed, at ease." Home is meant to give us an easy competence and familiarity. Clients have taught me how much they long to treasure what they have around them.

DO YOU ENJOY MOVING OBJECTS AROUND, OR HAVING A PLACE FOR EVERYTHING?

"BE CAREFUL OF WHAT YOU THROW AWAY."
—*Eleanor McMillen Brown*

As I have mentioned, I've been an admirer of Gabrielle (Coco) Chanel since I was nineteen. Chanel's taste in the decorative arts was a bit more elaborate than her taste in couture, but she had the same assurance and unquestionable confidence in decorating as she did in fashion. She said once in her measured voice, "An interior is the natural projection of the soul and Balzac was right to give as much importance to it as to the way people dressed."

Coco Chanel loved her home and was thought by many to be a homebody. The three rooms she lived in from 1954 until her death were a "magic grotto." Every detail was thought out with loving care. I never met Coco Chanel but I've seen so many of her well-known possessions and I know people who adored her. I'm fascinated that her ability to revolutionize how women dressed was only a part of her talent. If she had decided to become an interior designer instead, she would have become one of the best in history.

Looking at her favorite objects teaches us about her passions— Coromandel screens, mirrors, crystal, chandeliers, and gilt and lacquered wood. She considered corn her "lucky charm," and her collection of lions represents her astrological sign. For all her love of luxurious decoration, however, her favorite chair was a modest English eighteenth-century side chair with a shaped ladder back and a saddle seat covered in brown leather.

A successful businessman felt his house was crowding him. It had been purchased twenty years earlier when he and his wife Marsha were raising three young children and he was working around the clock climbing the corporate ladder. Now that Tom had "made it," though his children were grown and no longer lived at home, he felt the urge to live in a larger house with big open rooms and more surrounding land. A friend who sold real estate was notified to be on the lookout and to call when a great house came on the market.

Several months passed and Marsha and Tom went about their life as usual. When the phone call did come they were shown a house and both of them fell in love with it and bought it without showing it to their grown children or thinking twice. It was meant to be. The decorator who had always helped them select fabrics

"I HAD THREE CHAIRS IN MY HOUSE: ONE FOR SOLITUDE, TWO FOR FRIENDSHIP, THREE FOR SOCIETY."
—*Henry David Thoreau*

and coordinate colors was hired to help them turn this grand Southern plantation-style house into their dream house. It was purchased through an estate sale and had been lived in previously by an elderly widow. But something went wrong. Suddenly this nice, unassuming decorator began fantasizing that the Campbells were going to change their lifestyle and that Marsha would descend that wide staircase in a long green taffeta gown. The chandelier in the dining room was made for the set of the movie *Gone With the Wind* but it wasn't sold with the house and the Campbells had no intention of changing their personal style of living.

They are extremely private people and love the openness of the house with lots of French doors and sliding glass doors giving onto terraces with cascading lawn trees and a pond beyond. This house represents the culmination of a lifetime of hard work. Now, anticipating their children marrying and having their own children, the Campbells are thinking ahead to the joys of having their family come to visit. Marsha and Tom haven't changed their patterns at all, and their big, gracious house tucked away on a large open piece of land outside of Charleston is for their own pleasure and sense of security, not a statement to the world that they've arrived.

Everything got squared away in time. The well-meaning decorator who'd become overly impressed with the grandeur of the "estate" had lost sight of just who her clients were. Rightly so, she was gently taken off the assignment. The Campbells' three children love the new house and the mood and spirit of the "little house" has been maintained. The drawing room is a chintz-strewn music room and the house sings a youthful, charming, happy melody.

The Campbells had to christen the big house and have it bend to their less formal style of living. They, like most of us, live in space designed and built for someone else's life. Statistics illustrate that less than one percent of us live in spaces we have designed for our own style of life. The third President of the United States, Thomas Jefferson, is an exception. Monticello, a Palladian villa built as his dream house on top of a mountain, was an obsession for him for nearly sixty years. Professor Jack McLaughlin, in his biography *Jefferson and Monticello: The Biography of a Builder,* states that "those who construct their own shelter replicate themselves, at their deepest and significant level, in their houses." Apparently young Jefferson was so determined that his architectural vision would mirror his soul, he tore down the first Monticello after years of construction because he felt it failed to be him. He started all over again and the second Monticello was "to be the seat of domestic bliss and of Southern hospitality."

Jefferson tried to have his house reflect his personal style, and succeeded. Most of us have to turn a house, an apartment or a room into a space that satisfies our aesthetic, fundamental and spiritual needs. Contouring an environment to suit your unique needs is a basic human urge and must be satisfied in order for you to feel whole and empowered.

"IT'S NICE TO RETURN HOME EACH DAY TO SOMETHING INTENSELY PERSONAL."
—*Stanley Barrows*

SELECTING YOUR PERSONAL STYLE OF HOME

One of the main objectives of this book is to help you find a unique and colorful style that nourishes you and is beautiful in every sense of the word. Your house or apartment is a frame to house *you;* decorating should not be a makeover of the personality, it should reflect the authentic maturity of your life so far. The more at peace you are with yourself and the more you like yourself, the more fun this revealing and sensuous process will become for you.

There are many excellent magazines that help us see slices of other people's lives, yet they aren't really proper clues. We never know enough. Once I was lecturing and was asked why the magazines rarely give room dimensions along with the photographs. The reason is simple: most of the furniture has been rearranged for the picture and the way it is set up for photography doesn't work in real life. Dimensions would give this secret away.

Create your own reality at home. Through your imagination, your memory associations and desires, you can manipulate space and make it yours. You have to feel comfortable and the rooms have to flow together in a harmonious way so you'll feel continuous delight as you move around your home. The only way to develop a truly authentic personal style is to try to please one person—yourself. If you have a spouse and family, you have a partner or a team, but no one else should be allowed to enter into this quest. Once you determine the direction in which you want to move and you need someone to help turn your dreams into a beautiful reality, then you can share your thoughts with a professional.

Try not to seek help from non-professionals. Once you inquire of a friend, "What do you think?" you are evading personal style. What your friends think isn't relevant. You have a unique point of view. You're going to end up doing what feels best to you anyway, so don't confuse the issue. If you need to think through your concepts with someone, choose a professional, who is trained to listen well and guide you toward your fresh, pure style. Clients come to a professional designer with their ideal and then tell us how they want us to help them realize it. The question asked is, "How do I accomplish this abstract vision of my life so it becomes physical, tangible reality?" Ask yourself, "How do I want to feel in this room?" Then gather the building blocks that will bring your wishes together. Billy Baldwin understood that when people are comfortable in a room the room is real, and once a room is real it is alive. Often we lose our focus and become outer-directed, searching all around us for our own style, forgetting the obvious.

One quick glance at what we know of medieval days reminds us that the concepts of privacy and individuality are relatively recent phenomena. The idea of the single-purpose room is relatively new in historical perspective. When I began decorating in the early sixties period rooms were still being reproduced, and while they weren't scholarly replicas, they were put together to bring you back in time to an earlier age you never fully understood. Those who broke with the past fell for Art Deco and Art Nouveau styles that were extravagant and sensuous and left the past behind. These styles, however, were stage sets and therefore short-lived. An eclectic look made the most sense, but the emphasis wasn't on one's personal experience and passions as much as on a "look"

IMAGINE.

WHERE IS THE CENTER OF YOUR LIFE?

that implied a certain worldliness and frame of reference. There was a tendency to package nostalgia. Ralph Lauren markets "lifestyle." It wasn't his lifestyle and maybe not yours or mine; it was his dream of a family tradition he never had but sought.

I believe that one of the most unfortunate styles is minimalism. While I recognize that everyone is entitled to his own preferences, minimalism depresses me personally. If we can't live in our own bedrooms, bathrooms and kitchens where can we live? I remember having a fierce debate at the New School in New York City, at a panel discussion where I argued the virtues of personal clutter at home with an editor who sang the virtues of minimalism. Black leather sofas with tubular chrome frames, set in lonely fashion on industrial gray carpeting, lend an air of one who has no time to live. No time for home.

Personal expression through art, books, textiles, color patterns, rugs, objects and flowers is the way we show our appreciation and taste. Minimalism leaves one with sensual, visual, aesthetic and psychological deprivation. While the workmanship may be perfect and oh-so-expensive, it is uptight and lacks human warmth and charm. Minimalism for a home is deadly because real life is not allowed. It leaves me hungry. Real life is clutter. It messes up. Ah, but minimalism photographs beautifully. No people, no pets, no food, no color, no mess, no fun. Tom Wolfe's witty book, *From Bauhaus to Our House,* takes a real stab at "the leanness the cleanness the spareness of it all."

What do you love from the past? Is it old Windsor chairs and quilts and hooked rugs? Or do you adore Oriental rugs, needlepoint, Aubusson pillows and lace curtains at the window? I have an affinity for the French country style. My passion for French provincial furniture grew from my travels through France and visiting French families and decorating there.

For several years now American designers have promoted the English country look. What's wrong with an American or French or Swedish or Dutch or Greek country look? For a while in the seventies there was a Spanish look. If a department store has a special exhibition featuring India, suddenly there is an Indian look.

Beware of all these "looks" and styles which are trendy and

easily become tiresome and dated. I happen to enjoy chintz and find it refreshing in city apartments where we are starved for nature. When I read in the newspaper that chintz is on its way out I smile. Trying to pooh-pooh chintz is like knocking gardens. If chintz is romantic and pretty and if that's what makes you happy, how could you not think of using a chintz?

Billy Baldwin had the same chintz in his garden cottage living room in Nantucket that Brooke Astor has in her New York library. He loved the way the brown stripes and flowers emphasized his exposed wooden beams. After years of living with solids Billy got bored and wanted chintz. At the end of his life he changed his mind. We should use Billy as an example of how we can spend our whole life developing our personal style and then changing our attitude when the spirit has moved us.

KNOCKING DOWN WALLS

You hold the power to change the given physical configuration of your environment into a space that reflects your spirit and convictions. There are times when you have to redesign the actual space—knocking down walls and opening up ceilings. In some pre-World War II apartment buildings there is as much as three feet of "crawl space" above the plaster ceiling. Mechanics could repair equipment stored there. You could use this space to add height to your rooms or to hide air-conditioning ducts. If a wall becomes an emotional barrier, chances are it isn't entirely structural and most of it can be removed. If a wall has beams that need to remain, they could become free-standing columns opening up space to give you a flow of more light.

Approximately 90 percent of the walls that create individual rooms are arbitrary and were created for a different family to suit their individual needs. Other than supporting beams, most electrical, plumbing and air conditioning needs can be relocated.

Walk around your space and analyze how you feel about each room. When my daughters Alexandra and Brooke were toddlers, the kitchen of our apartment was small, yet I wanted to see them when they ate their meals in the next room; by knocking through the kitchen wall that had been a physical and emotional barrier, we were able to have a country kitchen divided by a peninsula. The girls appeared fascinated by my culinary experiments and I felt I was doubling the meaning of my time by being with them as I worked in the kitchen. Why have a wall isolate you against your will?

Think of walls as protection for privacy and as dividers. Remove unnecessary barriers. Think of all your rooms opening up to a sunny garden or a peaceful beach. Often there are walls blocking the light and view from your windows, so many halls appear cramped and dark. A Scandinavian photographer eliminated the halls in his apartment by having large rooms open directly onto each other. Long, skinny walkways with no windows or natural light depressed him. He needed to live surrounded by windows spilling in natural light.

The actress Marsha Mason bought a two-bedroom apartment in a building constructed in the thirties and proceeded to move every interior wall so the entire space opened to an incredible view and light. The few walls that were built act to accentuate the openness while adding to the feeling of security and privacy. The kitchen-laundry area, the dining room and living room are one sweeping space imaginatively laid out with steps, platforms and an island that divides the space without the use of walls. There is nothing closed in or hiding from the sweeping views. Even her dressing room is open to windows and can be closed off for privacy with curtains and sliding pocket doors. One bathroom has pocket doors at each end (the door slides into a wall) so when that room is not in use the surrounding light spills into the space.

If you can't knock down an entire wall because you need the two rooms to function for separate purposes, see if it is feasible to center the connecting door opposite a window so the open door can allow the window and light to be visible from the next room.

When my firm renovates for clients we always try to have walls placed so that the most natural light floods into rooms, and into spaces that don't have windows. Walls don't have to go to the ceiling. It is possible to divide space with a solid wall 60 inches high. Decorative folding screens can be painted differently on each side; arched openings can bring in light.

Walls are necessary for privacy, for quiet and for hanging art and shelving books. Other than bedrooms and bathrooms, many interior walls break up the flow of space and block light. Walk through your home and examine the location of the walls and analyze their function. A client did this and discovered he had a great view from a hall going into a bathroom. By eliminating a wall which blocked the light and view, he expanded his bathroom and made it appear even larger by mirroring the wall opposite the window and above his double sinks. Possibly you enter your house by a cramped entryway and you'd rather knock down the walls to free the space so that you'll walk into a grander, more open sweep. Jack Lenor Larsen, the world-famous designer and textile genius, has movable walls in his loft apartment in Manhattan, fashioned after the Japanese concept of flexible walls. Jack stores his objects and supplies behind these stretched China-silk wall panels, leaving pure, uncluttered wall surfaces. The overall effect is calm, serene and transporting.

It is perfectly possible that you are happy with your existing walls. If you are an art collector you will never have enough wall space to hang all your pictures. You need walls to house your books. The space under your windows on an exterior wall can be utilized for books and won't appear to take up the whole wall. We did this in our bedroom and installed a white ledge 22 inches deep with an apron depth of 4 inches under the windowsill so we can store books below and display books and magazines face up. On the walls on either side of the windows, paintings are hung.

Concentrate and study the walls that house your personality. Do they represent your personal style? A client who is extremely musical hangs quilts as art on his walls; the quilted cotton absorbs his sound and reminds him of his growing up in Kentucky. You may prefer to hang paintings or a collection of photographs. You may choose to amass sentimental pictures of friends and family on the walls of your study or office. In my husband Peter's law office he has one 20-foot-long wall filled with photos of friends

YOU ARE IN CONTROL
OF YOUR LIFE.

WELCOME CHANGE.

framed and hung from baseboard to ceiling. If you're a cook you may want to display your collection of copper pots and pans on the walls of your kitchen. If you are a playwright you may want to frame your Playbills and hang them on your bedroom wall. Or you may want to hang your basket collection on the walls of your breakfast room. We have a narrow bedroom hall we transformed by hanging a collection of flowered watercolors by Lord Alastair Gordon interspersed with Pearlware Wedgwood green, pink and yellow porcelain plates.

DO YOUR HOMEWORK

Be a sponge. Open your eyes. Get inspiration from everything around you. Open your world to a wider vision so you will have lots of imaginative options for each area in your home. One of my clients got the idea for the design of the raised panel doors in her library from the Christian Science Church she regularly attends.

A woman with great personal style keeps a running "dream house" file and edits it regularly so she distills her taste and style, using fresh inspiration from things she sees and clips out of magazines. Karen's "dream house" folder has beautiful over-door details, a carved shell motif on a cabinet, a photograph of a pretty chintz, some lamp designs, porcelain designs and furniture that appeals to her. Flipping through Karen's folder is fun because she only includes things she really loves. This is an excellent discipline because it is far easier to identify what you don't like than to pinpoint what you do like. Make a habit of noting everything that pleases you. Once you determine what kinds of styles and patterns you like, then it is often possible to find natural places to incorporate these ideas into your surroundings. The pink tone in a sunset sky could be the envelope lining color for your blue personalized stationery.

Put random details and beautiful pictures in your style notebook so you never waste an idea. Like having your passport easily available so that you're ready to go anywhere on the spur of the moment, gathering fresh ideas for a house or apartment is something you can do all your life. Whether you move or fix up where you live now, your clippings will help make the most of what you have to work with. When you are prepared, more serendipitous surprises tend to happen.

A widow friend met a man whose wife had died eight years earlier, and two weeks later she was totally swept off her feet when he proposed marriage. Jane didn't hesitate to accept and within two months she was planning the wedding and the honeymoon. Surprise! Henry insisted that Jane redo his house "to make it ours." She was prepared because of her style notebook and could happily barrel ahead.

In my *Book of Color* I wrote about starting a color box. Color is key to self-expression. To create a color box, put into a pretty box snips of fabric, yarn, scraps of paper—anything that represents your favorite colors—so all these tiny clues come together into a cohesive color scheme. The inspiration for *Book of Color* began with my own scrapbook of beautiful photographs, clipped out of magazines over a twenty-five-year period, showing how I always respond to color schemes in decorating that are inspired from nature. This personal scrapbook showed me how my own style has evolved over all these years. You too might paste some of the pictures from your inspirational folder into a private scrapbook of intimate delights. Paste your favorite picture on the cover. You can buy pads of white paper at an art supply store and glue your pictures in place with rubber cement. Over the years I've created dozens of scrapbooks with pictures too beautiful to throw away and divided the images up into categories.

These picture books need no words. The pictures express visual images that you relate to emotionally. If there is something you don't like in a picture, cut it out and throw it away. Crop ugliness and save only the essence of beauty. If you do decide to paste in your pretty pictures you will find that in time you will be defining a very original, imaginative and revealing personal style. Your own surroundings should become a mirror of the mood, colors and images you've gathered and put into these picture books.

WHAT'S THE MOST FUN THING YOU'RE GOING TO DO TODAY?

Stanley Barrows, an interior design professor and classical scholar who taught many of the top American interior designers, told me recently, "I advise people to concentrate on intrinsic values." As you look through the old *House & Garden* magazines (before the name was changed to *HG)* I'm sure you will agree that some of those pictures are breathtakingly beautiful and should be preserved. We rarely take time to reread a magazine, so having your personal scrapbooks adds hours of joy, both in the selection and in the review of page after page of revealing private delights.

ASSOCIATION

One of the richest ways to find your personal style at home is through association. You can be in a garden and decide that it has the mood and spirit you'd love to create for your living room. You can choose sun-drenched flower colors and use lots of chintz and botanical prints. Your house can be like a beach on a deserted island. Suddenly you become aware that your need for simplicity or an island escape far away from noise and pollution can be translated into wholesome, simple rooms at home. What you enjoy doing when you are away from home affects how you express yourself when you decorate. Your library can be done in rich greens, reminding you of the mountains. If you love the earthiness of the adobe houses in Santa Fe you can translate that feeling to Vermont or Washington or to a city apartment. Whenever you experience beauty that moves you, think about ways to translate the feelings to your home so that it is empowered with these happy associations. My love of Provence always finds expression in our kitchen. Even a blue-patterned Pierre Deux napkin or apron can symbolize the mood and spirit of that area of France.

There may be touches you'll want to retain from your upbringing even though you are a different person from your parents. Their style was of a different generation, another time. Most of the happy associations you have may be more recent in your life.

"WHEN I WAS YOUNG, WE *ALWAYS* HAD MORNINGS LIKE THIS."
—*A. A. Milne*

You will find a way of communicating these personal experiences into your style. I've found this to be particularly true of people who have traveled to exotic places and fallen in love with another culture, say Japan, although their parents may never have left Idaho. The greater your exposure, the greater your ability to bring colorful, powerful and meaningful associations into your home— regardless of how foreign they may be to your own heritage. They mean something to you because of your exposure through travel.

I remember the profound influence my trip around the world had on me when I was studying interior design. Suddenly I expanded my frame of reference from the confines of New England to France, Italy, Greece, India, Burma and Japan. And once I experienced the architecture and styles of those beautiful places, each with a unique spirit, I wanted my own style to incorporate some of the flavor and nuances of these places that touched my heart.

There's no such thing as pure individual style in a home. Houses are affected by the place in which they are located. They are likely to resemble the mood and attitude of community—say an island like Nantucket, built by whalers, with a symmetrical balance. Most of the houses on Main Street were topped by "widow's walks" where the wives would go to look for homecoming ships. Two hundred years later the inhabitants bring their own distinction to the interior of these classic houses and often change the inside so that the living room faces the water in the back of the house rather than the road, providing more privacy.

Wherever you are in one physical place, through your imagination you can create a richly individual feeling to your home. Throughout your lifetime experiences you have gathered bits and pieces of memorabilia that are profoundly meaningful to you. Because of their authenticity, your rooms become like your own flesh and blood.

When we leave our parents we begin our individual search for our real "home." I always lived in extremely old houses which my parents enjoyed restoring—sad, run-down houses that became bandbox preservations. In the past thirty years I have lived in four

"AN INTERIOR IS THE NATURAL PROJECTION OF THE SOUL . . ."
—*Coco Chanel*

IF YOU THINK SOMETHING IS WORTHWHILE, IT IS.

different apartments with none of the charm or history of the three old houses (one in Massachusetts and two in Connecticut) where I grew up. Yet I associate where I live now with the privacy, calm and beauty of the houses of my childhood. The apartments I've lived in and decorated in New York all have an informal country atmosphere which makes me feel comfortable and at home. I love lots of bare wood floors and shutters at the windows to suggest gardens beyond, and I have trees and flowering plants inside to give me the illusion I'm in the country.

However, my references are entirely different from those of my parents. I have a country kitchen inspired by many trips to the South of France, and our library-sitting room is our island escape. We walk into our library and it's as if we feel the gentle tumbling of the ocean waves which are in synchronization with our heartbeats; the noise, dirt and danger of New York are washed away. This room could be on a Greek Island, in Bermuda or in the Caribbean, and yet it is in a crowded urban setting. The windows overlook the back of another building which is so ugly we put in tubular incandescent light strips around the sides and top of the two windows and installed white shutters we keep closed. White roller window shades hide the black hole and bounce white light through the slates of the shutters. Sitting and reading in this room, listening to the tape we made of ocean waves, is as comfortable, private and relaxing as an island escape.

Use your positive association to bring your own heartbeat to your rooms. Make them breathe your fresh air, not stale air from another life. Bring home symbols and treasures you hold dear. Archaeological fragments, if you're allowed to take them, mean more if you went on the dig to Cyprus yourself. Display your trophies or your beautiful finds.

List all the really wonderful memories that pop into your mind. Look around *your* house or apartment. Be sure your home is alive with memories. Do you remember where you found a favorite pitcher or basket? The physical, tangible objects we gather can open doors to happy moments we've lived and can retrieve through these strong memory associations. Our possessions are a real part of our history.

HOW TO EDIT

"HOW MANY THINGS
I CAN DO
WITHOUT!"
—*Socrates*

The late Van Day Truex, designer, painter, former head of Parsons School of Design and former creative head of Tiffany, instructed his students to "control, edit, distill." Billy Baldwin, until his death in December 1983, was considered to be the foremost society decorator. His clients included Jacqueline Kennedy, Cole Porter and the Washington social leader Mrs. William McCormick Blair. Billy once said, "Beauty is always simple." Van and Billy were great friends and they were the biggest heroes to American designers and decorators because they shunned pretentiousness. They lived by Keats's famous words from "Ode on a Grecian Urn": "Beauty is truth, truth beauty—that is all ye know on earth, and all ye need to know." Both men understood that caned furniture can be charming in a New York apartment—it is simple, not grand, affordable and attractive. Van and Billy had seen the best of the best and their eye was so strict they only wanted to feast on true beauty. Both of them practiced editing in their work.

I learned how to edit from Eleanor McMillen Brown. She believed that "to develop in taste, quality and personality one is obliged to respect the past, accept the present and look with enthusiasm toward the future." She understood that eclecticism is the result of one's own experiences and one's own knowledgeable taste. One of Mrs. Brown's mentors, William Odom, who collaborated with her on acquiring fine antiques abroad in the 1920s, believed that one should not own a single thing that isn't beautiful. Odom did not accept something simply because it had romantic associations. He preferred to leave a space bare rather than clutter it up with a second-rate object. Under his tutelage, Mrs. Brown acquired classic eighteenth- and early nineteenth-century antiques, mostly from France and Italy, that graced her clients' houses and greatly increased in value.

Odom's taste was precise. Eleanor would watch him walk over to a table and, with a surgeon's concentration, rearrange the objects on the tabletop until they were in ideal harmony. "No one has a

better eye for arrangement than William Odom," she told her assistants. A living room tabletop might display a few books in a stack, a pretty box, a small painting on an easel and a small bouquet of flowers near a lamp. A dresser in a bedroom could have a small wood or lacquered tray, some decorative crystal bottles, a comb, brush and mirror set and some framed family photographs.

You want to gather all the romantic, nostalgic memorabilia you relate to and then edit out what you don't love, what is not beautiful, or what you've outgrown. Weed out the ordinary, the things that choke the objects you are most passionate about. The biggest mistake most of us make when arranging our tabletops is that we tend to put on too many objects so the eye doesn't register the main ones.

Your entire life is a continuous "work in progress." Your beginning is behind you and your end is before you and change is the only way in which you can express your personal growth and awareness. It is not a sign of restlessness to continue to refine your personal style. As you grow, your style must express you so your whole personality is integrated. Think what you have learned in, say, a ten-year period. You've traveled, you've experienced many personal changes and added some new objects and ornaments to your surroundings.

Edit your possessions. Take some of your belongings and either give them away, put them away for safekeeping or, in many cases, throw them away. Whenever you acquire something new make it part of your style to give something away. You don't have to be a minimalist to be a strict editor. Stretch yourself to live with the most beautiful things your eyes see and your heart tells you to truly love. Most of us are warehousing stuff we honestly can live without. I heard a story from a couple who bought their bedroom furniture at the Salvation Army thirty years ago and are afraid to replace it. "It might be harmful to our marriage." But the fact remains that their thrifty find at the beginning of their marriage no longer fits their lifestyle and greatly impedes their personal style. It's best not to be too blinded by sentiment while searching for style.

ENJOY THE CONTENTMENT OF DOING ONE THING AT A TIME.

"GRANT ME TO BECOME BEAUTIFUL IN THE INNER MAN."

—*Socrates*

HOW DO YOU LIKE TO DECORATE?

Elsie de Wolfe's amazingly frank and useful book, *A House in Good Taste,* first published over seventy-five years ago, was ghostwritten by Ruby Ross Wood, Billy Baldwin's boss and mentor. Early in the book the reader is told that we will be judged by our surroundings whether we like it or not. "You will express yourself in your house *whether you want to or not,* so you must make up your mind to a long preparatory discipline. . . . We attribute vulgar qualities to those who are content to live in ugly surroundings. . . . We may talk of the weather, but we are looking at the furniture. . . . A house is a dead giveaway, anyhow, so you should arrange it so that the person who sees your personality in it will be reassured, not disconcerted."

Develop a living philosophy so that your decorating mirrors your soul. Learn how to make the process wonderful through patience. Some people prefer to concentrate on one room at a time so the rest of their house isn't in chaos. The biggest mistake most people make is to rush and set unrealistic goals and deadlines. Everything takes much longer than you estimate. Budgets tend to expand as the work is delayed. Don't plan a party and then get everyone to turn themselves inside out to finish the work on time. Have an informal party as the work progresses. Enjoy the process. Savor the anticipation of the arrival of something new. Appreciate the joys of having your own home in which you can express yourself fully.

Professional interior decorators, designers and architects have a procedure so that a job advances in a logical sequence. If you are working by yourself, pace yourself. I have a client who likes to take the summer off from her house project. She does all her planning and thinking in nine months and enjoys June, July and August decision-free. She's the headmistress of a top girls' school and enjoys reading and traveling on her summer breaks. Come fall, she is rested, her well is full and she's ready to attack another area of her apartment.

Find your own method and stick with it. I am a born nester

and find great delight in daily rearranging objects and adding fresh finishing touches. I enjoy always being in the flow of decorating. From the most minor areas like my wrapping-storage area to systematizing our laundry space, I continue to make improvements. I have developed a high tolerance for confusion and unfinished projects because this is what I do professionally for clients every day. You have to make a mess before you create beauty.

Analyze your personality. Most people break down under the fine powder of continuous plaster dust. Living in a place while it is being renovated is difficult. Know your limitations. Be alert to indications that you are losing perspective. The more sensitive you are as an individual, the more emotional you may become about your surroundings. They are no longer spaces, they are vulnerable places that contain your essence. One bit of slipshod workmanship can set you off. Listen to your own voice. Be the loving, gentle person who deeply cares. Expect to be let down by others. Lower your expectations. Always remember that paid workers are working on your house or apartment because they need the income. It would be hard for anyone else to be as caring as you. They need encouragement, not tantrums. Let all the vibrations be positive, and when the house is put back together and the last worker has left, feel content that you have grown with the project and are blessed to be able to enjoy the result. I remind my clients that this process is a privilege and should be fun.

Maybe your personal style is to do a lot of the labor yourself. I have a client who is a successful businessman and a frustrated architect. John loves to work alongside the workers. Because he cares so much and has learned his skills well, he inspires A-plus workmanship.

Patience is always rewarding. Think through every decision thoughtfully. The most important aspect of decorating is to create a satisfying atmosphere. Take risks. You are not making a business decision. You are free to continue to improve your ideas and alter your thinking midstream. If you're screaming at the painters to finish and get out, you won't be in a good position to endear yourself to them and ask them to put on another coat of paint in the living room. If the color yellow is too harsh, the painters could

WHO ARE SOME OF YOUR STYLE MENTORS?

leave half a day earlier but you're stuck with disappointment for years to come.

Every Easter Mrs. Brown came to our home for lunch at the stroke of one o'clock. In March of one year we undertook to do a proper paint job on our living room walls that had never been properly cared for for over fifty years. No threats would rush these painters, and on Easter Sunday the steel door trims were stripped down to their gun-metal gray color and the walls were six different shades of color-tinted compound to point out areas that needed more sanding. We carried on by going directly to the dinner table and having wine there and after lunch we had coffee and a sweet in the library. Once you've done your best, understanding carries you far. Mrs. Brown was amused. "You really have good painters, I see. You know, dearie, preparation is ninety-five percent of a good paint job."

How do you react to the process of making improvements at home? If you find you have not been enjoying yourself, make some changes. Building your nest is what's fun. Finishing is never as exciting and is often a bit of a letdown. One of the signs of a creative person is never being satisfied with what's gone before, only what new improvement can be envisioned and executed.

START NOW WHERE YOU ARE

RISK ALWAYS
REVEALS REWARDS.

Begin your quest for personal style at home by evaluating exactly where you are now. To what extent do your surroundings express your present life? Are your possessions well thought out and lovely? Do they really please you? Do you find delight in most of what surrounds you? Do your possessions have harmony and rhythm? When you find your voice in your surroundings so the atmosphere itself creates pleasant rhythms and harmonies, you have found your personal style. When you discover your authentic voice, you automatically create a true atmosphere that sings.

Put on some favorite soothing music, light the lights, make yourself a refreshing drink and walk around your house or apartment, room by room. Let your eye flow from one surface to another. Examine the shapes of your chairs and table legs. Notice the color tones of the wood of your floor and compare it to the tones of your wooden furniture. Look at a tabletop and notice how you've personalized it with your chosen objects. Are you pleased? Do the objects you see represent your true self? Can you see yourself expressed through your favorite things? Can you describe a general style that you feel your personal style is emerging from? My style of decorating combines touches of English, American and French provincial designs. Most of the furniture and objects that you live with you might like, but you should sort through what is no longer "you."

PRIVACY

The ultimate luxury in life is to have and keep your home reserved for you, your family and invited friends. Have your private world of retreat saved for those with whom you are *simpatico*. You need a private haven where you can withdraw from the world and savor some uninterrupted moments of private pleasure and a sense of calm.

Guard your privacy. Reach out to others on your own terms. Be sure friends and relatives call ahead of time if they want to stop by. If it is not convenient for you to receive a guest, you have to learn to say no. Make definite dates with friends and relatives who come for visits so it is clear to them how long they are welcome. No matter how much you enjoy opening up your home to loved ones, preciously guard your time. As Napoleon said, "You can ask me for anything you like, except time."

Each of us is different in our need for privacy. Examine your individual needs. I am with other people whenever I'm away from home, so home is the only place where I can go to free myself of

WHAT IS MORE APPRECIATED THAN A DAY OFF?

obligations; home becomes my sanctuary where I enjoy my husband and daughters, where I can be contemplative and have some solitude. Home is also a sacred place where I share love with friends and therefore I am extremely protective of keeping a healthy balance between being alone and sharing time with others.

If you have a family, your house will be filled with your children and their friends. Children are adaptable and grateful for mere floor space. Your children, at a certain age, can entertain their own friends and still not completely invade your privacy. There are always doors to shut.

If you have a houseguest when deadline pressures in your work put you under stress, you will be exposing yourself in an unfair light. Yet your friend who comes to visit might be on vacation and have unlimited time to spend with you. What you don't want to hear is that you work too hard and look tired. Obviously you know how tired you look if you work as hard as you do. If you work at home and have a guest, it is impossible to try to work and equally hard to give in and be a hostess.

You might be better off letting a friend down by telling her it is inconvenient for her to spend the night than to do something you know is ill-timed. Trust your feelings. When you invite someone to your home, do it at a time when you can plan ahead to take some time off and can enjoy sharing meaningful time together. You be in charge.

Many people have confided in me how frustrating it is for them never to be alone at home. Having calm, private time at home alone or with your partner is essential to your equilibrium. If you live in a crowded city you feel a constant sense of crowding and claustrophobia. You long for the feeling of space, quiet and security. You have an opportunity to refresh yourself each day at home. Take it.

Ideally you should be free to be yourself at home, enjoying a place you find beautiful, where you have fun living out your daily rituals. Guard your privacy. It is your greatest freedom.

FIND PLEASURE IN THE LITTLEST THINGS YOU DO.

LIGHT

Nothing is more life-enhancing and joyful than natural light flooding your home. Natural light is energy and your life force. How affected are you by the weather? Does a sunny day help your disposition? What does a gray, rainy day do to your mood? I was in my friend Kate's office several years ago when the sky suddenly turned black and it poured rain. The sky flashed with lightning and there were loud, scary thunderbolts. Kate smiled. "Aren't you glad you love your work on a day like today?" A sunny day on the other hand, when the humidity is low and there is a refreshing breeze, can make you feel great joy in the mere fact that you are alive to appreciate it.

Light is life. You will continue to have dark, dreary days when you look around your home and it looks gloomy. Thanks to Mr. Edison you can light the lights and artificially illuminate your rooms. Studies illustrate that most of us are more content and happier on sunny days. Spend your money creating a cozy, sunny atmosphere at home so that on depressing days, when the weather is foul and you have to stay inside, you can spend your time well.

Just as it is wise to eat food closest to its natural state for better health and radiant skin, artificial lighting that most closely resembles daylight is best for your sense of well-being. Have good incandescent lighting on dimmer switches so you can make adjustments depending on the time of day and the weather. Good artificial lighting is preventive medicine. Years ago I had a client who refused to turn on the lights in her apartment during the day. Her apartment had no views and was, by its location, extremely dark. She was an unhappy person and I can't evaluate whether the darkness made her miserable or she enjoyed the darkness because she was so unhappy, but it made me extremely nervous to be there.

Analyze how you feel in different lighting conditions. Ever since I was little and spent time playing outside in intense sunlight, I've found it always dampens my spirit to go inside. I feel as if a gray screen has masked the true essence of the beautiful day. Sev-

"TO BE WORN OUT IS TO BE RENEWED."
—*Lao-tzu*

"MORE LIGHT!"
—*Goethe's last words*

eral years ago I was sitting in our living room reading the newspaper and I discovered I couldn't read the newsprint. There wasn't enough light. Whenever I read outside in bright light I can see so well it is a pleasure to read out of doors. I now wear glasses for reading and I've also placed stronger reading lights around the apartment because we enjoy reading wherever we are. Rooms that don't have enough good reading light tend to be somber. So many living rooms are useless because they aren't properly set up for intimacy and reading; they fail to be warm and comfortable emotionally.

If you have young children living at home, a light, sparkling atmosphere is not only cheerful but generates energy. Primary colors look best in well-lit rooms.

Bring as much natural light into your home as possible. Glossy white window trim surrounding clean windows magnifies light. Register how your rooms look and feel and how you feel when the sun shines through your clean windows. Work to perfect your artificial lighting so you can create the same sunny atmosphere when the sun is on a different side of your home. Make lighting allowances for rainy days or the dark of winter. Don't rely on the weather or chance for your light quality. Because without good light not only do your colors become dense and dull and your rooms lose their radiance, but your mood is saddened.

In the evening when the sun sets and you have experienced the light of day, it is natural to dim the lights, light candles, and enjoy conversation. Years ago, before the light bulb, this was part of the rhythm of the day. However, many of us enjoy reading and writing in the evenings too, so you should provide alternatives to candlelight. Seventy-five percent of my clients' houses and apartments don't have adequate lighting because they aren't aware of how dark their rooms feel. On a sunny day, go outside—say, to the garden, or to a beach or sit on a terrace—and then go inside. If the location of your windows doesn't allow the light to shine into your rooms—and of course it couldn't flood all your rooms with light at the same time—light the rooms artificially and see if you can create a warm, sunny feeling. Standing halogen lamps placed in the corners of your rooms flood light up onto the ceiling

WHEN YOU WRITE
NOTES, WHAT KIND
OF STATIONERY DO
YOU ENJOY?

(as if from the source) which then bounces down into the room. Work on your lighting room by room. Your rooms reflect your spirit and you want them to be bathed in light.

Use window shades for times when you are not at home, but when you are, let all the sunshine in and feel the joy of living in a sun-drenched home. Treasure these moments. Naturally faded fabrics can be part of your personal style. I have an early childhood memory of lying in bed smelling bacon cooking and watching dappling sunlight spill into my bedroom. The breeze blew the white eyelet curtains, which were like flags of white light dancing around the walls, casting patterns. No wallpaper could ever duplicate this sense of the moment. I remember feeling cozy under a colorful quilt as I awaited a delicious breakfast with my family before going outside in the glorious light to play.

KNOWING WHAT YOU LIKE

You pick up self-knowledge every day. Each selection, each tangible object you choose, becomes a symbol of your essence. The way to have your home alive and vital—filled with your passions—is to listen to the song in your heart. When you are expressing your inner life you will never convey lifeless materialism. Change your surroundings as you change and grow, declaring an important truth about your identity and your individual sense of what is lovely in the world.

Your home will reveal your state of aliveness, your sense of delight and excitement. If you enjoy life, your home can be charged with intensity and spirit. Whenever we love life, we find an outlet of self-expression.

Robert Henri, the great American artist and wise, inspired teacher, wrote in his book *The Art Spirit,* "There are moments in our lives, there are moments in a day, when we seem to see beyond the usual; such are the moments of our greatest happiness. Such are the moments of our greatest wisdom." We tend to recall our vision by some sort of sign. It was with these symbols that the

WHEN YOU ARE GENUINE, YOU ARE NEVER WRONG.

arts evolved. Signposts on the way to what may be. Signposts toward greater knowledge. Henri believed that art and life must always be in close relationship. He helped his pupils (and us) to gain artistic and aesthetic self-respect.

Perhaps you are a painter. Or you may be a potter, a weaver or writer. You may compose music, act, dance or produce movies or plays. You may be a gardener or a cook. You also decorate your home. Think about yourself as an artist and a student. Think about your life as a progress toward greater freedom of expression. Understand that you will never arrive at a definitive personal style for your home because it is a creative process. You will never be fully complacent looking back at what you've accomplished in the past. Your home will grow and become enriched as you yourself grow and become more knowledgeable. You never have to paint a portrait in oil or create a sculpture from marble, but you can have a living monument that can be your most creative achievement: a loving atmosphere at home. You can pour your artistic talent, your sensibilities and accumulated ideas and techniques into expressing yourself intimately and naturally where you live.

Mature people don't seek out approval or compliments. Your off-white might be warm and wonderful to you but dreary to me; my bright sprightly white might be too stark for you. Search your soul for your own truth. Your truth is not to be found in magazines, in museums, on television or at the local department store. Your sense of appreciation and beauty is deeply rooted in your being and becomes a philosophy, a way of life. You put all the meaningful elements of your life together in a harmonious relationship.

Architects and designers can guide you and help keep you on course. They can provide technical knowledge and expose you to options and help you translate self-knowledge into self-expresson. Your personal style at home must be real, and only when it is real and rings true will it be alive. So, be an artist. Experiment until you discover intrinsic beauty in all the elements around you. Look for the inner light. Love the pure form rather than the ornamental embellishments. Enjoy the stitchwork and quality of a handmade patchwork quilt rather than seeking Versailles brocade that may

VALUE YOURSELF.

SAVOR SIGNIFICANT DETAILS.

hold no real meaning for you. Search for intrinsic beauty and organic integrity. Understand that a handmade object, made with love, will have life and spirit and will bring you lasting pleasure.

Whenever you do something for pure pleasure, chances are it will be exciting and alive because it springs from your heart. Try to love and emotionally understand everything you select for your home.

DOES YOUR HOME SMILE?

When you walk through your front door and feel delight, then you've found your personal style of home. Rooms, like paintings, explain themselves. Home should welcome you and greet you warmly—as a mother greets a child coming home from school. Smiling rooms smell good—whether it's the smell of wax or the lilac in a vase on the hall table or the aroma of baked apples, cloves and cinnamon, room scents are as important as cologne, aftershave and perfume. You can experience the scent of peach, lavender, pine and roses by buying room sprays, scented candles, sachets, scented shoe trees and potpourri. You can now coordinate your room scents to your body scents and have your rooms smell as refreshing as an apple orchard or an arbor filled with lilac.

When your home smiles at you it is well-ordered, balanced and clean. There is nothing beautiful about dirt. When you have achieved a home that smiles at you it is original and is your own invention.

Think about the values that guide your life. Be sure they are translated symbolically in the atmosphere, spirit and mood where you live. Have enough personal mementos and objects around so they comfort you as well as inspire you. If you have been preoccupied, concentrating on other things, or if you have neglected your home, feeling afraid to express yourself freely, analyze the three basic elements that can guide you in your efforts—simplicity, appropriateness and beauty. Go to museums and auctions. Evaluate what you like and discard what doesn't appeal to you. Go to art galleries and exhibitions so you find artists' work that inspires you. Go to craft shows and examine the beauty of the artisans' execution of their materials. Play with your visual scrapbooks. Train your eye so you can judge as well as see.

Make your quest for personal style at home a happy, lifelong process.

OVERNIGHT GUESTS

DO YOU LIKE QUILTS?

What amenities do you have for overnight guests? Even if friends stay in a fold-out bed, their stay can be made more pleasant. You can treat them the way you like to be treated in a luxury hotel. Have a generous supply of fresh towels, pretty fresh linens with several extra pillows for reading in bed. Have a basket of toiletries in case they forgot their toothbrush or toothpaste. Also include sample-size containers of shampoo, conditioner, soap, hand cream, bath gel, powder, mouthwash and cotton balls and astringent. Add some perfume samples and a small sewing kit with scissors. Guests love to feel independent when visiting, away from the comforts of their own home. I stayed in a hotel recently that gave each guest a sampling of Caswell-Massey products including a small bar of my favorite almond soap. Naturally I thought it was there especially for me.

Next to the bed have a pretty enamel alarm clock, a pile of books and magazines, a scented candle, a bowl of fruit with a fruit knife and napkin, and a pitcher of ice water. Have a small arrangement of flowers with a welcoming note saying how happy you are to have them visiting you. In Milwaukee, Peter and I received gift-wrapped presents on our pillows. Our hostess gave Peter a small basket containing a local cheese encased in wax, and I received potpourri made from the flowers she grows in her garden. On a table between two comfortable reading chairs was a little dish of glazed cookies and chocolates.

Even if your friend is staying in a child's room, make a space in the closet with floral padded hangers with a sachet hanging over one to scent the closet, and have a terry-cloth robe for your guest. Have a full-length mirror on the inside of the closet door. An added touch that is always appreciated is an iron and a small ironing board (the kind you can buy to do sleeves) so your friend can set up the small board on the bed and iron out a wrinkle or put a crease in a pair of trousers.

Even if there isn't a desk in the place your friend is staying, have a stationery basket filled with art postcards, blank flower cards, a variety of stationery, some stamps and a fountain pen. If you have personalized stationery for your house, add that for your guest to use while staying with you. This thoughtful gesture makes it easy for your guest to keep up with his correspondence, even while lounging in bed at a friend's house.

If you are having friends over to meet your guest, give him or her a list of first and last names, nicknames and a brief description of each person. This way your guest can study it at leisure and participate with your friends more enjoyably. The same information is useful if you are all going out to a party.

COMFORT THE INNER MAN.

MAKE SOME GOOD MEMORIES TODAY.

BEING PARTY-READY

My friend Jane O'Toole who lives in Dallas was sitting under a hair dryer one day thumbing through *Harper's Bazaar* when she came across an article I'd written on entertaining. She teases me to this day because she stumbled across a sentence that made her burst out in laughter. "There's nothing to entertaining—you just have to be party-ready." Who among us is every party-ready? That is just the point. If I am an example of what gyrations we all go through before we entertain, it is a miracle we ever muster up enough energy and courage to have a party. But miracles do happen, and we gain enormous pleasure from sharing our home with our friends.

Think for a moment what being party-ready really means. For some people, perhaps, your home has to be "just right." For others you will want to be rested, tan and thin. Maybe you are party-ready when your flowers are in full bloom. Claude Monet always wanted to share the sight of his iris. So, time your parties according to your wishes and ideally your home and you are eager for the upcoming event. Entertaining, however, is not for sissies. If something can go wrong, it will, and unexpected things will surprise you. But when you are party-ready physically and emotionally, you're ready to plunge into the adventure with your whole heart. Fuses blow, toilets don't flush, a guest can't find her coat—and you can take it all in stride.

Recently I thought I was party-ready. The day before our annual August family cocktail party we had a Con Edison "brownout" due to a forty-three-day heat wave. We lost the power of our front elevator. I came home armed with flowers and vegetables from the Korean market and realized I didn't have a key to the back door. I sat in the lobby waiting for Peter, dreading the idea of our guests having to enter our apartment negotiating garbage cans and the heat and entering through our hot kitchen.

ARE YOU A
ROMANTIC OR A
REALIST?

To top things off, there was an ice shortage in the city because of the heat wave. I knew ice was an essential element. How many ice trays can a small freezer hold when filled with party food? Miraculously, a cold front came in, the weather cooled off, the front elevators worked and we were provided with plenty of ice to chill the wine and beer. The party was a great deal of fun, as always.

The best way to get party-ready painlessly is to have your home in fresh rejuvenation. Your windows should be clean—for your pleasure—so this isn't an extra burden. Your paint might require some touching up around the door trims and baseboards but you shouldn't have to call the painter in to touch up before a party. The painting can be touched up whenever you see it looks worn. Our library air conditioner was missing a part and because of the emergency of the heat wave, we weren't able to get the part replaced and the air conditioner reinstalled until hours before our party. Best to have your air conditioners checked in early spring before you need them. This is practical common sense and basic, but in the rush of life we often put off things.

Ultimately you shouldn't put on the dog for your friends and live less well day-to-day. When your home sparkles and is pleasant for you and your family day-to-day and you are feeling good, you have the basic requisites of being party-ready.

WHY ENTERTAIN?

People delight in being together. Entertaining friends makes you feel civilized. You can share your feelings for the goodness of life with people you want to please. Entertaining allows you to share relaxing, happy times with friends.

It takes a fair amount of energy to entertain. Yet if you orchestrate every detail so subtly that it appears to be effortless, you have succeeded. Miraculously, everything flows and moves in harmony like a melodious symphony. Once you set the stage then you should be free to enjoy yourself because you have created as close to an ideal party as you can. Usually the more thought you put into your party the more satisfaction you will have. Remember, the whole point of entertaining is to enjoy quality time with your friends. You never waste effort when you plan a party. However, it is best to pace yourself and keep things manageable so you won't exhaust yourself overpreparing and be too tired to enjoy your guests. The more you enjoy yourself, the more pleasure you'll bring to your friends.

One of the advantages entertaining has is to make you realize your capabilities. You don't merely play a part, you are the director, producer, writer, actor and stagehand. But it's not always possible to do everything yourself. Your circumstances dictate how much help you get from others and yet you are always acutely aware that you are responsible, you are in charge.

You create the atmosphere and visualize the flow of time. Entertaining brings lasting rewards; you realize you have made something happen that wouldn't be possible, in exactly the same way, without your gathering. It makes you happy to see friends meet at one of your parties and leave together!

Each party you give expresses your personal style of enter-

"SELF-CONFIDENCE IS THE FIRST REQUISITE TO GREAT UNDERTAKINGS"
—*Samuel Johnson*

taining. You are the host or hostess making all the arrangements based on your vision of fun, glamour, entertaiment or gourmet food. You are the provider, reaching out to others in generous, giving ways. The message rings true that you care and want to please your guests. In Charles Morgan's book *The Fountain* (Knopf) he said, "There is no surprise more magical than the surprise of being loved." Entertaining others is a loving gesture.

HOW SPONTANEOUS
ARE YOU?

Because you are giving to others, entertaining is a deliciously self-satisfying act. The sure way to have a great party is to want to give it for your friends. When you're doing something you want to do it is a self-fulfilling act. You may be a little tired the next day but you always feel transformed after your own party because you see your friends sharing in good times.

One of my good friends, Toby Rose, loves to cook. She is an artist and puts her creative zeal into cooking for friends. So often she tells me, "I made this especially for you because I knew you'd appreciate it." Even when she has only a few friends over it becomes comparable to a Chinese banquet. Toby loves seeing her friends enjoy themselves and her delicious food. I've been to her house for dinner and she's been cooking all day to please us. She enjoys the process and the results.

HOW TO THROW AN IDEAL PARTY

HOW COMFORTABLE
ARE YOU WITH
FORMALITY?

Peter and I enjoy giving "theme" parties. We give a party for a friend from out of town, a "first day of spring party," a family Christmas party, a "summer family party," a party to celebrate our anniversary or the anniversary of our company or we give a party for an artist or author. Even birthday parties need a theme besides someone's age. Instead of having a birthday party announcing your spouse's fiftieth birthday, why not have a Gatsby party and have people wear appropriate clothing recalling the twenties?

If you love wine you might want to have a wine-tasting party, which can be a great deal of fun and gives a twist to an ordinary cocktail party. Theme parties help people to open up because a common bond is understood. As a host or hostess the most important thing to consider is how comfortable your guests will feel. I, for one, never feel comfortable playing charades. Often, in an attempt to please, a hostess or host will act overbearing and create tension. Whatever your theme, which you obviously enjoyed dreaming up, try to realize that some perfectly decent people don't eat clams or are allergic to shellfish or are alcoholics and it is not thoughtful constantly to attempt to put alcohol in their glass. Don't judge. Serve. Provide for your guests' physical comfort and be watchful that they are having fun. If you have silly T-shirts or hats, let some friends feel comfortable taking them home as souvenirs to give to their children and don't force them to wear them at the party. Your gracious gesture will always be appreciated because everyone loves presents. It needn't send you into bankruptcy to have some little present tied in a ribbon. A pretty powder puff or bar of fragrant soap, talcum powder, or a little pocket notebook can be a nice reminder to a guest of the pleasant occasion.

The best way of entertaining is to provide lots of space for your guests to express their own personal style and not have to conform to yours when it makes them feel awkward and unhappy. That is never the intention so once the party starts, keep loose.

The greatest way to express your personal style of entertaining is to have parties in your own home. There is no greater compliment to a friend than to be intimately brought in to where you live. A simple lawn party at home or a wedding reception at your house is always more personal than when it is held at the country club or in a rented space. So much of our time is spent in large, impersonal settings that we should make every effort to have most of our parties at home. When we entertain at home the warmth permeates the air. Decorations are extensions of our natural style at home. So the ideal location is always where you live. This has an added advantage in that you can control the cost better when everything is in your hands.

If your home is small, select a pretty location for a large party, if possible. A friend threw a party for her stepdaughter, and when she saw the size of the guest list Betty realized her small house

"THE MANNER OF GIVING IS WORTH MORE THAN THE GIFT."
—*Corneille*

couldn't hold that many people so she rented a loft. Quite inno-cently the expenses skyrocketed because the loft was so ugly she had to install special lighting, put down a dance platform, paint the walls and use lots of flowers. This simple gesture to throw a party in a loft became a financial disaster. If a setting is pretty to begin with and has a nice view, you're halfway there. A tent on a lawn is cheaper than decorating a loft for six hours of fun. In the winter when parties have to be indoors in most parts of the country it might be cheaper to take over a room in a restaurant where you pay for food and drinks only.

To the extent you're able, have everything ready in advance. Parties are special and you should be with your friends as much as possible. Last-minute soufflés aren't appropriate unless you have someone in the kitchen making them. You want to entertain your guests and you can't be backstage and entertaining at the same time. You want to connect friends who have something in com-mon. It is always special if you can share something beautiful about yourself. Be there. Shine. Give a toast. Tell your friends individually how much it means to you to have them there.

Decorate according to the theme. You can be as silly as you like with your decorations because they won't offend a guest or hurt any feelings. Everyone loves balloons, and never be embar-rassed to have streamers or signs or a blown-up poster if the spirit moves you. This is your moment to make a statement. If you enjoy decorating you might create appropriate decorations to rein-force your theme. If there is no special theme, simply make things look pretty. Food should be seasonal and part of the spirit of the event. Most of us are fortunate enough to be well-fed and many of us are watching our weight, so food should be simple, yet attractive.

Music adds to our pleasure. Whatever your personal style is, music is always enjoyed. But unless you are having a concert, it isn't a good idea to have your guests stop talking in order to listen to a musician play. Let your music be in the background, no matter how great it sounds.

Above all, make sure this party is meaningful for you. You have to want this party or you won't find the extra adrenaline

"FRIENDSHIP ALWAYS BENEFITS . . ."
—*Seneca*

DON'T WAIT.

you'll need. When you really want to have a party, the anticipation, planning and hours of pleasure will add joy to your life.

INVITATIONS

Your invitation sets the tone. We enjoy receiving an invitation and marking our datebook, and most of us keep the invitation on our desk until after the party. Show your enthusiasm for your party and let your invitation set the tone for your coming cele-bration.

CELEBRATE NOW.

Your party theme should be announced by your invitation. If you're having a "first day of spring party" your invitation can be a bright-yellow-bordered 5 × 7-inch correspondent card with green ink so your friends can anticipate spring. Or, your invitation could be a Claude Monet garden postcard put inside an envelope. If you're having a publishing party for a friend's book, ask (with plenty of advance notice!) to have the publisher run you off some extra book jackets so your invitation can be tucked inside.

Whether you hand-write your invitations, have them engraved or have a calligraphy expert write them out, be sure they reflect your own style. You want you friends to sense a "ta-da!" flair and to feel your creative touch in every detail. If you want the invitations to be engraved, use a color dye evocative of you. When Alexandra graduated from high school she gave a party for her classmates' families and friends at a friend's large tower apartment. The engraved invitations were of pure white paper with pink engraving in a soft script. At the bottom of the invitation it said, "Dress: white." There were pink and white balloons, pink and white flowers and pink-and-white-cotton-striped chintz material was draped over all the upholstery and pinned in place. Everyone arrived dressed in white and anticipating a fun evening. The invitations set the stage and give necessary information.

If an invitation is especially meaningful it can be saved and treasured as memorabilia. Save your special-occasion invitations and put them in a drawer with a ribbon around them for safekeeping so the memory can be recalled. A thoughtfully prepared invitation communicates that your evening is a special occasion. It is best to send your invitations out three weeks to a month in advance. If you have certain people you need to have accept beforehand—say, the guest of honor—call ahead and once your friend has accepted, send the invitation with a note as a reminder.

MAKE AN INVENTORY LIST

Before you put the invitations in the mail, think about whether you'll need to line up extra help. Now you have to turn the promise and dream into a reality. Early planning saves you anguish, but I believe in doing a little work each day beforehand so that you are never overwhelmed with the pressure of entertaining coming on top of a full work load. Analyze whether you can do the cooking yourself or will need to rely on caterers. Can you buy some precooked dishes from local shops and have extra help to serve? If you're planning a wedding or an important celebration and need musicians, you've obviously met with them before you confirmed your date. Now you are committed. If you are having caterers help you, you have settled on the menu well in advance and have sampled the menu and been quoted a price. Yet if you are organizing the food at home and there is no printed menu, you can wait until you see what is fresh and what inspires you just days before your party. Remember, when you use fresh seasonal ingredients, you can't buy and prepare the food too far in advance or it will lose its freshness.

If you are having a seated meal, keep in mind simplicity, appropriateness and beauty and be sure the food will look attractive on the plate. When people are party-high, beauty is essential to whet the appetite and make the food represent the festive spirit of the occasion. If your kitchen is small and cramped it is best not to cook a pungent fish that may smell up the dining area. Whenever possible, make every effort to seat your guests. Even if they go

"RIPENESS IS ALL."
—*William Shakespeare*

DO YOU LIKE DRINKING FROM A STEMMED GLASS?

to a buffet table and get their food it is always appreciated when there is a firm table at the right height so that the meal and the company can be enjoyed unselfconsciously.

If you are serving a buffet, be absolutely sure the food speaks for itself. I can still remember my embarrassment thirty years ago when I was enjoying Sunday brunch at a friend's house and I thought the white sauce next to the roast beef was horseradish sauce. It had been placed on the server prematurely and was hard sauce for the apple brown Betty. Have your sauces related logically to the dish because there is no opportunity to put one's finger in to taste when guests are hovering. Just because you are having a buffet, there is no need to have too many different food choices. You should plan your menu much in the same way you would a served, seated meal. Most of us have gone to buffet meals at hotels, which are apt to be a spread of food that is aribtrary and over-whelming. Plan a menu you feel your guests will enjoy that is delicious and looks beautiful and you will be demonstrating far more personal style.

It is always wise to make a preparation checklist. Most of us have to go about our normal lives and squeeze our party prepa-rations into the interstices of the days before. A list keeps us focused and helps us not to overdo. I have more fun because I use my energies thinking about the fun of the event instead of wor-rying about the hundreds of details.

I have developed a master list that is custom-tailored so that every time I entertain I can review the list to help me remember odd details. I create an original checklist for each party, referring to the master list. But even when we plan carefully it is possible we can overlook a vital detail. Once we gave a large party at a friend's art gallery and Peter had rented wineglasses. A week or so before the party he received a phone call saying they were running short of the style wineglass we requested and they rec-ommended we call a party rental store. I telephoned and, it being Saturday, they were closed. However, I'd already checked off "glasses" and forgot to follow through. Minutes before the party the bartenders inquired gently, "Mrs. Stoddard, could you please

IT IS A BAD WORKMAN WHO BLAMES HIS TOOLS.
—*Proverb*

tell us where the glasses are?" I looked at Peter and froze. We both knew. Fortunately we were able to rush home and toss glasses into shopping bags.

First, take inventory and evaluate whether you have to rent anything. Most party rental stores have a minimum charge so plan carefully. Tables and chairs don't have to match. In fact, it is charming when you set up individual table settings in different rooms. We have friends who gave a bridal dinner for thirty-six guests in their apartment and they don't even have a dining room. They set up tables for six and eight in the living room, hall, library and guest room. By moving the twin beds against the wall and adding lots of pillows they turned a bedroom into a dining room with banquettes.

Your inventory list should include tables, chairs, glasses, plates, flatware, napkins, tablecloths, cups, saucers and serving dishes, bowls and even toothpicks. Remember that you may need forks for the first course, the main course, a salad course and a dessert. You can't hope to have the proper silver pattern and size for a mob, but you either have to have enough to go around or have people in the kitchen washing silverware between courses.

WHEN YOU NEED
INSPIRATION, WHERE
DO YOU TURN?

You can buy inexpensive folding chairs that stack for as little as thirty dollars, or you can rent them so extra seating isn't a problem. Inexpensive glasses can be purchased in quantity at a restaurant supply store. To make things pretty you can even make chintz slipcovers for the folding chairs, which can be most attractive. Places like the Pottery Barn have inexpensive white dinner plates so you can stock up. Buy extra wineglasses on sale and keep them in their cardboard boxes for easy storage so they'll be on hand when you give a large party. Each party you give makes the next one easier to plan. Hammacher Schlemmer has folding tabletops so a card table can become a round table for six or seven people. Your master list also reminds you of your inventory options.

If you have pets who might get discombobulated during the party you should plan to leave them at the veterinarian's or put them in a room away from the guests. What you don't want is to hear a howling dog scratching on a door and barking. A guest who is all dressed up may be upset to have a huge dog drooling all over her silk taffeta ruffles and it isn't the right atmosphere for guests to play with your pets.

Decide what liquor you want to serve. If you have a well-stocked bar and want to offer a spectrum of drinks, don't be thrown when someone wants a dark rum and orange juice with a splash of soda. You may have the dark rum and soda, but not the orange juice. You want to provide for your guests but once you have the basics, never apologize when a guest asks for something you can't provide. If you have bartenders serving drinks, whenever possible keep the bottles out of sight. Having all the supplies visible puts too much emphasis on drinking. If you don't have a bartender you can set up an attractive bar with fifths of gin, rum, vodka, scotch and bourbon and you as host make the first drink for your guest and then say it is a Rockefeller bar: the idea is they make their own drinks after you as host or hostess make the first one. Making a drink for a friend is a gracious gesture and a welcoming hospitality. This works well for a gathering of eight to ten friends; beyond that I suggest you consider a bartender to help.

If you have champagne, let your guests know right away. No polite guest will ask for champagne yet many would enjoy having a glass if it is offered. When we offer champagne we also offer mimosas (champagne with orange juice), which guests seem to like. It is a good idea to keep the drinks you serve simple with no mystery concoctions. We all have a different tolerance for liquor and when guests don't know how potent the punch is, it puts them at a disadvantage. Once liquor hits you it's too late. Avoid mint juleps or some sweet rum and pineapple drink you discovered on an island escape. Guests intend to be on their best behavior and as host and hostess we have to guard against serving sweet drinks that might taste good in a party atmosphere but might make friends feel hung over the next morning.

Many people with great personal style set up a wine bar and serve only wine and mineral water. If you enjoy wine, it is fun seeing the label and knowing what you're tasting. One of my neighborhood cafés has wine bottles all around the room above the banquettes for decoration. White wine bottles in a copper tub, on ice, are most attractive. Even if you offer a mixed bar, many people also enjoy setting up a wine bar. White wine is served as a preference at a cocktail party over red because it is considered to be lighter and also it doesn't stain when spilled.

If you are serving a meal at your party, be prompt. More than two cocktails is inappropriate and one is often plenty, especially if you're serving wine with the meal.

Have plenty of ice available. Ice is relatively inexpensive and is elegant. Serve ice water at the table with several cubes in the glass. After a dinner party serve each guest a glass of ice water with a thin slice of of lemon. This is a simple gesture. Whenever possible, serve drinks out of glasses rather than plastic cups.

YOUR FANTASIES
LEAD TO CREATIVITY.

WHAT TO WEAR

One of the most delightful things about entertaining is that you are the center of attention—yet, because you are serving your friends, you are not in any way considered self-centered. This is your production and for the few hours you have your guests captive, you and your environment are on display. Your clothes can become an aesthetically pleasing part of the background. Select your costume so you look good in the setting. Your dress should be becoming to you and the rest of the decor. Men should look comfortable at home and wear some color.

Let your clothes reveal something interesting. When Eliot and Roly Nolen came back from a trip to India they wore Indian silks at their next dinner party, which opened up conversations about the art treasures they saw on their trip.

Wear clothes you love that make you feel comfortable and attractive. Never wear something new unless you've spent several hours walking around and sitting down in it to be sure it's comfortable and fits well. You have too much to do when you entertain to adjust your straps or worry about a plunging neckline that shows your bra. Your clothes should send out a festive, colorful signal to your guests. Look glamorous and wear something wonderful. Try to look elegant because your appearance will set a graceful tone for your party. If you invite your guests to wear costumes that go with the theme of your party, indicate this on the invitation.

If you enjoy dressing up, do. It's accepted that the host and hostess can be dressier than their guests. If you are wearing a long dress or culottes, your female guests might want to join you. If you wear a short dress they might also. What you wear to your own party is telling. Be sure it has some flair and originality as well as color.

FLOWERS

Flowers are beautiful: they add color, texture, fragrance and they're alive. Most of us enjoy arranging flowers when we entertain. I have a friend who loves flowers and is passionate about arranging them. She can spend several hours creating pleasing bouquets to put around her rooms and on the table before a party. During the summer the flowers are from her garden and in the winter, when she has to buy them at the local flower shop, Jeannette feels grateful to her friends for providing her with an excuse to have flowers around the house. "I never feel guilty when I buy flowers I can share with friends," she confesses. "I really love them so I have a need for them year-round. Parties remind me how important flowers really are to me. No matter how hectic my schedule, I always enjoy the time I set aside to arrange my colorful bouquets. I feel the stress from my job melt away."

Flowers provide spiritual sustenance and nourish us as food does. Flowers can express your feelings of exuberance and well being and are a significant part of living beautifully. They should not set you back financially any more than food because you can budget for them and once you set a budget, enjoy making a selection that suits your mood, the party theme and the season. If you love flowers and value them as an extremely high priority in

"NOTHING TO EXCESS."
—*Inscription in the Temple of Apollo at Delphi*

your life, adjust your budget accordingly. It is perfectly possible you wouldn't mind marinating chicken; the money you save by not having a veal roast can be spent on flowers. Increase your flower budget in the dark winter months. I know lots of people who spend money on flowers by sacrificing other things because they give flowers such a high priority.

Flowers that you select and arrange have infinitely more charm than flowers that are arranged by someone else. Your selection of vase, the height of your bouquets, the colors and the combination of several of your favorite flowers will be extremely expressive. Always take time to arrange your flowers when you are entertaining at home and whenever possible when you have a party away from home. If friends know you love flowers and they want to send you some, it is a kindness to send them the afternoon before your party. In this way you can enjoy arranging them leisurely. If friends come to your party with flowers it can cause you to get flustered. It is not the time to find the right vase and abandon guests while you arrange flowers. If other guests missed seeing the flowers arrive, it could appear as though you weren't ready when your party started.

If you don't have a lot of confidence in your flower-arranging ability, don't worry. Let your eye and your heart guide you. Basically you want the container to be a support for the bouquet, as a lamp is to a lampshade, so have it small in relationship to the spread of the flowers. If the stems are pretty, as with tulips, roses, daffodils, pansies, or lily of the valley, a sparkling clear crystal vase can be attractive. I once saw dozens of daffodils resting in a see-through chemist's beaker arranged so the stems were in a swirling pinwheel design and it made a lasting impression on me. Fishbowls are often used by florists, and bowls in the shape of Chinese porcelain vases can now be found in inexpensive glass.

Playing with flowers is a great form of meditation, and time spent experimenting with vases and stem lengths should never be rushed. Think of the time as a spiritual experience and savor the creative act of rearrangement. Let your eye judge. If something doesn't sing, begin again. Our most usual mistake is to select too big a vase; then the flowers look dwarfed and skimpy. Far better

to have them exuberantly spreading out in all directions than looking restricted and rigid in the wrong vase. Even a clear drinking
glass can contain quite a substantial bouquet. Just because the
flowers you buy have long stems doesn't mean they wouldn't be
far more attractive cut short and sassy.

Mrs. Eleanor McMillen Brown arranged flowers in wide-
mouthed vases and often massed the same flower in a vase, her
favorite being anemones. The repetition of shape builds impact
and the variety of colors from red to fuchsia to purple and white
makes it a lush statement. You can do the same with a variety of
jonquils, roses or tulips. Édouard Manet painted the flowers that
his friends brought him at his deathbed. I suspect he arranged and
rearranged these bouquets to suit his artistic sensitivity. There is
an exquisite book entitled *The Last Flowers of Manet* by Andrew
Forge and Robert Gordon, about his last flower bouquets, which
is utterly delightful.

If a friend sends you a flower arrangement that was ordered
over the phone and it arrives looking as though it is better suited
for a wake, you must rearrange it so you can enjoy the lovely
fresh flowers. Everything is in relationship, one thing to another.
You shouldn't live with an arrangement you don't love. If you
receive long-stemmed Sonia roses from a friend and they come in
a plastic cut-crystal vase, you must put the beautiful flowers in a
favorite vase so you can feast your eye on them in great appreciation. Most florist shops lack style. There are exceptions and
those flower artists should be rewarded and revered the way we
revere artists, writers and musicians. Renny Reynolds is founder
and president of Renny Design for Entertaining, and I find his
passion for beauty expressed through flowers sensitive and full of
style. If you receive or give a bouquet of flowers by Renny, it is
invariably beautiful. I have been arranging flowers since my hand
was strong enough to cut and I have never fiddled with one of
Renny's flower arrangements. I've simply enjoyed them. Whenever you are not in control and you receive an arrangement, don't
be sentimental. If you don't like the way the flowers look, rearrange them.

I adore iris and remember having a seated dinner party for

TREAT YOURSELF TO
WHAT YOU NEED
AND WANT.

thirty-six guests when I had individual bud vases of purple and yellow iris. But by the time the first guest arrived all the iris had wilted. I now know to choose heartier flowers—tulips, daisies, lilies, roses, freesia.

SETTING THE TABLE

Setting the table is a symbolic ritual and is always a pleasure if you plan to have unhurried time. My friend Jane O'Toole thinks setting the table is the most fun part of party planning. Rushing could ruin the joy. As you set the table, put name cards in front of each setting and anticipate the conversation and magic of the party. Name cards are valuable for two reasons: you think through the best seating arrangement based on diplomacy and chemistry and your friends can glance at their dinner partner's name and be more gracious. I have a friend who puts the names of her guests on both sides of the card so people across the table can see the name as well. Make a list of all your guests and draw the configuration and shapes of the various tables. Place yourself at one table and place your spouse or guest of honor and go from there. I never mind whether I seat people of the opposite sex next to each other. I prefer to think of the wonderful discoveries two people will make because they have this time together rather than concern myself whether they're male and female.

Peter loves the table-setting ritual and this is something we do together. We arrange the placement of the tables first, usually a day or two before our party. We don't have a dining room so we borrow tables from our living room, library, hall and kitchen and put them in place in the hall and end of the living room. Ideally all the tables are in view so someone giving a toast can be seen and heard by all the guests. If your tables are of beautiful wood, you don't have to use tablecloths. For informal parties this can look charming, as you rely on napkins, placemats, flowers and pottery to provide the color. Suit your mood. Tablecloths can be so visually appealing, however, that you may want to use them

"TASTE IS MADE UP OF THREE THINGS . . . EDUCATION, SENSIBILITY, AND MORALITY."
—*Russell Lynes*

when you have seated parties. At one dinner party you can have cloths of different solid colors—yellow, pink and green. Each table can be different so that the whole impression is like a garden of color, texture and form. What solid colors would you select for your tablecloths? If you feel like having flowered chintz, buy remnants of inexpensive fabric that look compatible. Either have all the backgrounds white with colors printed on them or have them all colored. White stands out too much if all the cloths aren't white, but all other colors can blend together as harmonious background colors. If you have a theme party you could buy a bolt of inexpensive fabric and create a particular mood. We shouldn't be restricted by how many matching tablecloths or place settings we have. A friend who loves to entertain and who is a woman of great taste and style deliberately uses different plates when she entertains because she thinks it's prettier and more original. A talented decorator from Dallas uses cotton chintz tablecloths she's hemmed herself. The chintz fabric was bought on sale when a fabric house went out of business. All the fabrics were designed by an elderly French woman who creates Impressionist scenes on cotton. Combining these with color coordinated napkins and some fresh flowers creates a memorable table setting. When the tablecloths are not in use they can be stored on a shelf in the linen closet. Karen has white felt material cut the same size as her table so there is a padding under the covering. Square and rectangular cloths have fewer creases from being folded than round coverings. Love the elements you bring together. When you do, your guests will respond. You may want to try different napkins and rearrange the centerpiece several times before you are satisfied because there are no rules, only your eye. Play with different-colored napkins and possibly use several different colors.

If you are setting up extra tables, be sure there is room for people to move their chairs back and forth and room for someone to serve. The chairs should all be the same height. This may not seem important when people are casually seated in a lounge area but when sitting at a table it is important to have the seating uniform. Add a few cushions to some chairs if need be but give all your guests a fair advantage. When you place your name cards, check to see that the larger guests have sturdy chairs. Even if you have a strong chair, if the scale is too dainty a man who is six foot two will feel awkward. Just as with fashion, if things are too matched up, it becomes sterile. Odd chairs can be charming.

Each course should have its own look and selection of china. Being locked into one set of "good" china is a mistake because it becomes boring. Far better to gather plates and bowls that have distinction. For example, with a salad and cheese course you may want to use inexpensive Vietri pottery that originates from near Positano, on the Amalfi coast of Italy, or hand-painted pottery from the South of France. If you have used these plates and have enjoyed many memorable meals, they will have some chips exposing the clay. This adds character. New, perfect bone china is not necessarily attractive or impressive. It may be expensive but it is also lifeless. The ingredients of a good party don't depend on the expense of your china.

I disapprove of having "good china" which is set aside, high on the shelf, saved for parties. Immediately it gives a chilly impression because it has no life. If you feel uncomfortable using your "good china" when you dine alone or with your family or one or two friends, how will you feel when you use it for special occasions? There is no need to be a nervous hostess. I feel comfortable when I entertain but only if I don't put on airs. If you have some pretty plates, use them. We use hand-blown glasses for juice every morning. These go in the dishwasher. We have broken a few here and there in the course of time, but we appreciate them. At a party when there are many people and much noise, food and excitement, it is more difficult to appreciate these subtleties. If you never use better things for guests than you use for yourself and your family, you won't become anxious about entertaining. Your guests want to experience your natural style.

The key to greater ease when you entertain is to try to give generously of yourself and let your friends enter the intimacy of your family style. Whatever you enjoy as a style day-to-day is going to be far more interesting to friends than china, crystal and flatware that gets washed, dusted and polished only for special occasions.

"RESOLVE TO BE THYSELF."
—*Matthew Arnold*

"THE CONFIDENCE WHICH WE HAVE IN OURSELVES ENGENDERS THE GREATEST PART OF THAT WE HAVE IN OTHERS."
—*La Rochefoucauld*

Having friends over should be in the spirit of pulling up an extra chair. I laugh every time I recall a certain evening we went to a black-tie dinner for fourteen guests. When we all were ushered into the dining room, there were fourteen settings. The host had forgotten to count himself! Jack was charming and made a joke of it as we all squeezed closer to make room for another chair and place setting.

Let your imagination go free. Create a memorable still life with each table setting. Among the flowers, add objects you enjoy plus favors in front of each place. For example, I love porcelain vegetables and fruits and I distribute them among the flower bouquets. A tiny silver or colored shopping bag with a small gift— an elegant bar of scented soap, a blank book, some special candies, a small candle or some note cards—will add to the festivities. Everyone loves a present. One hostess buys inexpensive bud vases and makes a small bouquet of flowers from her garden, tied in a ribbon, for her friends to take home. When a guest sees an attractive name card, a present, interesting people at the table and original decorations, this creates the expectation of a special event. Set an unforgettable table.

> "THE HAPPIEST OF ALL LIVES IS A BUSY SOLITUDE."
> —*Voltaire*

QUIET TIME

How many times have you gone to a party fired up with enthusiasm, only to discover that the host and hostess are utter wrecks? We can only imagine what went on behind the scenes. The tension is so thick it puts a real damper on the evening. No amount of perfection is worth the angst and exhaustion. It is natural to have your nerves reach a crescendo just before a party begins because you have had to choreograph hundreds of details over several weeks and now the moment has arrived. Your friends will respond to the atmosphere. I enjoy keeping my party records in my Filofax so I can add to what I've done in the past and vary my menu and decorations. I can review my party planning on a train, at the office or whenever I have a minute. Just a glance can soothe me.

The best way to avoid jangled nerves is to have a quiet time before every party. One hour is ideal but a half hour is essential. You may sit in your bedroom and think about a toast you want to give or look at your guest list. You may have to redo a name card or two because one guest has the flu and another wants to bring a houseguest. This is a good time to review your party list so that any oversight is discovered.

Quiet time gives you an opportunity to appreciate the people who are coming and reflect on how much you're looking forward to seeing them. It is a transition period from working behind the scenes to the moment when you can enjoy the harmony you've created. While you are the one responsible for the success of the party, this quiet time provides you with some solitude so you gain perspective and can enjoy being a guest at your own party.

The hardest part of a party is getting it started. Once it begins to roll it's clear sailing. When you become a guest, you won't be nervous. Reviewing everything ahead of time gives you confidence that the arrangements are all in order and all you need to do now is to have a good time. If something goes wrong now, it is out of your hands. Some years ago we were giving a party and sitting at the table with our friends at a candlelight dinner when suddenly there was silence; our air conditioners stopped. We looked outside and New York was dark. Our dinner party ended with guests leaving through the kitchen door, each holding a knife for protection: that was the night of the second blackout in New York!

YOU FIND OUT MOST ABOUT YOUR ESSENCE BY TAKING ACTION.

One hot July evening we had a large cocktail reception and the lights went out. We had overloaded our electrical system with too many lights and air conditioners. We quickly lit small votive candles and put them around, turned the lights off and got the air conditioners back on. We enjoyed a cool candlelit evening.

Sometimes you have to rethink your preparations. Even the most careful planning should be reviewed under changed circumstances. One Easter weekend there was an unusually hot weather pattern and the temperature shot up to 90 degrees. We cooked the leg of lamb Saturday evening as well as the asparagus and served a cold refreshing meal the next day. Instead of gravy on the lamb we had a mint vinaigrette sauce and instead of hollandaise sauce on hot asparagus we made a lemony vinaigrette dressing. Our meal was fresh, cold and sensible.

One of my favorite bittersweet memories of entertaining was during the first summer Peter and I were married. We had rented a house in Nantucket on Orange Street. Billy Baldwin was in residence and we invited him for dinner. We'd been at the beach all day and on our way back from the beach we picked up our vegetables and zinnias from a farmer's stall on Main Street, our swordfish from the nearby fish market and our bread, warm from the oven, from the Portuguese bake shop down the road from our house. Once home, we were ready to prepare a special meal for our charming friend.

We made a vegetable casserole using zucchini, eggplant, tomatoes, peppers, onions and peas, layered with freshly grated cheese and topped with roasted bread crumbs. As I slid the casserole into the oven I lit a match and the oven didn't light. Peter tried. He looked at me and walked outside and tapped the gas container and it sounded hollow. We were out of gas! With only minutes to spare, we lit the charcoal and grilled some corn with the swordfish and grilled Portuguese bread. I chopped up the vegetable casserole so it was minced and made a delicious tangy dressing with orange juice, soy sauce, honey and lemon. The evening was memorable and Billy never knew about our gas crisis. He seemed to enjoy the raw vegetable salad.

During quiet time you have a moment to pause and reflect on the synergism of human relationships. Above all else, you have a moment to feel appreciation.

"AND WHAT HE GREATLY THOUGHT, HE NOBLY DARED."
—*Homer*

GETTING DRESSED

After the luxury of quiet time it is pleasant to take your time dressing. As host and hostess it is essential that you tried everything on several days in advance so you have what you need. Lay out your clothes the night before. Do your stockings match your dress? When you've thought about your clothes and are happy with what you're wearing, dressing is a pleasant part of any special occasion. Enjoy the last moments you have alone. Have fun doing your hair and makeup. These are restful acts when you take time to do them carefully and with grace.

YOU BE THE FIRST GUEST

When you are ready ahead of schedule you can walk into your own party and experience how it is to be the first guest. This gives you the confidence that everything is in order and you feel wonderful when you actually greet your guests. Let your eye scan the room. Maybe you need to put some matches next to a candle or adjust the lighting. I find I stand and putter initially, then sit down with Peter and we have a quiet moment together until the doorbell rings. It's fun and just a few minutes can make you excited with anticipation.

THE FIRST TO ARRIVE

You are now in an ideal position to let your guests know how glad you are to see them. The early arrival and you can have a special visit before you are needed to introduce other guests and supervise with drinks and food. Think of this moment as a small private party and make the moment enjoyable. Light the fire, dim the lights, light the candles and serve drinks. The party has begun and your guest has made something happen.

INTRODUCING FRIENDS

You as the host and hostess hold the key to helping your guests meet and have a good time. Introduce friends, clearly enunciating first and last names. If you have a friend who enjoys using a nickname you can add that. If you forget a name temporarily, you're only human. When you make an introduction it is nice to tell each guest a little about the other. This opens the door to thoughtful questions.

You as host and hostess know that each one of your guests is interesting. You have to be certain you make the atmosphere so warm and congenial that your friends respond by opening up. As a guest you have to assume that the people all have an interesting life and a story to tell. When people don't enjoy cocktail parties, one of the reasons usually is because there only seems enough time for small talk. Yet when someone is properly introduced, they have a chance to get to the heart of their interests and mutuality. It's fun to go around and sense where you can add a few encouraging words and inform guests in conversation of their common interests. It could be that one guest's daughter goes to Princeton and another's son will be going there next year. These tips from an alert host help the flow of conversation.

Take a shy person around, introduce him to your guests and stick around him for a while until he feels comfortable. Being at ease in a room full of strangers is a learned art. Some people have to muster up their courage to introduce themselves. At the beginning of a party, when you see people sitting down, it is usually a sign either that they are shy or have a bad back. If a friend has just had a knee operation and is sitting down, bring guests to her and explain the situation. A little sympathy is a good opener, especially considering that your friend is probably in considerable pain and is a brave soul to be there.

STAY OPEN TO YOUR FEELINGS.

BE YOURSELF

Your personal style depends on your being totally natural. You should move about at your party with great ease. Because you have invited people who interest you and whom you want to please, the key to your party's success is your being pleased. Enjoy yourself. If you see an ashtray filled with ashes, you can whisk it away but if it doesn't bother you, leave it alone. If you are enjoying a good conversation with a particular guest, don't feel guilty savoring a special moment together. If you are happy, that is the best barometer that your party is successful. Guests will always appreciate your naturalness. They come to your party because they like you and if you put on airs you create a false impression. If you are entertaining someone of prominence, he or she wants to fit in with everyone else. People of position and power usually are remarkably humble and generous, whereas insecure people never feel they are quite good enough.

If you are proud of your house and a guest wants to see the rest of it, take them on a little tour. You have time and should feel free to do whatever you feel like doing so you enjoy yourself. Showing a writer your study or an expectant mother your nursery is a gracious act and never inappropriate.

Peter has a young granddaughter named Julia. She is invited to many of our receptions with her parents and because she has come to these parties since she was only a few months old, she enjoys herself enormously and our friends enjoy her. We usually have parties where we invite guests from different generations. It makes the older people feel young and young people can observe and learn from the more mature guests.

If you are a family person it is natural you'd want some of your family to be at your gatherings. My parents included us when my sister and brothers and I were young and we have included our children in our parties. Our children, in turn, include us in their parties.

When I was in my early twenties I was at a cocktail party and had a most interesting time talking with Ali McGraw. She is a charming, outgoing person and puts on no airs. I was at a dinner party several years ago given by a well-known American novelist, and Jacqueline Onassis was there. If everyone had been themselves they could have made her evening a lot more relaxed. Everyone wants to be real and human and have a relaxed, fun time.

As the host and hostess, obviously you are going to serve delicious food. Serve some of your favorite dishes, no matter how humble. An artichoke is a lovely thing to eat and is attractive and tasty. You don't have to have smoked salmon if you'd prefer to have a green salad or cold tomato-basil soup. If you financially stretch yourself serving wines and food that are out of your price range, this too is pretentious. Far better to serve chicken cooked your favorite way than to have baby rack of lamb and become miserable because you've exceeded your budget.

CONVERSATION

There is an art to asking questions. Ask leading questions. For example, "What kinds of things do you like to do in your leisure time?" Or, "What country do you prefer when you travel?" Questions that can be answered with a yes or no should be avoided. When you show a genuine interest in others they are apt to become more interested in you.

A well-known truism is that one should avoid discussing religion or politics in social settings. These are not laughing matters. Try to keep the conversation upbeat. Talk about art and literature, gardens, international cuisine and architecture. Anything cultural will keep the conversation on a positive plane.

Fundamentally, human beings share many of the same yearnings and dreams. When you feel comfortable with yourself you can go anywhere, enjoy yourself and feel at peace. Part of personal style is trying to make the world a better place. Inquire of the person you are having a conversation with what is their most important mission. Enjoy listening. You may hear a surprisingly inspiring tale. Look for and find an uplifting slant to a serious conversation. If a guest gets bogged down in discussing a problem, inquire, "What do you feel the solutions are?"

A party is where we should celebrate the dignity and greatness of each other. We need to take breaks from the pressures of our careers and commitments. Just because you are beautiful or handsome and have a wonderful wit and light touch shouldn't negate your seriousness. You have to be yourself even if some people are acting in a frivolous manner. Being serious and aware and also fun-loving and amusing is, depending on your mood and the circumstances, a useful social skill.

PARTIES WITH STYLE

Think back on all the parties you remember where there was great style. My mind is flooded with images of tenderness and affection. People with their own style have a flair for making other people feel special. They honor their guests. If you have warmth and genuine feelings of felicity and grace, these will be expressed to those around you. You convey a certain point of view that is unique yet universal. All the rituals you've performed to bring the elements together in harmony will create a magical environment. Parties are shared moments with friends and loved ones.

ENJOY EXPRESSING YOURSELF.

SPECIAL KINDS OF PARTIES

There is such a range of types of parties you can give, it is good to remember that every time you entertain doesn't have to be a formal banquet or a huge financial drain. A lovely kind of party is an early breakfast for busy professionals who appreciate being together and not missing work. Omelets are inexpensive and quick to prepare. You can offer six or eight ingredients and let your guests tell you what kind of omelet they want. You can have a memorable breakfast party for as little as a few dollars per person.

Brunch on weekends is a relaxed, enjoyable time to entertain. You can serve some simple dishes which you've prepared in advance and slice a ham or turkey. Arrange a buffet that is visually appealing and unusual. Have some fun garnishing platters and decorating the table.

I have several friends who enjoy giving teas for their female friends who are all in stimulating careers. Bringing these talented, busy women together at the end of a working day before they go home makes a cozy, relaxed atmosphere. Very little is required for preparation. Tea, coffee and wine are offered and there may be an orange cake or banana bread available but food is not the emphasis. Everyone talks and listens intently and there are usually several people who don't know the other guests, so all get reintroduced to the careers of the other women.

The ritual of a tea party elevates these gatherings to a gracious level and yet the conversation is often serious. We air our concerns about never having enough time to ourselves. We work all the time. We want more balance. We rarely discuss these concerns when we are with our spouses. We also have time to discuss our travels, what exhibits we've seen, what we're reading. I find that even the shyest among my friends feels comfortable in this warm, supportive setting.

Peter and I have friends who love chamber music and in the winter they have Sunday afternoon concerts in their apartment. We're served coffee, tea or wine and there is elegant finger food set up buffet style in the dining room for a reception before and after the music. This is a wonderful way to spend a Sunday afternoon, listening to great music among friends.

When a friend has written a book it is fun to give a publishing party. Publishing firms are conglomerates, for the most part, and can't always give each author close personal attention. Everyone loves an autographed book written by a friend. These parties are always electric and a great deal of fun. If you have a friend who paints, you may want to have an exhibition of his or her paintings at your house. We have artist friends who live in England and often give a party in their honor as well as an exhibition of their work in our home when they are in the States.

BE PLAYFUL.

DON'T JUDGE; BE.

If you have a large house or apartment you can offer to give a party for your friend who is running for political office. If you belong to a group that has invited a speaker to come to town to lecture, having a reception for him gives the community a chance to meet and greet that person individually.

Be on the lookout for excuses to have a party. We can never celebrate life too much. Giving parties is our way of expressing that living is a beautiful gift we want to share.

THE PARTY ISN'T OVER

Peter and I never give a party without having a post-party wrap-up. We put our feet up, have a bite of food together and talk about our friends. We remember the delicious food, the conversations, the laughter, the toasts and the chemistry among our guests. This is a poignant time because the party is physically over, but it is inside us and, we hope, inside our friends. We laugh at the funny moments—the waiter who made a corny penguin out of a potato and black olives as a garnish for the shrimp, not our style but his. We remember introducing two unmarried people and hours later seeing them leave together. We remember the joy of the moment when we come together and we know we can never repeat the occasion. Looking around, we see the flowers, the sparkling reflections of polished silver, the flickering candles, and we appreciate for the moment how the surroundings gave actual pleasure through beauty.

Each time you entertain, you and your friends are enriched and you will have a memorable bond among you. Having this relaxed, happy post-party wrap-up reminds you that the party isn't over. It has given pleasure and has opened doors. The spirit of your gesture lives on.

WE ARE NOT
PREPARING FOR LIFE,
WE ARE LIVING.

GRACE NOTES

❧ Whenever possible, have the real material and not an imitation. A white picket fence should not be made of plastic. A window should have mullions dividing the glass, not click-in dividers. Wood countertops should not be made of Formica to look like butcher block. Silk, cotton, wool, wood and marble materials have integrity and are real.

❧ Emalj white semi-gloss paint is ideal for all trim in your rooms, doors, baseboards, windows, cornices. All rooms in your house can be linked together by this flow of white paint. This is refreshing and will add sparkle and expand the space.

❧ When you group your collections together, stage them well and they'll become more interesting. Put all your eggs in one basket!

❧ Have a brass knocker on your front door that speaks to you and makes you love coming home.

❧ Set up your desk near a window so you can look outside and daydream.

❧ When you reupholster your chairs, have them put on a swivel so you can sit comfortably and take in the whole room or face a window to catch more light.

❧ The next time you arrange flowers put them in two or three different-sized pitchers and group them together.

❧ If you have a carved armoire and you like leaving the doors open to display your favorite collection of pottery, reverse the hinges on the doors so the carving and richness can be enjoyed and not hidden.

❧ Bedrooms can be living fantasies when you consider using white eyelet, white Emalj paint trim, pastel colors and soft flower petal colors from early spring. Men as well as women love flowers and love the color pink. For inspiration, think of the colors of a baby's nursery for your master bedroom.

❧ Stenciling is easy and fun to do. Consider stenciling the risers going up your uncarpeted back staircase. Or possibly you have a room that would be enhanced by adding a ribbon stencil around the ceiling line to act as a cornice molding.

❧ Put a bright-colored silk tassel on a key to an armoire or a table drawer to add romance and color.

❧ When using chintz, use it lavishly—on chairs, sofas, curtains and cushions—so you can walk into a room and feel you're in the most beautiful garden.

❧ Let nature inspire the colors you select for your rooms. Think of your rooms experiencing the same quality of light that you enjoy when you are out-of-doors on a clear, sunny day.

❧ If you love quilts and have more than one, display them. You can hang them on a wall using Velcro—a synthetic that comes in two strips you can buy by the yard. It works on the principle of negative-positive—each pair locks together. You attach one strip to the back of your quilt and the other to your wall. Or, you can fold some in a stack in a bedroom or hall, or store your quilts in an armoire, folded like towels, to add color and pattern. Why hide them away in the linen closet?

❧ Colorful French wired taffeta ribbon is now available in some home specialty shops and looks wonderful when tied in a bow; you can use it to hang botanical pictures or to twist around a chandelier chain.

❧ Mirrors bring light and sparkle to a room and they open up space. Place a flower arrangement in front of a mirror and it will double in volume and drama.

❧ If you decide you want some assistance from a decorator to help you pull everything together, do your homework first. Have a clear-cut idea of the mood you want to achieve and have some of the questions we asked earlier answered. Pictures of details you like that you've ripped out of magazines will help confirm your points.

❧ Make comfort your trademark. When you are physically and mentally comfortable, a room becomes a world to you and others.

❧ Dark floors and dark Oriental rugs absorb light. Lighter floors allow for a play of light.

❧ Rooms are alive. Furniture is meant to be moved around. Seasonally rearrange your furniture. Bring a sofa over near the window in the summer so you can enjoy the sunlight. Arrange a cozy setting by the fireplace for winter evenings.

❧ Our rooms have to be useful. We have to be able to do things in them. If you love to paint, set up a spot in your living room. Set up a sewing table. A weaver's loom. A writing table. Perfect, symmetrical rooms don't help us live as fully as do real rooms that provide spaces for us to pursue our interests.

❧ Furniture has personality. When something catches your eye and you feel pleasure, chances are it will have a sweetness to its character. Look at a table or a chair. Do you feel a certain spirit?

❧ Feel the smoothness of surfaces. Let your fingers touch underneath a tabletop or run your hand down the leg of a table or chair. Touch the carving of a mantelpiece. Delight in the softness of an old quilt, the coldness of marble, the smoothness of a walnut tabletop.

❧ Start a collection of baskets, old books, antique pillows, stamps, boxes, decorative porcelain or fountain pens.

❧ Paint the inside of a cabinet a rich blue or hunter green to show off your porcelain collection. Light the shelves by taping Christmas tree lights underneath the shelves.

❧ Rest small paintings on easels and put them on tabletops. Stretch silk, velvet or a piece of marbleized paper on the back, like a surprise lining of a jacket.

❧ Line the drawer of a table in a pretty fabric. Or use an antique lace placemat. This little touch will give you lasting pleasure.

❧ Read Alexander Liberman's *The Artist in His Studio*. This book provides an intimate glimpse into the lives of many favorite artists—Cézanne, Renoir, Monet, Bonnard and Matisse. We get to know them through their environments, their art, their belongings and their passions. Monet's garden, for example, at Giverny, still exists and is open to the public. Liberman brilliantly documents the artist's presence. This book was published in 1960 by Viking in paperback with black-and-white pictures and is now available in an edition with color photos published by Random House.

❧ What you leave out of a room is as important as what you put into it; corners don't need to be filled. Let them breathe.

❧ Encasing fragile decorative porcelain, crystal or jade behind glass doors makes a room look and feel like a museum. If you display a fragile collection in a secretary or armoire, open the doors and let the objects come alive.

❧ Sunbathe for a moment by an open window to feel the warmth on your face and the pleasure of the light spilling into your room.

❧ Be sure you have a favorite chair. There are often times when you will want to sit in it and just think. Will the chair you select for your own be of wood, leather or upholstered? Comfort involves meeting physical and emotional needs. Claim one chair as yours.

❧ One of the reasons many people find it so risky to plunge into expressing their personal style at home is that they don't have the overall scholarly knowledge of what is the ideal. Yet our homes aren't museums and our possessions are for our own delight, so we should seek decorative objects that satisfy our eye and our heart. Remember, lots of museums may have "the real thing" but you may feel it stiff and boring no matter how much you respect the quality. The Newport desk-bookcase that fetched $12.1 million at Christie's is beautiful but I wouldn't enjoy it as much as my own pine highpiece.

❧ Mirrors expand space and can be used to replace a painting, or used architecturally to fill a wall space entirely. In our living room we placed mirrors in two recessed wall areas and now it appears that we have four windows instead of two, which is attractive and also doubles the light.

❧ Think of the hardware on your doors as you would the buttons on a blazer. I love buttons and hardware! Just as you can transform an inexpensive dress by replacing simple plastic buttons with brass Chanel-style ones, the same idea can be applied to hardware. A door or a kitchen cabinet can be made noble by replacing the hardware. Have knobs and handles that feel good to your hand.

❧ Invest in your happiness. Unless you are a serious collector of museum-quality furniture and objects, buy from your heart, not for investment. Buy something beautiful you will live with every day. My clients who buy what they love never sell their treasure, no matter how much it escalates in value.

❧ What are the things that make your rooms sing? What delights your eye? What signs of your personality gleam through?

❧ What rooms in your house have books? Do you feel more comfortable in a room that has lots of books? Do you feel they're decorative and friendly as well as informative?

❧ If you had to be photographed in a chair, what kind of chair would you see yourself in?

❧ What are your favorite semiprecious and precious stones? If you told me lapis lazuli and sapphires I'd assume you like to use blue in your home. If you said malachite and emeralds, I'd think you'd want some green in your home. Look for these consistencies in your preferences.

❧ Prepare a place for a guest. The greatest way to flatter a friend is to be ready when she arrives. By setting the table and preparing some food and drinks ahead of time, you create a celebration instead of the appearance of a chore.

❧ Shutters give a protected appearance to a room and suggest a view of a garden beyond. They never block light the way a heavily curtained window treatment can.

❧ Doing things with your hands soothes a confused mind. While you do something useful and pleasurable you gain a sense of relaxation. Hands provide us with healthy ways of self-expression.

❧ If you see a detail you like in someone else's house, edit it in your mind to make it suit you. Visualize how it will look. You store these images and retrieve them when you have an opportunity to put them to use.

❧ When you have more than eight people to your home many guests will stand for drinks because they'll want to be part of other guests' conversation, and a good seating group never seats more than eight. If you have a large room with more than one seating group, the same chemistry applies. Providing for eight people to sit and have conversation is ideal.

❧ There is a fine art to placement. When resting a book or several books on a table, extend the edge of the book beyond the surface. This adds vitality. don't line up the edges with the table but place some books at an angle beyond the surface of the table. Fantan-Latour's Impressionist still-life paintings beautifully illustrate this dramatic tension.

❧ Use drinking goblets or tumblers for flower bouquets. What could be more charming?

❧ When you have a round table, throw a white square cloth over it for a fresh look. You can use an attractive pink or pale-blue dish towel as a cover for an end table in a bedroom. Freshen up a draped table by putting a white lacy cotton square cloth on top.

❧ Apricot-colored walls bring out the patina of the wood of your antiques and give a room vitality and a warm glow.

❧ If you have an odd chair or table, a piece that is a bit unusual in proportion, paint it the same color as the wall and it will not stand out as much.

❧ Take the plunge and trust your first instinct. Don't kill the romance by questioning or analyzing. Trust your chemistry with furniture and objects.

❧ Use dressmaker touches for tablecloths: sew a double ruffle along the bottom edge. Use a shirring cord—it's easy. Buy tape that has drawstrings in it like a man's bathing suit or pajamas. You pull the ends according to how much fullness you want. When not in use you can untie and loosen the cord so the cloth will lie flat in the linen closet.

❧ Another tablecloth idea: Buy bolts of fabric inexpensively and cut generous cloths with pinking shears and balloon the bottom underneath, hiding the rough unfinished edge.

❧ A bare painted wooden floor is refreshingly simple and clean. Try white, pale mist-green or a fragile yellow color. Why buy an expensive rug for a guest room? Cotton rag rugs near the bed look charming.

❧ Change something in your house every day. Rearrange the movable furniture and objects.

❧ When you redecorate, switch fabric. Try a new scheme. When your chintz wears out, use it as an opportunity to try something new and different.

❧ Paint an old oak chair a pastel tint. Put cushions on the back and seat, tied on with bows of the same material.

❧ A room will be more exciting when you mix things together rather than matching.

❧ When you give a dinner party, remember that place cards are festive and useful. It is easier for your guests to be outgoing when they know someone's name.

❧ Flexible seating makes a room "give." When you are alone reading the newspaper in the sunshine or having tea with a friend or having a party, your living room can never remain rigidly arranged. Chairs are meant to be pulled up and moved around. Some architects will never realize this truth.

❧ A round or oval ottoman in a living room can be an ideal place for a host or hostess to perch and join in a conversation with a guest. Because an ottoman usually has no back, several people can sit on it together.

❧ Do you have a favorite piece of furniture? I do. I have a Regency carved fruitwood table with a marble top I bought in Provence in 1963 for $275. We eat at this table, I write at this table and my pleasure with it increases every day. While my life continues to change and this table has moved with me, it is an important element of continuity that will be with me wherever I go. In 1963, $275 seemed like a lot of money. In fact, it was almost my entire net worth. My favorite table is now worth $20,000 in dollar value; to me it is priceless.

❧ I once had a gardenia plant in full bloom in my living room that made the room so inviting I would go just to sit, absorb the sweet scent and look around at the art and beauty. We now have lemon trees and when they flower the same thing happens.

❧ Wallpaper is an imitation. If you have a great view and some personally selected art, wallpaper is not necessary. If you have no view—in a powder room or a bathroom, for example—and want to add gaiety, wallpaper is ideal. Stripes work well with art and don't compete with nature.

❧ Do you like colored drinking glasses? I do, Peter doesn't. I enjoy hand-blown glasses with candy-cane bands of color. I adore the pale green, amber and blue tints of the bubbly glass from the South of France at Biot. We should all drink out of our favorite kinds of glass. They need not match any more than it is necessary to drink the same things.

❧ If you were to describe your Garden of Eden you might gain clues to your style of decorating. If you like formal, symmetrical gardens with clipped hedges, you will probably like the same balance in your rooms. If, however, you enjoy the helter-skelter freedom of an English garden, you might find you like less structure and more freedom in your decorating. Do these correlations match up in your life?

❧ Do you like poster beds? Do you also enjoy bed hangings? Have you ever slept in a four-poster bed? How did you feel?

❧ Have you noticed that most ads for sheets and photographs of bedrooms show unmade beds, sensuously rumpled and cozy? Before you make your bed, see how it looks. Maybe it's your personal style not always to make your bed.

❧ Primroses—yellow, orange, raspberry, pink, purple—are so honest and satisfying. Pot a bunch and put them in a soup bowl for your table centerpiece. What could be easier, more charming and less expensive?

❧ We all love to use our fingers when we eat artichokes, lobster, corn on the cob, fried chicken and shrimp in the shell. Even asparagus is fun to eat with fingers. Finger bowls are so easy—warm water and a slice of lemon—and add a practical, refined touch.

❧ Enjoy feasting your eye on antique porcelain and getting inspiration for color schemes for your home—tomato-red, grass-green, China-blue, butter-yellow and white.

❧ Marbleizing is easy to learn. Isabel O'Neil's book *The Art of the Painted Finish for Furniture and Decoration* can help you get started. Remember: when marbleizing, expect the unexpected!

❧ When you go to a museum, go for pleasure. Delight your eye first. Look, and enjoy what you see. Don't look at labels first and read what you're about to see. If you don't like something, move on to something you do find amusing or beautiful and you'll naturally want to read the label to learn more.

❧ Blue-and-white-striped slipcovers can turn the spirit of your house into that of a summer beach cottage.

❧ By moving your objects around you actually see with a sense of renewal. Suddenly something your eye got used to in one setting becomes a dramatic sight in another.

❧ Serve ice cold strawberry soup with a few flower petals floating on top. Put a pint of strawberries in the blender. Squeeze in the juice of two lemons and four oranges. Put in a teaspoonful of honey and blend until liquid. Serve in a big all-purpose stemmed glass.

❧ Some sheets are as beautiful as an expensive fabric. You can use a king-sized sheet as a shower curtain simply by buying a plastic liner and clipping the rings to the top hem. Instant decorating, instant satisfaction.

❧ Trellises can give you the feeling that you are in a garden. Possibly you can conceal some lights behind a trellis painted green—in the ceiling or on the walls. A gazebo is born.

❧ When you serve yourself or a friend a drink use a pretty cotton or paper napkin to add a personal touch.

❧ Have a fire laid and ready to light a match to. Who knows when the spirit will move you to sit by a cozy fire—alone or with company.

❧ Have a scented candle burning in the front hall.

❧ It's fun to have pretty mints or Godiva almonds out in a jar or candy dish on an end table. Even if you don't eat them you'll notice they need replenishing.

❧ Think of your house as having four seasons. Which is your favorite? When you break the year up into three-month sections you become inspired to infuse some of the season's most enjoyable charms into your surroundings. In the summer, lift up the rugs and have bare floors; slip-cover in inexpensive stripes. In the fall, have a basket of apples on the hall table. In winter, decorate festively for the holidays. In spring, clean!

YOUR GRACE NOTES

THREE

Your PERSONAL STYLE OF APPEARANCE

FINDING SUITABLE CLOTHES
FOR YOUR LIFESTYLE

hen you're really comfortable with your style you'll *feel* comfortable. Ideally, once we get dressed we won't have to think about what we're wearing. What counts is our presence. How do we radiate and project our essence? Our eyes and smile reflect character and posture more than clothes do. Some of the finest people I know can't afford to buy new sets of clothing each season, and there is no way their authenticity and integrity could be hidden.

When you think about a friend, you usually see her animated. You envision gestures; there is a vitality flowing through her body. People always tell me, for example, that my pictures don't do me justice. I'm complimented by the negative reaction to a photograph because it is hard to project people's radiance or twinkle in a picture. Our afterimage of a friend is of her energy and vitality, her kindness, her warmth. To remember clothes before the person is tinsel.

Peter reminds me that we wear one set of clothes at a time so we don't really need to overdo. Having too many shoes or too many clothes is like overeating. Why should our closets get fat? We should enjoy the process of selection throughout our life and not ever have a stuffed wardrobe. I enjoy a soft, tailored look and my clothes have to make me feel happy. I think of clothes the same way I think of rooms. I like cheerful, happy people, clothes and rooms.

WHO'S STOPPING YOU?

Think of your clothes as sunny days. What would you wear on a rainy day to cheer you up? If a red coat would put a smile on your face on a gray day you might find the same is true on a sunny day. Use clothes to live out your fantasies. Do you like wearing clothes that evoke an earlier age? What designers do you identify with? Do you think of yourself as a tailored, outdoor, sporty person? So often the style you choose for your clothes has a similar spirit and mood to your decorating style. What is your color palette in decorating? Open your closet. Do you see a correlation between the colors in your rooms and those in your closet? Is there one color you see as a link—say, your favorite shade of blue or red? Are there certain types of materials you like to wear as well as to use in your room?

One client loves sweaters and knits and prefers woven textiles to printed patterns in her decorating. A friend loves flowers and has chintz in her rooms and flower patterns on her dresses and scarves.

General guidelines for our appearance are similar to those for the rooms where we live. We want to be clean and of a piece—well put together. Our clothes should also mirror our spirit. You use the same logic when putting an outfit together as you do when selecting fabric and furniture. You can combine different-period styles of furniture but probably wouldn't think it appropriate to mix Shaker and a Louis XV inlaid marquetry commode. Dress for where you're going to be. Even if you're going to a dressy cocktail party you don't have to wear a frilly lace cocktail dress or a somber dark suit. You can wear an elegantly tailored red dress and pearls and look striking, because that's what makes you most comfortable. A man in a blue blazer is appropriately dressed for all cocktail parties.

No one wants to be distracted by quirky styles and extremes. Clothes should wear our own face, not that of the designer or manufacturer. There might be occasions when you want to dress so that people will stop on the street to stare at you, but those occasions are special, not part of every day, and even then your personality should shine through the costume. All extreme clothes are costumes. Most of our lives are spent doing everyday things, and so most of our clothes should fit into the categories of the ways we spend our time.

Stylized, overdone rooms can look like stage sets and make us feel uncomfortable. Whenever style is created to impress others instead of to give personal pleasure, it is artificial and not authentic. Be cautious about trying too hard with decorating and with your clothing. We don't have to appear nonchalant when we prefer attractive, well-fitting, well-tailored, colorful, simple, casual clothes. Think of Jacqueline Onassis, who can wear a simple black wool dress; when she travels she packs a few colorful silk scarves to spice up her classic dress. When you think of her you see her face, not her clothes. Once clothes dominate, one becomes a mannequin.

Who are some women you admire and find attractive? Chances are you'll name women who have something more to offer than a perfectly toned size 8 body. Just as the furniture in your living room doesn't have to be perfect, your clothes and your body don't have to be either. There is beauty to old, well-polished shoes and a well-traveled handbag. Just as the patina on a wood table adds warmth and character, men and women with character usually age gracefully.

Your clothes should suit your life. If you decide to buy a fancy full-length white raincoat, you will be able to walk in the rain and stay dry but you will also be noticed. Think of the connections between the way you decorate and the way you dress. Those links are always there. If you enjoy wearing casual clothes, chances are your rooms will have the same ease and informality. I can look

TRUE ENJOYMENT IS A NATURAL STATE OF BEING.

at the way someone dresses and usually be able to translate that sensibility into their decorating.

When you are home in the evening alone, what do you tend to wear? When you have friends over do you like to get dressed up? Do your male friends wear jacket and tie?

If you have found your color palette in your decorating, see if your clothes have the same color scheme. Is your decorating style nostalgic? Can you see touches of the past in your clothes? If you adore ruffles and lots of rich fabrics in your decorating, chances are your clothes will reflect this love. If you only use natural fabrics in your rooms you will probably seek them for your clothes as well.

YOUR DREAM STYLE OF APPEARANCE

Studies prove that when we feel good about ourselves we tend to be more outgoing and self-confident. Honestly evaluate your appearance. Without being hard on yourself, are there areas you feel you should work on? Weight is a constant battle for most of us. Good muscle tone and firmness make us feel better. Many of us feel tired and stressed from our work, which is reflected on our faces. Yet each of us has an image of how we'd most like to look and feel and we can quietly and steadily work toward appearing our best.

EVERYTHING IS A CLUE.

If you make some shifts in your appearance—say you put a colored rinse in your hair to cover up the gray—do you feel better? I have a brunette friend who has a white streak in the front and it is striking. A friend lost twenty pounds before his fiftieth birthday and he looked ten years younger. It was excellent medicine for his half-century mark because he felt so good. "Even my tennis improved. Going down to my fighting weight made me feel youthful and I began to cover the court better." So, weight loss for George also shed years. "People come up to me and tell me I look so young—that I never age—and it makes me feel great."

Study your body and make the most of what you have. Within

reason, you can hone, firm, tighten, tuck, and contour your structure. You can improve your posture, lift your chin, throw your shoulders back, walk with your feet straight ahead and carry yourself well. What you can't do is shrink your bones in an attempt to emulate Audrey Hepburn. Use your knowledge of your body to help reinforce your appearance. If you feel a bit soft and see a few rolls around your tummy, do the "pinch an inch test means ugly fat" and firm up the loose flesh. Ease up on chocolate and ice cream, do some sit-ups, and you'll catch a small warning before it becomes a real problem. When I was young I could fast for a day and lose five pounds. Not anymore. Weight is easy to put on and becomes increasingly difficult to take off.

Everything you do to help yourself feel good radiates outward. If you have a pedicure, few people see this yet you feel great. If you have a facial, you feel a radiant glow and want to smile and have eye contact with everyone around you. You don't see your face, others do; but you feel that your face has shed layers of stress and tension. Don't you always get a lift from a haircut? You work out to some favorite tapes, early every morning. You work up a sweat and then you shower, wash your hair, blow it dry, dress and go to work. All day you feel great and have lots of energy. Or you swim laps three times a week and lose weight. You walk to work. You do yoga in the evening.

No one else knows your regimen. Most people who look and feel wonderful do certain things to pamper themselves—like having a manicure or a workout, a massage, or time in a steam room. They follow an exercise plan to help them maintain and improve their bodies.

All of us have off days. We may eat a bit too much or our hair doesn't look quite right. We pretend it doesn't matter how we look because we want people to respect us for ourselves. But we know better; everything matters. We should try to look our best whenever possible because we are so personally affected by our own appearance. Question yourself when you are not feeling your best and analyze what you can do to feel better. Just wearing that raspberry coat to work could turn a gray day into a cheerful one for you and others.

PROJECTING THE IMAGE
OF WHO YOU WANT TO BE

"EACH MAN THE
ARCHITECT OF HIS
FATE."
—*Appius Caecus*

One of my favorite illustrations by Norman Rockwell from the old *Saturday Evening Post* is of a ten-year-old girl dressed in a white eyelet nightgown, sitting in front of a huge gilt-framed mirror with a magazine open on her lap to a page showing an elegant woman. This little girl's doll is resting against the mirror. She has styled her hair and put on lipstick. Her fingers are tucked under her chin to hide her childish nails. Her ungainly feet grip the edge of the mirror. Here, in an intimate moment, Rockwell lets us wonder with her. Who am I? Will I be pretty when I'm older? What will I do when I grow up? This lovely, tender scene is all about becoming.

This illustration reminds me of attending my godparents' daughter's wedding in Framingham, Massachusetts, when I was thirteen. I was just home from summer camp where my uniform was shorts and T-shirts, and I wore my hair in a ponytail. My mother took me to a dress store where I tried on a crimson A-line Ann Fogarty dress which made me look twenty-one. My nails were a wreck so I wore white gloves, and Mother lent me a black hat with a veil. I was photographed at the wedding reception to capture this scene for all time. I was trying to be grown-up and sophisticated. Thanks to a girdle flattening my tummy and some high heels, a Grace Kelly page-boy hairdo, a borrowed pair of gold earrings and Chanel No. 5 dabbed generously behind my ears, I looked and felt like a young woman. Clothes have a powerful effect on us and while that wedding outfit was a real style stretch, I remember what fun I had and how glad I was to have dressed up for the occasion.

In that case my clothes added to my confidence because when you're thirteen your social skills are somewhat limited. I was an awkward teenager inside a beautiful dress and I felt as radiant as the bride.

Now, all these years later, I think my clothes reveal my true self more than they did at that August wedding, but that memorable event taught me that it's sensible to pay attention to what we wear. Depending on our selection, we will feel comfortable or awkward.

A friend went to law school after her youngest son was in school full-time, and her uniform at the local university was blue jeans, a sweatshirt, sneakers and a knapsack to hold the weight of a seeming ton of textbooks. Lorraine wanted to fit in to the prevailing dress code. Once she passed the bar exam and was accepted at a large law firm, she went shopping to purchase her serious career wardrobe. Guess where she went. Brooks Brothers. Lorraine took an elevator to the women's clothing floor and bought a gray flannel suit and a navy blue pinstriped suit. She bypassed the cotton blouses with a ruffle at the neck and zoomed over to the counter where she bought some button-down shirts. There was a rack of silk ties for ladies, the kind you tie in a bow around the neck. Lorraine was entering a male-dominated world and she wanted to look serious. The shoes she bought were no-nonsense, low-heeled, with a wide stacked heel.

Happy with her investment, she went the extra mile and entered a fine leather store and bought a natural-colored briefcase and had L. G. Matthews stamped in gold above the sturdy handle. Now she was set. Lorraine could be a great lawyer. She was one of the guys.

I don't know exactly how long it took before our lawyer rediscovered she was a woman, but her unisex look was relatively short-lived. She found out that once you are a lawyer, the worst sin is to act like one and—heaven forbid—to look like one. Half of her clients were female and she felt out of place with her masculine look. What really saved Lorraine was her sense of humor. While on an airplane shuttle to Washington she looked up and laughed. To herself she admitted, "Oh no, I don't look like me. I look like a stewardess and they wear airline-issued uniforms. I paid hard cash for mine and it's all wrong!"

How do we learn to see ourselves first as we really are and, second, as others see us? How can we project an accurate image of ourselves? To begin with, ask yourself what you most like about your appearance. Are you satisfied with your posture? Your hairstyle? Do you feel comfortable with your makeup? Does your wardrobe give you pleasure? Gisele Masson, who with her late husband Charles Masson founded the restaurant La Grenouille in New York City, is one of my favorite women. She exudes personal style in everything from her love of her family to her passion for her native Brittany, where the poplar trees sway to the music of the wind. Gisele tells me that she loves her life. She loves to laugh, and she dresses in clothes that are unique, colorful and spirited. She is thankful for a full, beautiful life and this is the precise image she projects. Several years ago I discovered that she had been born into a family of fashion. Her mother, aunt, grandmother and uncle all sewed; they did embroidery and beading. Gisele grew up with the understanding that you create beauty with your hands. "I learned about style in fashion and cooking and the beauty in pleasing proportions of everything," recalls Gisele with sparkling eyes.

I asked Gisele what she wants most for her two precious grandchildren, Flavia and Charles. "I want them to find strength in their marks of individuality. Individuality is a strength. Flavia is three and she has the good sense of knowing exactly what she wants. She loves music and nature. She loves books. Recently Flavia moved some pebbles from a fountain in Old Westbury Gardens in Long Island and rested them on a path, putting water on them . . . 'The pebbles will sleep better,' she said. With nature she is far away. It is inside her, she was born with it and it has developed."

Gisele epitomizes the essence of style because she radiates the richness of her whole being. The best way to project the image of who you want to be is to simply be that free spirit. Gisele is inspiring because *she* is inspired. After her husband Charles died, she didn't feel lonely. Smiling, she looked into my eyes and told me: "You're never alone when someone loves you."

"SIMPLICITY IS THE WHOLE SECRET OF WELL-BEING."
—*Peter Matthiessen*

EVERYTHING YOU WEAR SENDS SIGNALS

Change should represent growth but sometimes circumstances change and you'll go through periods in which you lose touch with your style. My daughters remind me that my style has been fairly consistent except for the period just after I married their stepfather Peter, a prominent lawyer. Apparently I was so concerned with fitting into the life of being married to an older, more established man, I dressed as though I were his age! At the time I wasn't aware of what I was doing. I was thirty-two and so much in love with Peter. I looked around at his friends and tried to blend into the scenery. This period of sudden aging lasted about two years. I woke up one sunny spring morning and it became clear to me: I wanted to be the person I was when Peter fell in love with me! I wanted to recapture my own personal sense of who I was, which required a more fun, youthful, colorful way of dressing.

Never make the mistake I did of trying to fit in. "Proper" clothes are boring and don't make a statement. Be willing to stand out. Wear a fun blue hat. If the spirit moves you, decorate the hat with a garland of fresh field flowers before going to a niece's wedding. Consider the event a play, act your part brilliantly and honestly. Cast yourself as the interesting character you are. To be yourself you will express originality. When you see yourself in a new, different light, as with my awakening to the reality that I was pretending to be prematurely old, leap upon the opportunity to make a constructive change. In my case, I had to give some clothes away and start again. I felt that I shed years simply by recognizing I'd made a mistake and then doing something about it.

What is the message you are conveying? Is it truly you? Clothes, just like your home, are an extension of your essence, revealing *your* character. Everything should connect to *your* center.

My friend Gisele Masson made me feel better when she told me she had also experienced a style crisis when she came to America from France in 1949. "I'd seen George Patton's army fight so

ALL FORMS OF SELF-EXPRESSION ARE LINKED.

bravely; I saw that symbol which impressed me when I was eighteen and I wanted to go to America. Immigration took four years and I finally got a six-month tourist visa. When I arrived in New York I had only thirty-five dollars. The immigration officer said, 'Happy landing,' and, because I only had thirty-five dollars, cut my time down to two months. It was terrible!"

Fifteen days before Gisele came to America on the *Nieuw Amsterdam,* she'd met Charles on a blind date. When, as a complete stranger, he first called and asked her out, she felt he had some nerve. How forward! But friends knew him and told her he was a gentleman and attractive. She agreed to have dinner and it was love at first sight. Tenderly he inquired, "Are you sure you have enough money to go to America?" Charles gave Gisele the address of his sister who lived in Manhattan and who worked in a restaurant. Gisele arrived on July 13 alone in Newark, New Jersey, called his sister and went to live with her in her apartment in Manhattan.

"Soon Charles arrived and took one look at me. The humidity had gotten to my long hair and I didn't know how to style it. I felt like a mop. Charles was eleven years older than I and more worldly and he loved beautiful women. He told me I wasn't wearing the right things. 'Your hair is wrong. Your jewelry is wrong,' he observed. I'd lost my feeling. I loved America but I didn't know how to be myself. Charles helped put me on the right track. I decided I was going to find myself again. I felt uncomfortable. I loved everything but I didn't know how to fit in. I knew Charles was right but I didn't know what to do about it. It took me a year to put it all together."

I asked Gisele how she did it and her story was enchanting. "Being a newlywed, I did what Charles asked me to do. He bought me a pink hat and I felt uncomfortable but I wore it anyway. Charles was the headwaiter at Le Pavillon and the manager from Christian Dior went there for lunch." Charles arranged for Gisele to be interviewed with Dior as an executive secretary. "Immediately I got the job and I felt so comfortable. I felt I was back in my own skin. The first day they had a sale of hats from the models. I bought three hats—one lavender chiffon with a pouf, one black

> ". . . IN EVERY
> GESTURE DIGNITY
> AND LOVE."
> —*John Milton*

and one red which I wore on the side that had a shocking pink bow with the tail sticking up! It was wonderful. Yet I hardly wore hats. I had no place to go. No money, no clothes. The next day I bought two suits." Gisele spent more money in two days at the fashion house of Dior at 730 Fifth Avenue than she'd earn in a month!

"I owed all that money. I was in debt but there was such elegance. There were Dior's own models. Everyone was well dressed. The manager wore a hat. We all worked with hats on. Mr. Dior came two times a year. He saw me and told someone in French, 'She is nice, jaunty.' I did errands for him. I'd go to Klein's department store and buy gray towels. Mr. Dior loved pearl gray. He was a simple man. A genius. You could feel it." The legendary Dior, who revolutionized couture in 1947, had a magic style, which was a certain glamour combining simplicity with richness. "He looked like a king. I was there for three years before becoming pregnant with my son Charles. I had a black dress. I wrapped myself in shawls." Dior had a tender attitude and wrapped women in feminine, romantic, simple shapes, flattering to the figure. "Dior is where I learned my personal style. I found myself. I bought fabric and started sewing baby clothes. Charles was with me at home and I sewed."

REVEAL YOURSELF.

Gisele once lost her way, I lost my way. I am touched to hear similar stories of people getting off track in their individual searches. It helps give us the courage to look at ourselves afresh.

GAINING CLUES FROM PEOPLE YOU ADMIRE

We all need role models for inspiration. Examine the appearance of those you admire. Would you like to wear their style of clothing? Or, is it *how* these people wear their clothes that you like? Is it their originality? Do they wear monochromes, earth tones or bright colors? Notice the fit and tailoring of their clothes. Do they wear solids or patterns? I discovered I love polka dots and I enjoy any fabric that has polka dots. I buy colored polka-dot ties for Peter whenever I can find a bright one that has big, wonderful circles. My favorite tie is sky blue with one-quarter-inch red dots. The women Claude Monet painted over one hundred years ago wore polka-dot ribbons on their straw hats and on their dresses in the garden. French fashion designers are using them today. Polka dots make me feel perky and happy. I wear a white sarong with hot pink polka dots over my bathing suit at the beach. I find color and a perfect circle of white, black or another color a flawless, dazzling design. What are your favorite fabric patterns? Do you like woven materials—say, woven tweeds or twill? Do you enjoy wearing silk?

I'm tall and never knew how to deal with the "yo-yo" hem lengths fashion insists on changing each season. An elegant older lady, Natalie Davenport, the former decorator for the late Babe Paley, always dresses the part of refinement and taste. I observed over a twenty-five-year period that her suits and dresses were always the same length, just below the knee. People around her were wearing "hot pants," or hems were down to the ankle or up around the thighs, but Natalie had established her own style.

Keep a fashion folder of clippings of everything that looks stylish that you feel would look good on you. If you see advertisements that entice you, make it a priority to set aside some time to try on the clothes. We learn through molding these different shapes to the reality of the contours of our own bodies.

Study the length of a sleeve, the width of a lapel, the line of a skirt, the length of a jacket. Check the fullness of a skirt or trousers. Study which colors and textiles attract you. Edit out all the shapes and colors you don't like so you can bring into sharper focus what pleases you.

WHAT TO LOOK FOR

Each time we try on something we learn more about which style of clothing flatters our body. Don't go by size. Some of us have clothes in our closets that jump four sizes. It is not important how tiny our waists may be if our hips require a size larger. To save yourself aggravation, first try on a size bigger than you think you are. You can always reduce sizes. Psychologically you'll feel slimmer. If you buy a size that is larger than you'd like it to be, rip out the size label. It's for your knowledge only. Forget about it because one of the secrets to expensive designer clothes is that they try to flatter the woman's ego by calling a size 12 an 8. Deception has a short life because when we try on an inexpensive piece of clothing, it usually is cut small.

The fuller and baggier your clothing, the more it appears as though you are solidly packed inside. When we are overweight we tend to untuck our blouses and wear oversized handbags. Full hips with a small waist, for example, look narrower when you have an A-line skirt. A soft straight-line skirt flatters my body more than a flared skirt that adds layers of bulk over my hips. The cut and fit of your clothes can add or take away more than ten pounds.

I saw an ad for a snappy pink-and-white-striped boxy linen jacket and felt it was meant for me. But when I tried it on it fell straight over my waist and was the width of my hips, making my figure disappear. I've learned I need clothes that flatter my waist because I have big hips, full breasts and broad shoulders. When my waist is accentuated, the proportions all fall into place.

Once a friend called me—she'd found two classic dresses she knew would look good on me. One was a rich plum-colored linen and the other a raspberry-red wool. I ran to the store and tried them on. No size fit me. I'd try on bigger and bigger sizes and the larger the dress size that fit my shoulders, bust and hips, the more the waist was lost. These dresses were so attractive on the hanger but made me fight back tears in the dressing room!

We tend to become emotionally attached to colorful, attractive materials and because color speaks louder than form, we don't immediately pay enough attention to the cut, line and proportions. When you do find a piece of clothing you are drawn to, pause

THERE ARE NOT LIMITS, ONLY POSSIBILITIES.

and study how it is cut. When you discover you need to wear long jackets that cover your fanny, never compromise and buy a short jacket. If you look best with a fitted arm, don't even try on a shirt that has a big, flounced sleeve. If you find you are not at your best in a sleeveless or strapless dress, edit these models from your wardrobe. A friend who has a great deal of style only wears dresses and blouses that zip or button in the back because she finds the smooth line more flattering than the possible gapping and pulling across her full breasts. Another friend wears silk blouses tied in a bow at the neckline to direct the eye away from her sagging neck.

Examine how much cleavage you want to show with your daytime dresses. More than a little is inappropriate. Often a dress can be raised a little by taking a tuck in the seam at the shoulder. Notice sleeve lengths and styles until you have a few that are attractive on you. A friend bought a designer dress with accentuated full shoulders and sleeves and found it didn't look as good on her when she gained weight. The sleeves became overpowering, so she had them taken in and replaced the larger shoulder pads with smaller ones.

Short women do best in dresses and suits because one color lengthens, whereas two different colors cut you in two. Separate blouses and skirts, if they match in color, are attractive also. Vertical stripes are slimming. Horizontal stripes draw your eye outward to make you appear heavier. If you want to wear horizontal stripes, like a wonderful blue-and-white-cotton Marimekko shirt, have it fit you well so the shirt is snug against your body. Push up the sleeves.

White looks larger than a dark color such as navy or black. Try to avoid wearing a black top with a white skirt or pants because most American women with heavier hips and thighs (in contrast with, for example, oriental women) would look out of proportion. Better a white blouse and a black skirt or pants because black reduces the size of the widest part of the body. A friend whom I've never considered slim wore a white fitted blouse and a straight black linen skirt to dinner one evening and looked dazzling.

HOW TO BUILD YOUR DREAM WARDROBE

If we all had magic wands we would open our closet doors and every piece of clothing would fit perfectly, buttons and hems would be reinforced, there would be no spots, everything would be pressed to perfection. Each item would look smashing on us, flattering our contours. If you don't have a magic wand, honestly evaluate each item in your closet.

THERE YOU GO.

The French interior designer Andrée Putman, who wears black day and night, loves America and American women. "But there is one thing that deeply shocks me—American closets. I cannot believe you can dress well when you have so much." Her own closet consists of a free-standing eight-foot-long copper clothing rack. "At a certain time of your life, you should have almost no choices." She admires the legendary furniture designer Jean-Michel Frank, whose wardrobe consisted of forty identical gray suits. "I love the idea. To me, it's perfect—the ultimate." Andrée is a minimalist and you might find her ideal of utter simplicity too extreme but it makes a powerful point. Many Americans have overstuffed their closets.

Forty percent of the clothes in one's closet can be eliminated entirely and 20 percent need some form of alteration or repair. Usually only 40 percent are ironed and ready to wear. The best way to build a dream wardrobe is to empty everything from your closet and try on each item in front of a full-length mirror.

Our clothes have to suit our bodies as well as our lifestyles. Where and how we live should determine the kind of wardrobe we assemble.

Many of us go from early morning through the evening in the same clothes. A fashion magazine editor in chief wears dresses with jackets in the daytime and at night she removes the jacket and changes her earrings. A suit can always hide a dressy blouse that can be appropriate for evening. If you go from appointment to appointment all day and then often have to get through the evening without changing your clothes, select materials that can withstand heavy wear and tear without showing wrinkles. A lovely linen dress is an ideal selection to go from shower to cocktail reception, but if you put it on at 6:00 A.M., take a train to work, and then go to a reception before dinner and the theater, you'll wish your dress were made of some miracle wrinkle-free synthetic fiber.

Build your dream wardrobe around *your* life. If you rarely go to black-tie events, you needn't have more than two dressy dresses at a time. A consistency of your image and point of view should be reflected in all your clothes. Break up your clothes into four categories: work, social life, leisure time and intimate time. A literary agent may dress conservatively in dark colors for work, but his clothes take on more color and individuality when he dresses for friends, when he is spending his free time away from the office and when he is at home with his wife. Think of these four categories as you build your wardrobe. What is your work? How do you dress for it? What do you do socially? How do you spend your free time? If you love the outdoors and sports this calls for a different kind of wardrobe from what you wear on city streets. It's useful to remember that you don't have to be with someone else in order to have attractive at-home and sleep wear. One third of our lives are spent in this category of clothing!

Your ethics are expressed in your clothes as well as in your actions so be sure they represent you well. Having a huge closet full of expensive clothes doesn't necessarily imply an ideal wardrobe. A few well-selected, quality items can be both satisfying and practical. We wear only one category of clothing at a time. By focusing on your style and limiting what you buy, you can have several color changes and save time and money. When I go to a beach resort I wear white pants and a colorful tunic blouse every night. Simple, easy and nice.

Our jobs dictate the type of clothes we wear at work. If you are a research doctor working in a laboratory all day you cover up your own clothes with a smock. Yet it is important that your clothes fit you well and are well-ironed and fresh. When you wear

STYLE NEVER
PRETENDS.

clothing that is baggy or drab it will affect your spirit, which generally affects your performance. The interior decorator whose romantic evening clothes are so feminine and full of ruffles and lace could reexamine her work wardrobe so it better reflects her personal style and superb color sense. Her clients would enjoy seeing a bit more flair in her costumes when she is in the business of dictating taste and style.

Our time among work, social life, leisure time and intimate time overlaps. It is just as important for you to love the clothes you wear around the house when you are alone or enjoying family time as it is when you are out among clients and friends. Remember that you are dressing to please yourself. The best wardrobe is one that makes you feel wonderful all the time! When clothes are varied to meet your many different engagements and when each piece of clothing has your stamp (even the ones others don't see), you will have clothes that suit your life.

Ideally, your wardrobe should be timeless. Some of the best-dressed women in America have silk blouses, scarves and handbags that are at least twenty years old. Fashion designers make their money from the insecurity of women buying the latest status symbol. By sticking with your newfound personal style, noting new additions and eliminating some of the items that are tired and worn, you can make a far more stylish and appealing fashion statement because it will be your own. Chanel is one of the few designers whose look has remained relatively consistent over the years, so one feels comfortable building a Chanel-styled wardrobe that is classic and always right. Chanel has been copied inexpensively and people who can't afford designer clothes can adopt the look at reasonable prices. Today's balloon skirt will soon be yesterday's news. That's not to say it isn't fun to have a funky balloon dress, but because it's a frivolous, amusing "look," when it fades you may want to retire your dress. Spend your real money on *your* personal style and pay little for fashion-whim follies that never last. A tailored Chanel style is timeless, elegant, feminine and confident.

"MEN SELDOM GIVE PLEASURE WHERE THEY ARE NOT PLEASED THEMSELVES."
—*Samuel Johnson*

TEN TIPS TO FINDING YOUR PERSONAL STYLE
OF DRESS

1) Be Practical

Your clothes have to work for you throughout the year. If
you are on a limited budget you can't have a wardrobe of "dry-
clean only" clothes. If you loathe ironing, have some clothes that
are wash-and-wear. If you are hard on your clothes, be sure to
reinforce the buttons and hems. If you have a skirt and jacket you
enjoy wearing separately, try to wear the skirt the same amount
of time as the jacket and always clean both separates together so
they will age as a suit. Once I bought a suit with a straight skirt
for work that had bias binding around the bottom of the hem and
I made the mistake of trying it on in a cramped fitting room
without walking around the store. I wore this skirt to work one
day and discovered I couldn't walk. My legs were bound in this
narrow skirt that had no give. I made a back slit which allowed
me to walk, so my mistake wasn't a total loss. Only you know
what use you put your clothes to. They have to function well for
your style of life.

2) Value

Mrs. Brown believed we should have some really good clothes
and then some inexpensive "numbers" we can replace every few
years. I always feel I get good value when I spring for something
a bit out of my financial reach, knowing it should be with me for
years to come. Once we figure out which style slacks are the most
flattering, which line of skirt suits our build and which types of
necklines we like on our blouses and shirts, we can afford to make
a few serious investments each year. Indulge when you find attractive things in your size, because you are spending your money
on clothes that will give you lasting pleasure. Beware of sale signs;
we never get value out of an expensive dress that has been marked
down if it doesn't fit well and is not in a fabric or color we really
adore.

Love each purchase you make. Clothes you rarely wear, like rooms you frequent only on very special occasions, are cold and never as comfortable and friendly as clothes you hate to take off. Try to hit the mark with each item so you get value from having one great blue blazer instead of having three "just okay" jackets. Make every clothing decision a major one. Keep reminding yourself that what you select will affect your mood, and that it is better to have fewer, well-chosen things than to compromise.

3) Variety

Many well-dressed men and women who find a suit (or dress) they like buy it in several different colors and materials. If the cut and fit are attractive on you, the different colors will make the outfit appear different yet the shape will add to your sense of style. I have a friend who loves to wear seasonal uniforms. She simplifies by buying her clothes in multiples. She has only a few different models of dresses and suits and has a wide selection of color variety, in solids and prints. If you find a sweater that is attractive you might like to add several different colors to your collection. Color is an ideal way to add variety to your style of dress, and it makes a strong statement about how you see yourself. Wear simple lines that best complement your figure and repeat them in a range of colors that look good against your skin and hair.

Use the seasons to give you color and texture variety. Just when you cannot stand your winter clothes another week, spring does come. Wear materials seasonally even if you live in California and don't have four seasons. Wear rich textures and colorful patterns and tweeds in the winter, and fresh pastel seersucker, lightweight silks, linen, piqué and Swiss cottons in the summer.

Envision the different activities in your life. For summer you need clothes for the beach in addition to bathing suits. You need sarong cover-ups, T-shirts, shoes and colorful tote bags. Men's dark business socks and leather briefcases at a beach resort are unattractive. You need clothes for leisure as well as for work. You might wear a sundress around the house in the summer because it is comfortable, refreshing and light. You don't necessarily have to be in the sun to decide to put on a sweet sundress. Have some surprises, some twists, some brilliant colors and color combinations in your closet. Put a priority on the things you most love to do and then add spice and style to the different categories. If you love the beach but try to avoid the sun, have a variety of attractive tops in pastel stripes or solids to put over your bathing suit. Collect ribbons and scarves to wrap around the brim of your straw hat. Reserve pastel flat shoes, ballet slippers or sandals to wear to the beach so they're special and not part of your everyday shoe wardrobe.

4) Accessories

Take advantage of every opportunity to add a personal touch to your clothes so the total look is refined, coordinated and has your special flair. The simplest basic black dress can change personality if you add pearls or a silk scarf; or it can have a gold belt, a black leather or suede belt, or, for fun, a wide hot pink or hot orange belt. So if the spirit moves you, your accessories can be in primary colors to contrast against black. Try twisting a colorful silk scarf around your waist for some punch, tying it in a sash at one side. Twist your double strand of pearls around a colorful ribbon or scarf and tie the ribbon in a bow at the back of your neck. Your jewelry should be in two general categories: real and fun fake. Pearls, a gold necklace, some gold bracelets, a few pairs of earrings, an inherited family crest ring, a tie pin, a gold watch—these are serious accessories that we can enjoy every day. Jewelry pieces with colorful stones and diamonds—pins, necklaces and earrings—tend to be for special occasions. Be careful, however, not to overinvest because they can become dated if not carefully selected. It is fun to wear real jewelry when you're all dressed up but if your lifestyle doesn't call for it, except on rare occasions, you may want to concentrate on plain jewelry you can wear every day. Simple gold earrings with semiprecious stones, for example, are attractive and appropriate for daytime use.

Fun fake costume jewelry is colorful and adds glamour and style. Givenchy has a beautiful selection of colorful glass stones set cleverly in brass, and rhinestones set in blue lacquer to give you the chic without the worry or expense. It is fun to have jewelry

DO YOU ENJOY ORDERING FROM CATALOGUES?

enhance our clothes and in the evening when we get dressed up, amusing jewelry adds to the festive spirit. In the summer or when you travel on vacation to the tropics, a collection of silver jewelry looks good against your tan and gives you a refreshing change.

Hats, gloves, belts and scarves are fun style accessories. You gather these items over years and they're there to choose from when the spirit moves you. Accessories should add sparkle and panache to your classic tailored clothes. Thirty years ago the late Mrs. William Paley walked in from the rain to a four-star restaurant in Manhattan and when she took the colorful silk flower-design scarf off her head she hesitated and then folded it lengthwise and tied it loosely around the handle of her pocketbook. She started a style. Think of all your accessories as opportunities to express your personality and mood.

5) When to Buy

Buy clothes, shoes, handbags and accessories as you go along, when something catches your eye and, most important, when you are in the mood. Wise purchases require time and patience and if you are too rushed you will not do yourself justice. Buying out of dire need is always costly. With rare exceptions, there won't be any surprise events in your life when you have to make a special purchase for a particular event. Take Thoreau's advice: "Beware of all enterprises that require new clothes." Let your personal style guide you so your wardrobe accommodates all areas of your life. If you go to only one or two dressy dances a year, one great evening dress might be all you need and you can change the feel of it with a jacket, a shawl or imaginative jewelry. Plan to add a few pieces to your wardrobe. Buy a few items at the beginning of the season so you can enjoy having a wide selection and wear your clothes for a longer time.

Again, be wary of sales. Thomas Jefferson warned us, "Never buy what you do not want because it is cheap. It will be dear to you." The clothes that others have picked over and passed up might not be right for you either. Designers and manufacturers goof and often they produce clothes that aren't right on most bodies. If you are buying marked-down clothes be more particular than ever because you can't take final-sale merchandise back and if, once home, it isn't right, your thrifty gesture becomes a painful mistake. Everyone likes a bargain, but we usually pay for what we get. If we are lucky, we can get exactly what we want on sale. When we purchase something we adore, chances are it will bring us lasting value.

6) What Will Affect Your Choices

Most salespeople are on commission and dealing with them as you negotiate a variety of sizes over your hips can be traumatic. Shop where people are nice to you. Friends may offer to help you select some clothing but they don't know your body flaws or finances and may lead you astray. Your spouse may think of you as a "doll" or a "fox" but may not have a realistic picture of how you feel in the clothes he selects or how your wardrobe has to coordinate and serve you. If you just ate a big lunch you will be puffier than normal. However, it is never wise to buy new clothes after you have starved yourself for two weeks. One woman did this and became so excited that she'd dropped a size, she stocked up on size 8 only to be disappointed a few weeks later when she resumed her normal eating pattern and her clothes became too tight. Be realistic. You'll gain a few pounds and still want to fit into your new clothes. If you want to celebrate weight loss, buy one great item, not six. Build your clothing inventory slowly.

Designers forecast future color trends and there will be whole seasons when you look around hopelessly for wonderful colors and you end up with black and white. Far better to wear black and white than ugly colors you hate. When designers all decide on beige or "neutrals" I happily boycott the stores.

Try never to buy clothes when you are feeling blue. Don't translate your gloomy mood into things that don't represent you at your best. Far better to browse in a bookstore and buy an inspirational book when you're feeling down. The book may help you snap back, but the clothing mistakes you'll inevitably make can only prolong your sadness. When I look in my closet and clearly recognize a disaster, I hold it up and wonder how I ever could have been so depressed. But since we are all different, some-

"CAN ONE DESIRE
TOO MUCH OF A
GOOD THING?"
—*William
Shakespeare*

one may find it a happy surprise on the hanger of a local thrift store. Cut your pain by eliminating the mistake from your closet.

7) Wear What You Love

I know a stylish man who carefully selects each day the clothes he feels will support his positive hope for the day. Even when he discovers he's having a bad day, Edward is humored by his colorful tie, his striped shirt, the tassels on his well-polished loafers and his colorful silk scarf. We should always wear clothes that we love, especially if we're going through a sad time. Our clothes should remind us of who we *really* are. When we wear clothes we love, it shows on our faces, in the way we carry ourselves, in the way we walk and in our gestures. People respond to our cues and act more pleasantly. Clothes are signals of our ideal and we should enjoy putting these revealing clues on our bodies. Love your clothes and enjoy expressing yourself through them. It's far better to wear just a *few* outfits you love than many different clothes you don't feel wonderful wearing.

8) Inventory

Twice a year—perhaps in September and March—remove every article of clothing from your closet. Try everything on and arrange your clothes into categories. If you've lost weight you may have to shorten some of your dresses or get them taken in. There could be a silk blouse you haven't worn in ages that is really snappy. Try it on and find a skirt, slacks or a suit that goes well with it and hang them back in your closet together as an outfit. Begin grouping jackets with skirts and slacks. Individual style requires that you spend time trying on different combinations of clothes until you find what looks best. If you do this each September, you'll have a fresh start for the fall and winter season. Repeat this evaluation again in March or early April. Bring out your spring and summer clothes and retire your winter clothes behind cleaner's plastic and place them in the back of your closet.

Take time to try on each sun dress, party dress, bathing suit and tennis dress. Our body weight shifts as we age. You want to be confident that everything that is hanging in your closet is

CUT YOUR LOSSES.

pressed and clean as well as comfortable. A little tuck here or easing a button there can give you the reassurance that last year's clothes are better than new. Clothes need to be worn in order for them to become you. As you take stock of your wardrobe, take note of how many years you've enjoyed certain outfits and then analyze why. When clothes are well made of good fabrics, with clean, simple lines and with colors and patterns you adore, they will have a long, happy life with you.

9) Flexibility

Certain key outfits in your closet can go from morning till midnight. They travel well, are comfortable and you can wear them in the city or in the country and you are always correct. Think of the flexibility of a blue blazer for a man and a great-fitting pair of white Katharine Hepburn-style trousers for a lady. The white trousers go from a dock in the South of France to dinner in the Berkshires to Bermuda and back home by a fire with a cashmere sweater or a sensuous silk blouse and pearls. Think of how many different places you and your clothes can go and be appropriate. The more flexibility we get from our clothes, the fewer of them we need. I know an elegant man who never wears cotton sport shirts when he is in the country being casual. He prefers to wear his colorful striped shirts with white collars open at the neck and sleeves rolled up, and he wears these with an ascot or silk scarf tied at his neck. He enjoys the soft ironed cotton and the smooth way it fits. His business shirts can double for leisure because there is a variety of colorful stripes to choose from.

SPONTANEITY LEADS
TO SERENDIPITY.

10) Color Choices

Color is the cheapest, easiest form of change and can have the most powerful effect on your mood. It is wise to pay no attention to color trends in fashion. Each of us has to find our ideal colors. Many of us have discovered what colors look best on us based on our hair color, the color of our eyes and complexion. However, we have to go farther than that when putting together our wardrobes. There's only so much time and money and we can't have shoes and bags to match every dress that looks good on us. Select two basic neutral colors for shoes and handbags. If you wear a lot of bright primary colors, black accessories are ideal. If, however, you wear mostly autumn colors, brown accessories are best. Choose between navy and black. It is expensive and time-consuming to have both. I enjoy wearing bright blue and red so I have eliminated brown and navy accessories, focusing on black. Changing your purse every day is a bore. The fewer colors you have in your accessories, the simpler things are. Black shoes and handbag look wonderful with bright blue and red. If you prefer navy blue to black, navy is excellent with red and green.

Wear bright, clear, lively colors, especially in the brilliant light of summer. Experiment. Don't pay attention to the advice you may have received when you were young to wear dark colors so no one will remember what you wear. It's wonderful to be re-membered. I have a friend who has a red suit that makes her glow. Every time I see Amanda in her suit I am thrilled. Wear colors you enjoy, colors you look good in that lift your spirits. I bought a baggy camel-colored wool coat one winter and felt like a rat. Work on gathering together a pleasing color palette that truly becomes you and makes you feel radiant.

DRESSING UP RATHER THAN DOWN

You can always take your jacket off or roll up your sleeves, but if you are underdressed for an occasion, it can make you feel self-conscious. If you receive an invitation that says "informal," that doesn't necessarily mean it's a barbecue. Informal could mean not to wear black tie! When we are attractively and appropriately dressed our options increase; when you are visiting someone for the weekend, possibly you'll be invited to have lunch at their country club or dinner at a restaurant.

Dress attractively even if you are only going to see the dentist or the doctor. You'll cheer yourself up and your day won't be so dreary. Remember, only you know you're going to do chores or

LET'S DO IT.

have root canal work. Dress beautifully and smile. Something magical might happen!

Often we go to buy groceries after work on our way home when we still are in good clothes. We won't ruin our good clothes by doing a few local errands. I find I'm in a better mood when I dress attractively even if I am doing something routine. I dress to please myself. If you feel like wearing a bright cotton shirt while you unpack book cartons, do. It will add some grace and elegance to a necessary task. It is especially important to dress well when visiting a friend in the hospital because it adds cheer.

At home, put on fresh clothes that make you feel good. Some of my clients wear jeans at home. I hate jeans. I feel fat, uncomfortable and restricted in them; I wouldn't wear them if I were to paint a bathroom. When I do paint I wear a pink-and-white-striped jumpsuit that puts a smile on my face. When I'm home relaxing I enjoy wearing white pants. Home is sacred and while we don't ever need to be formal there, it is nice to look fresh, colorful and attractive. Always dress with the idea that every moment counts and your clothes can improve these moments.

YOUR APPEARANCE IS YOU

It makes you feel good to look your best each time you step outside the house. Try not to be in the position of having to apologize or explain your appearance. A neighbor of ours was fired from his job and he immediately began to dress sloppily when he went out to walk his dog, which made us all feel sorry for him. He sent out powerful signals of rejection. Once you're dressed and you've examined your appearance in a full-length mirror, forget about the way you look. You know you look your best and now you're free to go about your day unselfconsciously. Focus on others. What you do to care for yourself is what others see. Express positive energy. When you give yourself your best, you share this with others.

Planning carefully and anticipating each day as a fresh opportunity to express yourself helps you flow from event to event with a real sense of confidence and pleasure.

INGREDIENTS OF A WELL-ROUNDED WARDROBE

What everyone wants is a dream wardrobe that can take them anywhere in the world. You want clothes that represent your best self-image, and your style doesn't depend on quantity. Have fewer, well-selected things that complement each other so that you can wear your clothes interchangeably and can enjoy having all your clothes as your favorites. You should always feel you can select the best from each category so you are saluting each occasion as an event.

Try not to overload your purchases in any one year. It's always exciting to look forward to a new season. Think of your clothes as you would a garden. Buying fresh new clothes is like planting seeds that will blossom in future moments.

COATS

❧ One heavy winter coat should be colorful and loosely fitted so you can wear it with a wool suit. On freezing cold days you'll need to wear both and shouldn't have to struggle to get it on, ripping the sleeve lining. A perfect blue, a cherry red or a plum would liven up the darkest day of winter.

❧ Spring coats usually get little wear so buy only if you find one you can't resist. Come spring we usually want to shed our coats. If you do buy one, be sure the coat is long enough and has a deep enough hem to have flexibility over the years.

❧ You need one long evening coat which will cover your bare shoulders and look elegant when you wear it over a long dress. Quilted velvet or Thai silk is richly textured.

❧ Try to find an attractive, colorful, lightweight, water-repellent raincoat so that it can double as a dinner coat. This is excellent for traveling also, and could replace a long coat.

❧ Have your coats coordinate with your shoes and boots. If you wear a lot of navy, a navy blue coat will be practical. If you have one good daytime winter coat, keep it simple—black, navy blue or red—and use lots of different-colored scarves to spice it up. Spruce up last year's winter coat with some smart brass Chanel buttons.

JACKETS

❧ Be sure your jackets look equally good with straight skirts and slacks. Check to be sure they are long enough. Jackets usually look bulky over a full skirt.

❧ Determine where you will wear a jacket. Men like sport jackets and blazers, but for women who wear suits and dresses, jackets may not be necessary except for the country. I know a well-dressed woman who has a collection of polka-dot and patterned short fitted jackets she wears interchangeably with solid-colored skirts. A velvet or silk moiré jacket with a sash can be useful and attractive to wear over a silk dress for evenings.

SUITS

❧ Have your daytime suits dressy enough so you can wear them into the evening with a contrasting colored silk blouse. For men who must wear the same clothes into the evening, choose a dark-tone suit and take with you to work a fresh tie, shirt, and white linen handkerchief to tuck into your jacket pocket.

❧ One dressy suit, say black brocade, is elegant for black-tie events when you don't want to wear a long dress. Add jewelry and, if it suits you, put a bow in your hair and you'll turn a basic black suit into something more formal.

DRESSES

❧ Silk dresses are always appropriate and elegant and can go any-where. They're flattering and feminine. Once you find the line that is best on your body you can enjoy a variety of different colors, both solids and patterns. You can press them after each wearing and dry-clean them after three or four wearings. I use Goddard's spray spot remover on my dresses (and Peter's ties) to save money on cleaning bills.

❧ Dresses that are belted at the waist are generally flattering to your figure and make you look taller. Try wearing a contrasting 3-inch-wide colored belt—yellow for a purple dress, hot pink for black, blue for red.

❧ Most day dresses can be worn through the evening. A formal dress for a special event can be completely simple in silk in a lively color and it will look sensational.

SKIRTS

❧ If you have good legs, don't hide them underneath long skirts. Enjoy finding an ideal length that makes you feel good.

❧ You need skirts of only two weights—lightweight wool for fall, winter and early spring, and cotton, cotton piqué and silk for spring, summer and early fall. A heavy wool skirt makes your body appear out of proportion when worn with a silk blouse. A suit, however, can be of a heavy material because it balances your body contours.

❧ When you find the cut of a skirt that fits you ideally, stock up. Buy (or have made) one in black, one in white, and one or two in other colors that coordinate with your blouses and jackets. No matter how many skirts you have in your closet, invariably you'll reach for the one that makes your figure look best. Skirts have to fit right for you to feel comfortable. They should be loose enough so they don't leave heavy creases when you sit down. Knit skirts are practical because they never wrinkle. However, be careful not are practical because they never wrinkle. However, be careful not to hide behind them. I gained a great deal of weight one winter when my knit skirts stretched to meet my weight and the elastic waistband expanded upon command!

SWEATERS

❧ Long cardigan sweaters with a contrasting band of color and brass buttons can act as a suit top. If you like knits, look for knit suits or skirt and sweater sets.

❧ One-of-a-kind hand-knit pullover sweaters with lots of different yarns and stitchwork are works of art. These pretty sweaters are rich and sensuous when worn by the fire on winter evenings or on long walks in the woods.

❧ A cardigan can be carried and put over your shoulders at dinner and is more attractive than a tailored jacket over a silk dress.

❧ Pullovers—with the exception of cashmere—are usually for casual occasions and sporting events.

❧ Be sure the sweater is as long as or longer than a tunic blouse.

SLACKS

❧ Slacks are a true barometer of how you are maintaining your weight. A fluctuation of even a few pounds can make them tight or loose. Many of my friends use their slacks rather than the scale as their guide to weight control. Most women look more feminine and sensuous in dresses and skirts. However, I know a lot of women who have less than ideal legs but who look great in slacks. Slacks are comfortable, they give us mobility, they're casual, they make us feel young and they keep us warm. Whenever I wear slacks in the winter to keep warm I am reminded of leggings as a child. Evaluate whether you look best with blouses tucked in or in longer tunic overblouses that tend to give the body a slimmer line. If you have full hips and a full fanny, select a blouse that just covers your buttocks. Have the legs of the trousers tapered.

❧ Black slacks make us look a size smaller. White slacks, while they make us look neat and crisp and nothing is smarter, add a size to our appearance. When we feel good in white slacks, we probably have our weight under control. Corduroy visually adds about eight pounds. Men can carry this off better than women. If a woman is flat-chested, this material will be too heavy for slacks. Lined tapered silk slacks appear slimming. If you have a full figure, avoid bulky wools and plaids in your slacks. Wear color and pattern above the waist. If you have nicely shaped legs wear narrow tapered pant legs to accentuate them.

❧ If you try on slacks at home and they feel tight, put them away and every so often try them on again. When they do fit you again, you'll look attractive in slacks. Help yourself slim down; don't gain a whole size or two without putting up a fight.

SCARVES

❧ Most of us love large, colorful silk scarves but don't quite know how to wear them. Having a drawerful of vibrant silk scarves you rarely wear is a waste. You can twist one around a straw hat. They are fun tied around your waist. To add color you can tie one around a handbag. You can wear scarves over your head to protect your hair when it rains or is windy. They add spark when tucked inside a coat or a suit. Use a mirror to experiment draping a scarf over your shoulders, tied in front. Study the way others do it and how it looks. With a plain, high-necked dress or blouse, a scarf should be draped around the shoulders. Scarves look good tucked inside a silk blouse or a cardigan sweater and tied at the side of the neck.

❧ I most of all enjoy touching my silk scarves and looking at the beauty of the colors. I can remember where each one came from and when I received one as a gift. They are an important part of our wardrobe. I love seeing men wear silk handkerchiefs in their suit or blazer pockets. It's sassy, dapper and fun.

BELTS

❧ Accentuate your figure by wearing a belt. They add a certain elegant refinement and splash of color. Enjoy having them hang in your closet as decoration. Anytime an ordinary matching belt comes with a dress, turn it around so the buckle is in the back.

❧ Experiment with belts. They can be expressive, colorful and amusing. A man can have an elegant brass, gold or silver belt buckle on his leather belt which adds a note of refinement. Colorful horizontally striped belts are fun for summer.

GLOVES

❧ Gloves have dropped out of grace. Except to keep our hands warm, gloves are rarely worn. They are so elegant and comfortable, we should think to wear them more often. Buy a few pairs of short white gloves and carry them to a wedding or tea. Some people wear one glove and hold the other. If you are at a reception where you will be shaking hands with lots of people, you'll be glad for your gloves! They are a gentle, genteel refinement and were once so fashionable. If you are inclined to wear gloves, they are always proper and graceful. I especially like white kid gloves. When I went to work for a decorating firm in the early sixties, we all wore hats and gloves to work. I wish we would revive this custom!

HATS

❧ Who doesn't remember Jackie Kennedy's famous pink pillbox hat made for her by Oleg Cassini? Now wide-brimmed straw and silk organza hats are in vogue. Wear a pretty hat for a festive occasion.

♣ Try on hats the way Gisele Masson did when she discovered mountains of hats at Stern's in 1949. Put one on and then act the part. Smile, model and have fun wearing a hat. They can be sassy, provocative, and can make you look ravishing. And afterward, what is more fun than to put your hat away in a scented flowered chintz hatbox?

SHOES

♣ Shoes can make or break your total look. Everyone notices your shoes. They should fit your foot as well as suit your personal style. You can't go wrong with a classic Chanel-style two-toned low-heeled pump for daytime.

♣ Shoes give us foundation. Twenty years ago Gucci pumps with brass decoration on the heel were the rage, yet they crippled your feet. Be sure your shoes will also get you where you want to go. The wise old saying "If the shoe fits, wear it" still applies. Your discomfort from an uncomfortable shoe will show up on your face and even in your voice. When I was in high school my feet grew so fast I pretended I had a smaller foot when I went to the shoe store for my loafers. On the theory that I would look better in a smaller shoe, I scrunched my toes up. Little did I know how painful this would be. When you find a shoe that fits you well, don't change.

♣ Many well-dressed career women wear elegant flat shoes in the daytime. Not everyone has pretty toes, so open-toe shoes are inappropriate unless your toes are good-looking enough to be on public display.

♣ Women frequently now wear sport and walking shoes to work and change once they get to the office. Beware: you are seen by more people when you are walking to work in sneakers than you are when sitting behind a desk. Old, well-polished shoes can be comfortable for walking and still suit your sense of style. New York observer Georges Gilbert lamented the decline of style.

"When I see women shod in dirty white sneakers, wearing turquoise blouses, red slacks over blue socks and possibly a yellow sweater, I shudder . . . and I mourn, as I witness the requiem of style."

❧ Keep your shoes in good repair and always have them well polished. Scented shoe trees help them to keep their freshness as they keep their shape. Never wear a shoe two days in a row. Let the leather breathe. Wear stockings with leather shoes; your feet and your shoes will be thankful.

❧ When shopping for shoes, go alone when you are not tired. Spend time walking around the store in the shoes before you make a purchase. Vow never to squeeze into a pair because you want your foot to look smaller, they are the perfect color or they are on sale. Take it from me, it isn't worth it!

HANDBAGS

❧ Well-dressed women with personal style carry attractive handbags. You carry the keys to your house or apartment, wallet, cash, credit cards, driver's license and makeup, glasses and notes and perhaps pills and address book inside your purse. You may also carry your office work in a tote bag. A tote bag can be checked or left with your coat, but your handbag is a large part of your image.

❧ Scale is vital to style. If a daytime handbag is too tiny it is just as awkward as one that is enormous. Pay careful attention to proportion and experiment so you can fit your essentials neatly into an attractive handbag.

❧ I never like having more than a few good handbags at a time. I rarely leave enough time to change purses when I get dressed. If the colors clash I will make the extra effort and change purses. Change handbags seasonally, not daily. In the evening you usually take out of your daytime purse only what is needed that night so you can carry a smaller purse when you are dressed up.

❧ Purses you use often become dated and beat-up. It is best to buy one that appeals to you, use it regularly and then replace it. The current trend is shoulder bags so that your hands will be free. Shoulder bags are better for your back than carrying weight at the end of one arm. I now have a Chanel-style shoulder purse just large enough to hold a file folder, which makes it possible for me to eliminate carrying a tote bag.

❧ Weed out the inside of your handbag at least once a week. Keep all cosmetics inside a plastic-lined cotton zipper pouch. Buy a small-size lipstick from Chanel for your purse so your bag doesn't have to bulge. When you find your bag is bulging, that is a sign to take time out to organize the stuff you accumulate as you rush around. Throw things out. File your receipts. Save your change in a jar for your travel fund and think about your week. This ritual of useful puttering helps you organize the inside of your handbag, and in the process you also get organized mentally. I recommend carrying your Filofax or engagement book in your purse or tote bag during the day so it is always with you. You can put in fresh refills and take out unnecessary pages as part of your handbag-editing ritual.

❧ Smart, colorful museum-art shopping bags can accompany your purse and they look fresh and lively. If you know you are going to pick up a few small items at the pharmacy, carry a pretty shopping bag with you so you never have to be seen with an ugly plastic sack. Advertise yourself, not a store.

UNDERCLOTHES
❧ Most of us can be organized about our suits and dresses, but somehow our underwear drawers look oddly like the rag drawer in the laundry room. By paying attention to these private pieces of clothing, you add to your pleasure when dressing and undress-

ing. The fit, line, shape and cut of your bra affects the way you look in a blouse. If you have large breasts a "minimizer" bra can actually reduce the size dress and blouse you wear. Usually one breast is larger than the other. When you buy a new bra, adjust the strap immediately to make the accommodation.

❧ In your Filofax, write down the brand name and size of the bras and underpants you wear and your favorite stocking brand, size and colors. There is no need for your underwear to chafe or make you itch. Why remember all these details? Thoreau observed in *Walden,* "Our life is frittered away by detail . . . Simplify, simplify." When you restock your underclothes, simply bring your Filofax with you to the store. Or better, save time and call in your order on the telephone and have the store deliver your items. Buy exactly what you've discovered suits your figure best.

❧ Arrange your underwear neatly and keep tabs on what items are losing elastic and life. Things wear out and there is no reason for you to sag simply because your bra is stretched out of shape. Plan on replacing these items every six months.

❧ Whether you live alone or share your life with someone else, underclothes should be as attractive as they can be so they make you feel wonderful. Look inside your drawers and be sure everything is as you want it to be. Discard all the items that aren't right for you now. No day should get off to a bad start because you have to pull and tug at your underwear. These ill-fitting items fool you into thinking you have plenty of your necessities in clean supply. Better to be spare and have only the best-fitting undergarments, ready to wear.

AT-HOME CLOTHES

❧ It is hypocritical to look nice only when outsiders see you. If you live alone you should please yourself and if you live with a love you should look appealing because you have pleased yourself. A night at home should be an opportunity to wear sensuous clothes you adore that are not proper to wear in public because they are too suggestive.

❧ Examine your pajamas, nightgowns, bathrobes and peignoir. If clothes are an extension of our inner selves then it follows that our intimate, at-home clothes should be fresh, attractive and good-looking. Send out your best signals even when no one is looking at you. Dress beautifully at home. You will feel comforted and uplifted, appreciating your time at home far more when you dignify it with lovely personal clothes.

❧ Indulge in some really elegant pajamas—silk or soft cotton with contrasting piping. A young woman bought some blue-and-white striped pajamas and ended up wearing them in the evening on a Caribbean vacation. Fantasize and wear a white gossamer embroidered nightgown under a silk peignoir and spend a candlelit evening enjoying your solitude or your mate.

❧ The clothes we sleep in should be soft and lovely. Never let your sheets and pillows be prettier than the clothes you wear inside the bed! You, your intimate clothing and a pretty bed are all one statement of your real personal style.

"BEWARE OF ALL ENTERPRISES THAT REQUIRE NEW CLOTHES."
—*Henry David Thoreau*

HOUSING YOUR CLOTHES

Take good care of your clothes. Never dress in such a hurry that the process is unpleasant, because dressing is a delightfully private moment. In the morning you are fresh from your dreams, rested from a good night's sleep, and when you dress you are anticipating the adventures of a new day. The way you house your clothes makes an enormous difference in the way you look, feel and act.

People who have found their own style are apt to be neat. Clothes deserve to be respected and properly cared for and your closet can be turned into a small room where you enjoy spending private, sensuous time.

No closet is too small. In the eighteenth century in France people were taxed by the amount of rooms they had, and closets were considered rooms. To avoid taxes on closets the French invented the ideal solution: the armoire! One armoire is ample space for a marvelous wardrobe. A closet is grand by comparison.

After you've stood in front of a mirror and tried everything on so that every item in your closet is in good condition, ironed and ready to go, you may find your once-crowded closet looks roomier and better than ever! It is discouraging to have unironed clothes crumpled all together so you can't see what you have.

If you haven't worn something in three months, chances are you won't have the confidence to put it on. Remember also that clothes have associations and evoke strong memories. If you ever have a horrible time in a suit or dress it will probably permanently spoil your enjoyment of it.

Spend time in your closet. Group your clothes seasonally and according to the use you put them to. For example, all dresses you wear to work should be next to each other so that at a glance you can immediately see what your options are for work. What fits your mood? The weather, the kind of day you anticipate, who you're seeing, how formal or informal you need to be, determine your selection. Flipping through your shirts, suits or dresses should only take seconds if everything is placed in good, logical order.

Next to work suits and dresses in the closet, you can have cocktail clothes—a dark or silk suit and silk dresses and designs that are meant for social life, glamour and dancing instead of career. At-home clothes should be together so that at a glance you see your selection and can make the best choice. Sports clothes should have their own space.

Every time you buy something new, eliminate one item from that category. If you buy a new pair of trousers, give an older pair away. Always upgrade but don't clutter. If you bring home a new pair of shoes, eliminate a pair you know are over the hill. Stockings, too. A tiny run will be a big run by the end of the day.

Keep reminding yourself that you are expressing your individual distinction through your careful editing of your wardrobe. Your style evolves and many of the clothes you once wore are no longer you. Cotton blouses you once wore to the office, say, can be placed where you house all your sporty country clothes. Make some shifts and eliminate the extraneous. What you pass on to a thrift shop is never a waste.

Think of your closet as a room devoted to making you look and feel your best. Set it up according to the way you live and the way you want to look and feel. Try not to share a closet. Nothing could be more personal.

Have matching hangers. Place sachets in your lingerie drawers. Have strong lighting and mirrors to light up your wardrobe and you. Keep your shoes in see-through shoe boxes or on shoe ledges so you can see them at a glance. Carpet your closet in a colorful wool that is cozy on your bare feet. Or use soft, colorful rag rugs that are easy to clean. Hang chintz curtains to hide suitcases and storage. Let flowered boxes and hatboxes decorate your shelves.

"YIELD AND
OVERCOME . . ."
—*Lao-tzu*

USING A PERSONAL SHOPPER

Busy working women find using a personal shopper enormously useful because it saves time and money and also eliminates frustration. Department stores have shoppers who can gather appropriate clothes from all different departments that fit your body type and personal preferences in the way of style and line; you try them all on in a fitting room. When new clothes come in that your personal shopper thinks you'll like, she'll put them aside for you and call you. These professional shoppers are trained and can see something on the rack and know how it will look on you. This service costs nothing and can be most helpful. You pay only for your clothes and probably have a wider range to choose from throughout the year than you would if you kept going to different stores looking around.

FINDING A SEAMSTRESS

Knowing of someone who sews and can measure you and do fittings can be a blessing. Often we know what we want in a suit or dress but can't find it at a reasonable price in the stores. Sometimes we buy a great-looking blouse and after wearing it for several years wish we could have it in a few different colors and patterns. Or we have one ideal straight skirt we want duplicated in a variety of materials. If you enjoy selecting materials and having your clothes custom-made for you, find a seamstress.

Word of mouth is best. You want someone who cares about helping you flatter your figure. You'll spend some time being pinned and tucked. Find someone who makes you feel good. Get a rough estimate before you do the detailing. When you fully design a piece of clothing and ask for the price, accept it graciously. The dressmaker knows how many hours she will take to make your outfit and she wants your repeat business. I've found seamstresses quote fair prices and from my experience they save you money. Not only do you get just what you want, things no one else has, but your seamstress usually has a low overhead so her prices will usually sound quite reasonable.

When you have a fitting the seamstress (or tailor) usually makes things too big. You can always take something in but you can't add more fabric. Be specific about how tightly you like your clothes to fit. Don't ask, "What do you think?" because chances are you might not see eye-to-eye about fit. Many people like to wear their clothes loose but I feel this adds bulk. There is no perfect fit; there is an ideal fit for your body and how you feel wearing your clothes. You must make this final decision.

DO YOU LIKE
NEEDLEWORK?

YOUR CLOTHES GARDEN

The more pleasure we have in life, the more we will enjoy expressing our individuality in the ways we present ourselves to the world. Just as flowers bring us a great deal of happiness, our clothes can too. Think of your clothes as a garden in bloom all year round. When you tend to your wardrobe in much the same way you'd care for a garden, your personal style blossoms.

"A GOOD STYLE
MUST, FIRST OF ALL,
BE CLEAR . . ."
—*Aristotle*

GRACE NOTES

❧ When wearing a pullover cashmere sweater over a blouse with slacks, put on a belt. This is elegant and shows off your figure.

❧ Wear tinted stockings—very sheer when wearing silk and more opaque with wool. This gives a flowing grace to your appearance.

❧ Wear a fresh flower in your buttonhole or in your hair. It won't live forever but it looks spirited and makes you feel more alive.

❧ Tie a vibrant-colored sash at your waist that has another lively color on the reverse side so you add touches of two colors to a solid-colored dress.

❧ Wear brightly colored wool scarves twisted at the neck with your winter coat.

❧ Stop going to a store where the saleswomen are snobbish and condescending. Tell the manager.

❧ Order simple items like sweaters or a bathrobe through mail-order catalogues. You can return anything that doesn't fit and save yourself a hassle in a department store.

❧ Try wearing bright-colored eyeglass frames. Sunglasses too. Turn a necessity into a colorful personal touch. Coordinate them to what you're wearing. I have yellow, red, blue, green and lilac and they make me feel happy.

❧ Superb posture gives you an air of confidence and makes you look thinner.

❧ A shine on your shoes puts a Gene Kelly spring in your step.

❧ Your hands tell a lot about you and your character. Be sure your hands reflect your intelligence. Perfect long, well-manicured nails might not be right for your lifestyle, especially if you love to garden. It's far more attractive to have artistic hands that create than a model's hands that can't function. Which women do you admire most? How do their hands look?

❧ If you are a romantic, use clothes to live out your fantasies. Wear an antique lace blouse and an heirloom pin. On evenings at home change into a smoking jacket and silk "at home" pajamas.

❧ An outdoor, athletic look can be disarmingly refreshing. If you feel like tossing a sweater over your shoulder, do.

❧ When a jacket lining wears out, have it relined in a vibrant purple or red silk.

❧ Add a dash of panache to a rainy day. Carry a bright chintz umbrella. Tired of your old drab trench coat? Replace it with a bright red or blue water-repellent coat. Or buy a chintz slicker.

❧ Have a signature piece of jewelry. Lauren Bacall wore a gold ID bracelet given to her by her beloved Humphrey Bogart. I wear a hand-hammered gold necklace with interconnecting circles that Peter gave me when he decided to marry me. I also wear a small gold crest ring on my baby finger that is the identical match to rings my daughters Alexandra and Brooke wear. What's your signature piece of jewelry?

❧ Before you finish dressing, add one final touch—the pièce de résistance—say, a wide pink belt or a silk sash around your hat or handbag. Look in the mirror and decide what will give the extra punch to your outfit.

❧ Check in strong light for spots and dirt on neckties before and after each wearing.

❧ Chanel favors a hemline that comes to the middle of the knee. If you feel your legs need a little firming up above the knee, work out on an exercise bicycle.

❧ Remember, even fashion designers, like writers or actors, are always experimenting. Use your body and your spirit as your guide and enjoy the process of discovery.

❧ Try the free samples of perfume and cologne given out in stores and buy a small bottle of the ones you like. Vary your scent when the spirit moves you because it will stimulate you. Save all your perfume bottles. They can be refilled or used as bud vases. What are a few of your favorite perfume scents? Have you had one favorite all your life? I still enjoy the floral jasmine scented fragrance of Chanel No. 5 today. This was the first perfume to be made with chemicals; before, perfumes were created with oils from flowers.

❧ Line a long black-on-white polka-dot evening coat with yellow silk for a dash of personal delight. Wear it over a simple plain long black dress.

❧ Babe Paley, known for her simplified-yet-elegant fashion sense, summed up her style in one word—"neatness."

❧ Locate an ideal place to put on your makeup. If you're a romantic and enjoy sitting at an attractive dressing table, have good lighting and display your pretty accessories—framed family pictures, cut crystal, silver, enamel, bottles of rose water and perfume as well as powder puffs, compacts and lipsticks.

❧ Put all your cosmetics you use every day in a basket in the bathroom. Cover the basket with an attractive patterned cotton napkin. When you are all set up you save time.

❧ Do you like fur? Many women prefer a great-looking fitted black cloth coat to a bulky, too long, furry, expensive coat. One client who moved from Summit, New Jersey, to Dallas, Texas, told me that after she bought her house she next bought a fur coat because it is a uniform in Dallas. Yet she had needed a warm fur coat far more in New Jersey than in Texas. Furs are fading from grace. How do you feel about that? Have one loosely fitting wool coat you can wear a heavy suit underneath for warmth.

❧ When wearing a red suit or dress, go the whole way and wear stockings with a red tint and gold-and-red earrings. Think of looking tall, handsome Givenchy in the eye, and smile!

❧ There is generally a close connection between the way we dress and the way we decorate. If you wear ruffles and like silk and brocades, you'll probably enjoy those sumptuous materials in your rooms. If you consider yourself a tailored dresser, you'll probably enjoy simpler textiles and details in your rooms.

❧ In the summer, brighten your watchband. Select red, blue or green.

❧ Starting the day being well turned out gives you a good feeling that can carry you through a hectic schedule. You compromise when you get dressed and wear a shirt that has a cracked button or a tie that should be at the dry cleaners or a skirt that needs ironing. Begin your day as fresh as your dreams.

❧ Pure natural materials breathe. Wool, leather, cotton and silk are comfortable to wear and they adjust to our bodies and get softer the longer they're worn. I recommend dress shields to save the life of your good clothes.

❧ It's hard for us to part with an old solid-color scarf even though we haven't worn it for several years. Perhaps it could be used as a table throw in the living room or bedroom to add some elegance and color to a brown wood surface. Some of my clients throw silk scarves over a lampshade to add a touch of romance and spice to a dreary hotel room. The light bulbs in hotels are such low wattage that there is no fear of fire and it looks colorful even if the light isn't turned on. Before you give up on a scarf, use it to line a drawer.

❧ Stripes on the diagonal zing.

❧ Buy a two-dollar lint remover—a roll of masking tape with a plastic handle so you can give a last-minute whisk to your clothes.

❧ Fun, colorful striped grosgrain buttons can spruce up a plain solid-color dress. Buy some ribbon wide enough to cover your buttons and ask a local upholsterer or tailor to make them up for you.

❧ Generally shoes should be darker, not lighter, than your dress or trousers.

❧ Treat yourself to some lovely underwear. The things closest to your skin matter a great deal.

❧ Clean hair instantly gives sheen and a feel of exhilaration to the new day.

❧ When you wear your hair up, use a cheerful ribbon or colorful combs. Experiment. Mix together two different ribbons.

❧ Clean fingernails and toenails make you feel as though you've just been swimming in Bermuda.

❧ There should be a predominant color in your wardrobe. What is your signature color? Red? Blue? Black? Mine is bright blue. Think of your favorite colors, the colors that look best on you. Select as your main color choice the one you feel represents your spirit best.

DARING TO BE *Yourself*

YOUR GRACE NOTES

FOUR

Your Personal Style of Work and Communicating

REALISTIC EXPECTATIONS ABOUT YOUR WORK

would like to think that we can earn a living doing what we love to do. A dancer can get paid to dance, an artist sells his pictures, a writer becomes a bestselling author and an avid gardener opens a thriving flower shop. I'm realistic enough to know that this often isn't the case. Many people work at one job or profession in order to pay the bills and gain freedom to pursue other interests. A sculptor does catering to earn extra money, a journalist does waitressing in the evenings.

That's okay. To assume that work is meant to be fun and challenging all the time is unrealistic. No one in any field escapes difficulties and discouragement. The way to lessen the negative aspects of a job is to keep a clear picture of the fact that you're being paid to work, not to love every task you're asked to perform. I've found that I make the most potentially frustrating moments

WHAT DO YOU MOST
LIKE TO DO?

175

tolerable by trying always to be myself and do my best in every given situation. I have spoken with people all across the country and without exception they tell me how hard they work. None of us has idle time on our hands. Work is not meant to be easy. There will be times when you don't like what you're doing. But once we accept this fact, we can bring our own style to everything we do and see that our work adds strength and muscle to our character. We may not love our work but we must love ourselves enough to do our very best.

Even if you love your work you will have lots of surprises. We decorators all have moments when it seems a client is trying to drive us mad. We may love to decorate but our patience can be tested regularly.

When faced with a crisis I try not to take it personally and I remind myself that I'm the same person I was before this problem happened and I'll be the same person afterward. If we keep our sense of humor and try not to let things get under our skin we have a good chance of surviving. Our attitude about ourselves is revealed in all parts of our lives, especially in our style of work. I once had an assistant who in time revealed a poor attitude about her work. She was sour and sloppy. For some reason she thought that everything should be fun, which resulted in inefficiency and chronic complaining. "I never get to do anything I want to" was her lament. She hated filing and when she Xeroxed she usually put the document in the machine crooked so that you couldn't read all of the copy. She fought everything as though her duties had to be attacked as in a battle. She wished only to be away from the office, taking clients to see beautiful furniture and rugs, and was miserable doing necessary office tasks. There was no pride in work or satisfaction of a job well done. Her grudging attitude affected everyone else. Any changes in schedule or clients' decisions threw her into a rage. "That's ridiculous," she angrily screamed around the office. In brief, she hated her job and quit my firm miserable. Everyone but this lost soul knows that she hates herself.

This young woman didn't understand that everything is connected. If you approach all the details of life with sloppiness and mediocrity, that defines who you are. If all the small routine procedures are taken care of well, then the bigger, more important things fall more easily into place. All the little things we all have to cope with frustrated this person because she felt too talented to do clerical work. She was above work and therefore never experienced enjoyment. Instead of feeling a wonderful flow from one well-done task to another, happy to be useful and pleased to do every job well, adding a personal touch to her work, she fought herself at every turn. I believe this is not something that will change without a complete change in attitude because no job can be the cause for such depression and misery.

HOW DO YOU SPEND
AN IDEAL WEEKEND?

Think of the people you meet in your travels who take pride in what they do—a cheerful bus driver, a funny waiter, a helpful salesperson or a cheerful doorman or checkout clerk in the grocery store, or a porter or a secretary. People can enjoy themselves doing a good job no matter what their work is, as long as they don't feel that what they are doing is beneath their dignity. I've met hundreds of women all over the country who bring their energy and enthusiasm to their work no matter what they do. Whenever we are being true to ourselves we can hold our head up high and not feel we are being defined by the nature of our task. Nothing should be considered below your standards. If you deliver packages in your free time to earn extra money so you can do some extra things for your children, I'm sure you can find this part-time job satisfying. You can elevate a job to your standards by your attitude and character.

People whose style is to do their best and put their all into everything they do, always trying to be useful, will be able to earn necessary money and, as a bonus, feel good about themselves. Think of a mother raising children and how she can never choose her job description. She does what has to be done each day. She does everything herself or she gets someone to help her but she is fully responsible. A job is like that. The people who give lip service to work but don't want to do the dirty work are people who probably need a trust fund or a rich spouse or both. I respect people who do their job well, no matter what their work may be.

There is a dangerous mystique about work. Some people have

the notion that work should be glamorous. They think success has no grubbiness. This is a myth. The owner of a small independent bookstore lugs heavy book cartons around, dusts off shelves, has sore feet and works six long days a week.

Barbara is a petite, brilliant, artistic lady who is a Chinese scholar. While studying in Taiwan several years ago she lived with an excellent cook who lured her into the kitchen and she got hooked. With some of the most subtle recipes under the sun she dreamed of opening a restaurant that would reflect an intelligent, elegant art to Chinese cooking. Now, at her Half Moon Café in San Francisco, she helps wait on tables in a pinch as well as taking care of all the administration details and most of the cooking. She wants to serve the best Chinese food in the whole city and she understands that by working hard she is accomplishing her goal. She'd do anything to succeed. Barbara didn't embark on this ambitious undertaking thinking it would be easy.

Look for the clues and serendipitous events that open your mind about work and add new challenging dimensions to what you already know through experience. Barbara's own experience as a Chinese expert led to her vision of the restaurant. I owe my being a decorator to flowers, because I wanted room interiors to feel as fresh and pretty as my earliest childhood memories of my mother's garden. What you have to offer ultimately is your own experience.

THE EXCITEMENT IS
THE PRESENT.

Look at your everyday happy experiences. I've had a lifelong love affair with ribbons and enjoy using them for everything from trimming sweaters, curtains and pillows to tying packages, making bookmarks and hair ribbons and tying together favorite letters. When Alexandra and Brooke were young I'd braid their hair and put sassy generous bows over the ponytail ties. This was a most satisfying, pleasant daily ritual. I'd iron my ribbon collection and hang the pair of eighteen-inch strips over hangers and put them in their closet.

One morning as I was braiding Brooke's hair, Alexandra was selecting her ribbons and a set for Brooke and when I looked over to see which ribbons she had chosen I had an "ah-ha" moment of awareness. Those ribbons, woven together, would make a breathtakingly beautiful tablecloth. I'd been hired to design a table setting incorporating china, crystal and glass for Gorham Silver Company and had been trying to dream up a unique idea for how this table could be so lovely it would be captivating. Ribbons. I could weave ribbons together. The same ribbons I used on the length could be repeated on the width. Colorful polka dots, stripes, taffeta plaids, moiré, grosgrain ribbons made the ideal statement to show off the new Gorham line of china and crystal to go with the silverware. A daily ritual I celebrated privately at home with my young daughters gave me the idea I needed for an important professional assignment.

More often than we may be aware, the solutions to our work come from within the initial experiences that occur right where we are. Try to make these connections, allowing one satisfying area in your life to link with the others. Let a need in one area be satisfied and resolved because of your awareness of the connections.

For instance, Russell Baker in his wonderful autobiography *Growing Up* describes how in high school he was late for an essay assignment and so he wrote an essay for his own amusement about his family and the first time they ate spaghetti. The essay, "The Art of Eating Spaghetti," was read aloud in class the next day and his classmates laughed—not at him but at the way he described the experience. He was amazed and felt he'd found his style, his voice.

WHERE WOULD YOU MOST LIKE TO LIVE?

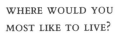

QUESTIONS REVEAL CLUES

What kinds of things do you do to amuse yourself? What seemingly unrelated interests could be combined into your field of work? Do you enjoy helping people? Do you like working with your hands? How disciplined are you to work on your own? Do you feel comfortable doing several projects at once or are you more linear, wanting to start something and finish it before beginning something else? How good are you at handling pressure?

Are you willing to work long hours in order to succeed? Do you consider yourself goal-oriented? How conscientious are you? Do you feel a lot of your identity is connected with your work? Is your work a way for you to maintain your own identity? Is it important for you to make a personal mark? What are the kinds of work that come easily to you?

Think of all the things you have a knack for and do with grace. Did you have to work hard for your grades at school? What were some of your biggest hurdles? Did you give up easily when you were doing poorly? Did you tend to tackle the hardest subject first or leave it for the last minute? Did you enjoy participating in classroom discussions? Did you sit in the front row or in the back? Did you attend classes regularly or did you cut a lot? Do you consider yourself a conqueror? Are you determined to do well? Tenacious? Do setbacks overwhelm you? Can you turn a problem into a challenge?

Do you seek outside help when you feel stuck? Do you believe that everything you do well will benefit you and help you? Can you laugh at yourself? Are you process-oriented as well as interested in results? How well organized do you think you are? What are some tasks you loathe to do? What are some of the most pleasant tasks you perform?

Were you brought up believing in the work ethic as a family trait? Do you feel you are lazy? Overly conscientious? Do you get headaches or stomachaches from too much pressure? Do you believe in giving back to the world what you've been given? Do you think of yourself as a teacher? An enabler? An inspirer? Do you believe your chosen work can make a difference?

How creative are you? How important is earning power to your sense of self? Do you equate salary with self-esteem? Do you feel you have enough self-confidence to accomplish your goals? How well do you take criticism? Do you admit when you mess up? Do you try too hard to please? Is excellence a goal or are you a perfectionist? How tolerant are you of others' errors? Do you enjoy completing a task? Do you procrastinate when starting some new project? Do you function best under deadlines or do they make you push yourself too hard? Do you respect people who

IF YOU COULD
APPRENTICE TO
ANYONE, WHO
WOULD IT BE?

have more talent and skills than you do, or are you jealous? Do you compliment someone who does a job beautifully? Do you thank them?

When is the last time you got lost in your work when you were in the flow and lost all track of time? When is the last time you had a vacation? Did you bring work with you? Do you take office work home on weekends? Does time vanish or drag when you are at the office?

How efficient are you? Do you have an entrepreneurial spirit or do you thrive on having a strong boss who leads you? When is the last time you were out sick from work? When are your happiest, most productive hours when your work seems to be the most enjoyable? Morning? Afternoon? Do you get enough sleep? When faced with something you have questions about how to handle, do you ask for help and guidance from others?

Do you feel comfortable with your work load? Overwhelmed? Are you using all your talents? Are you appreciated? What do you want to be doing in five years? Do you like computers?

What motivates you to do your best? What do you do for pleasure that one day you might do professionally? What are your secret dreams for your work? Do you want to validate your existence with a form of self-expression? What steps are you taking to lead the way? A mother of two young daughters quit her demanding job at a law firm to spend more time with her children. She's studying interior design through two correspondence courses, hungry to learn all she can. Nancy is painting their house and enjoying using it as a laboratory as she learns new techniques.

Do you like working independently or as part of a team? When you were a student did you enjoy a large school or a small one? Do you consider yourself a leader? What were your favorite courses in school? Do you have dreams of eventually starting your own business or do you like working for a large corporation? What do you like the least about your job? Do you enjoy your coworkers?

An enlightened fourth-grade teacher came to a talk I gave in La Jolla, California, on the subject of color and after my talk she told me how expressive her students are when describing how

WHEN YOU GO AWAY, WHEN DO YOU START PACKING?

HOW WELL DO YOU SLEEP?

much they love color. When she told me all the fun projects they are doing I realized what an enlightened woman Margaret is and how rare. She truly loves her students and feels privileged to teach them. I wish we could clone Margaret to bring joy to more fourth-graders.

Do you find an office atmosphere confining? Would you prefer to be out-of-doors? Do you enjoy selling? In design firms there are people who see clients and enjoy selling them beautiful things and there are people who prefer to stay in the background and do drawings, furniture arranging and color schemes. Do you enjoy business meetings? Do you feel you are growing in your job? Are there lots of challenges and new skills to learn?

BRINGING YOURSELF TO THE WORKPLACE

To the extent that you can, personalize your physical environment so that it works for you. If you're a salesperson in a store, this won't apply but at least you can have a small suitcase full of personal necessities to keep at the store, or have a locker with some pampering necessities. If you're in a position to personalize your own office, think of the ways you can enhance your time there. My husband Peter is a lawyer and finds it less fatiguing to move around during the day than to stay at one desk. So he has two large desks and a stand-up desk in his office. John Kennedy had a bad back and had a rocking chair in his office. The head of a corporation had a heart attack when he was young and became quite smart about how he could take care of himself and also maintain a full work load. He kept a sofa in his office and took a twenty-minute nap in the afternoon, putting a "Do not disturb" sign on his door and turning off the telephone.

My office has to be pretty in order to be productive for me. I can't be creative in a dump or a sterile atmosphere. Aesthetics make me feel comfortable, more so than efficiency, although I believe it is possible to combine both. For example, I sit in an antique ladder-back chair and my desk is French provincial because

"THE FORMULA FOR COMPLETE HAPPINESS IS TO BE VERY BUSY WITH THE UNIMPORTANT."
—*A. Edward Newton*

I am affected by the way they look and I respond to their warmth and charm. Because I'm an interior designer, having an office as beautiful as my living room makes work more enjoyable. I have flower paintings on the walls, porcelain fruits and vegetables and lots of beautiful boxes which I use to store projects as well as to feast my eye. I doodle with colored pencils I keep in a cup on my desk and I collect inkwells and pens to make my work a pleasure. Even a clipboard is wrapped in wide taffeta ribbons. I try to always have a few flowering plants on my window ledge and, when possible, flowers on my desk. Why do I create a homey atmosphere at my place of work? Because these touches are me and so it is natural I'd want them surrounding me forty-eight-plus hours a week.

A woman from Reno, Nevada, had a vision of opening a bookstore in Carmel, California, but in her dream she saw a fireplace. She quit her job in finance, moved to Carmel, found the spot and within six months Blake Bookstore opened its doors. Going there is like going to someone's charming home with a well-stocked library—one enjoys chintz, color, ruffles, a crackling fire and unusually attractive green bookshelves. Marsha laughs and says, "Sometimes I have to put the air conditioner on to cool the store but the fire is cozy and inviting and my customers come in and sit and read." Next to food, what's more important than books? Marsha is thrilled she can earn a living doing what she wants to spend her life doing: reading and recommending good books to others. She has a mission to expose her customers to good books in a gracious, cozy, cheerful atmosphere.

WHAT BOOKS HAVE
YOU RECOMMENDED
TO FRIENDS
RECENTLY?

MR. KEATING

In the movie *Dead Poets Society,* which enjoyed unexpected success, Robin Williams beautifully portrays Mr. Keating, a passionate teacher willing to risk his job for what he believes in—teaching students to feel literature in their own way. He wants learning to become an emotional experience. Mr. Keating could have been my art teacher, Phyl Gardner, who got me passionate about life and art. She would run out in the rain when my mother would have worried I'd get my feet wet. Peter had a teacher, Don Large, who taught his classes to use the unusual word in the usual place and the usual word in the unusual place. With some students Don Large formed the equivalent of the Dead Poets Society—a literary magazine called *The Andrean*. My daughters had an English teacher, Mr. Bird, who would stand up on his desk Keating-style and turn Shakespeare into a cool guy.

Mr. Keating opens minds and hearts and has soul. He wants his students to do their own thing, to be original and not accept anything as it is.

One of his exercises in self-expression helps the boys to feel what is right for themselves. He has everyone form a circle and begin walking. He questions them when they begin marching in unison. Why should you follow in someone else's footsteps? He persuades them to walk the way they feel. You can walk like a chicken or you can exercise your right not to walk.

The Mr. Keatings of the world are rare. Have you had an inspiring teacher, someone who opened you up to the possibilities of life, who tapped into your heart and made you think and question and become? I hope so. One is all you need to believe in yourself.

I've learned over the years that we can teach ourselves to walk in our own way and grasp life and then run with it, loving every minute. We can inspire ourselves.

WHAT PROFESSOR
WOULD YOU MOST
LIKE TO STUDY
WITH?

WHAT PROJECT ARE
YOUR ANXIOUS TO
BEGIN?

PEOPLE WHO LOVE THEIR WORK

When Rosamond Bernier lectured at the Design & Art Society, Ltd., on "At Home with Matisse, Picasso and Henry Moore," she showed many pictures of the artists' work and pictures illustrating their inspiration from their environment. Many of the paintings were of the rooms where the artists lived. Artists paint what they know. The Impressionists show us the ordinary scenes from their own fields and gardens and how these became their inspiration.

We're all fascinated by the ingredients of success, and what I've discovered is that all the successful people I've ever known do what they love to do. They are being true to themselves. The best way for people to express themselves is to be themselves. Just as a book is created out of a need, so many of our ideas and inspirations come from right under our noses. We can learn to tap into what we are naturally drawn to and find ways to continue to do what we love and make a living at it at the same time.

Emily Dickinson is a brilliant example of how our territory for creative ideas is inside us and how we can mine it without going anywhere. When we use our own experience to move us to bring forth the talents that are inside us, we can take real pleasure in our work. Some people are blessed and know at an early age what they want most to do in life. Others take a more winding path and have moments of realization that make them change their course.

A successful photographer, Lilo Raymond, took her first picture when she was nineteen. She was near the seashore in Maine so she bought an inexpensive camera and began to take black-and-white pictures. It was instant passion. Then she studied photography and hated it, never taking another picture for twenty years. Lilo married and divorced twice in this period and taught tennis for ten years in New England. "I floated about. I wasn't motivated. I went from one thing to another. I had been a Jew in Nazi Germany and it affected me. I could only concern myself with survival and never returned to Germany.

"I worked hard—working becomes a style of life—and then I bought a camera. I was a finished person. I'd lived long enough and I knew what I liked."

I've worked on shoots with Lilo and her eye is brilliant. "When you look in a camera I think it's total instinct. I respond to things. I don't think it through ahead of time. One quarter of an inch can make a difference so there is a method of feeling it out. We all have a limited amount of subject matter. I like natural, organic things. I now have a home in upstate New York. I really love

"... THE READINESS IS ALL."

—*William Shakespeare*

living in the country. I love to photograph flowers, trees, still lifes. Simple scenes. All organic, everyday things that are connected to people but I don't have to show people. I show evidence of people."

When Lilo was photographing an all-white still life for my *Book of Color* she looked into the camera and saw that something wasn't right. Amidst the lace, pearls, mother-of-pearl and white lacquer boxes, the stems of the white freesia jumped out at the eye and ruined the picture. We removed the flowers and the scene became soft and sensuous and beautiful. Lilo's lifestyle is work. She takes simple pictures that speak for her love of this world. The book designer at Doubleday saw some of her work and said, "Wow, she sees the world as a beautiful place." Lilo uses a camera as her tool in order to capture her feelings.

Alan Campbell was headed for a career as an architect when he was at Princeton but he changed his major and studied modern European history and became a diplomat in the foreign service. Alan remembers how he felt when he was struggling to decide on his major. "How do you know what to become? You don't know what all the possibilities are." Alan went straight to New Delhi from Princeton and had been around the world several times when his classmates hadn't even begun to jump into life and get their feet wet.

Alan jokes about how he "floundered" his way into the successful textile and wallpaper firm he founded in 1976, Alan Campbell Incorporated. "I'd always drawn and painted for myself, my family and friends. I enjoyed making things. I became fascinated by textiles and batik in India and Indonesia and Sri Lanka and having watched others do it, I began myself."

At home at night and on weekends Alan worked on creating his own batik designs, which required dipping fabric into the bathtub. He showed his original batiks to the decorators Albert Hadley and Sister Parish and soon Diana Vreeland, Mary McFadden and Oscar de la Renta bought his one-of-a-kind designs. Most of his work was done for Halston. Suddenly orders were piling in and he realized he only had one free bathtub! Alan had a moment of insight, an "ah-ha" vision when he realized what

"ALL INTELLECTUAL IMPROVEMENT ARISES FROM LEISURE."
—*Samuel Johnson*

he'd do. He needed more space and more bathtubs. He proudly claims that his firm, Alan Campbell Inc., started in earnest as a cottage industry in a rented cottage on Long Island. A team of like-spirited friends and he expanded their creativity. "I couldn't spend the rest of my life in dye pots so I started my firm. I wasn't nervous. I don't know why. The timing was right. I had moral support from friends and family, I had financial support due to a man who got us going and I was able to do what I most like to do. There hadn't been any outlets before for my loves and now there is. One can never look back. I think everyone should try to utilize their talents." Alan is doing what he loves to do.

We've all heard stories about people who have been lucky to happen upon a successful career. A reader from California told us that she made a wonderful lemon cheesecake that her friends enjoyed so she began making it for them as gifts. One friend was having a huge summer party and begged Brenda to make twenty cakes and bill her. She did and a successful cheesecake business began.

A mother of two young daughters went to the flower market in New York once a week to provide seasonal blooms for their apartment. She discovered that for five dollars you could get a substantial bouquet. This was in the early seventies. She was lamenting to a friend the fact that more people couldn't have inexpensive flowers year-round when her friend laughed and suggested she buy for friends as well and charge them. Her thriving flowers-by-the-week business began.

Someone who continuously renews my faith in the virtues of being passionate for one's work is Alice McAdams, who works for the antique firm Stair and Company in New York. Alice is a young, perky, vivacious woman who has a twinkle and a quick laugh. Her mother is an artistic person, a painter. Alice went antiquing with her mother and thought the shops were dark, dingy and dusty. She felt, at the time, that she had no inclination toward antiques. At college she studied French and child psychology and took lots of student teaching courses. She thought perhaps she'd teach French to young children.

After college she was slow in getting organized but eventually found a position in a small law firm answering the telephone. The firm expanded and they let her do a little decorating. "I began decorating for friends, helping them with fabrics and color, rearranging furniture. My parents were friends of the Stairs and I asked Mr. Stair if he knew of a decorator I could apprentice to without pay. It was 1977 and the prestigious New York Winter Antiques Show was about to open and Mr. Stair was short-staffed. 'Why don't you work for us for a couple of months? I know you don't know anything about antiques but I can teach you and while you're helping me out you'll meet the top decorators from all over the country.'" Alice laughs. "I'm still here and I owe everything to Mr. Stair."

DO YOU LOVE YOUR WORK?

"THERE IS ONLY ONE
SUCCESS—TO BE
ABLE TO SPEND
YOUR LIFE IN YOUR
OWN WAY."
—*Christopher Morley*

When you love what you're doing and are passionate about it, it shows up in your work. You actually gain momentum and energy from your intense enthusiasm for what you love to do. When you immerse yourself, when you lose all track of time, when you are in the flow and would rather be doing what you're doing at that moment than anything else—that is a feeling of exhilaration and great joy. How can you get to that place? How can you maintain the intensity and the passion? How can you have fun when you work hard?

People are usually happier when they are performing some useful function. In Hans Christian Andersen's words, "To be of use to the world is the only way to be happy." The more positive your attitude about your style of work the more you will accept the relationship between effort and reward. Tolstoy reminds us: "One can live magnificently in this world if one knows how to work and how to love, to work for the person one loves, and to love one's work." If you love your work and take pride in it you will gain psychological rewards as well as accomplishments that will, in time, lead to recognition. But while recognition is the result of excellence, it can never be the goal. In 1853 Henry David

Thoreau was informed by his publishers that *A Week on the Concord and Merrimack Rivers* had sold 216 copies since its publication four years before, so they sent him the remaining copies. He wrote, "I now have a library of nearly 900 volumes, over 700 of which I wrote myself." Doing a good job has its own rewards. In the case of writers, most of us would admit we would write whether we were paid or not, and at times we do write and are not paid. Van Gogh sold only three paintings in his lifetime, yet he compulsively painted to the end. Critic John Ruskin said, "The highest reward for man's toil is not what he gets from it but what he becomes by it . . . In order that people may be happy in their work these three things are needed: They must be fit for it. They must not do too much of it. And they must have a sense of success in it."

The woman who taught me a great deal about work is Eleanor McMillen Brown. In her interior design work, she had one foot on the business side and the other on the creative side and always, as if cross-country skiing, kept the two in parallel. One without the other is irresponsible and a waste of opportunity. Eleanor Brown had innate talent which she developed through design school and travel. She studied business administration and must have been a pioneering liberated woman in 1922 when she started her own firm. Much later, after her firm was a huge success, she became a trustee at Parsons School of Design and she'd teach classes there. In discussing how to make a proper curtain estimate, she'd list on the blackboard the fabric, the lining, "Don't forget the interlining, the valance, trimmings, labor and installation." She valued all the steps important to achieving excellent results.

Mrs. Brown's favorite word to this day, after a century of wisdom, is "success." Her father was a successful businessman from St. Louis who invented the American stove. She looked up to her father and took pride in her own ability to make her enterprise run through the good years and the Depression years. Success was a tonic. She had great talent she was utilizing, she had her firm under her strong control and she had her pick of the good decorating jobs both here and abroad. Her business was a huge focus in her life and was her anchor during a divorce and

> "TELL ME WHAT YOU LIKE, AND I'LL TELL YOU WHAT YOU ARE."
> —*John Ruskin*

after the deaths of her two husbands and several close friends, including her mentors William Odom, Van Day Truex and Billy Baldwin.

"You have to be in training to be a good decorator. You need lots of sleep and a good pair of shoes," Mrs. Brown would say. Several years ago Peter and I went to visit her with her old and dear friend Elisabeth Draper, who is also a grande-dame decorator about to turn ninety and still working full-time. Mrs. D told Eleanor that she was looking for an assistant. "Betty, are you *still* working?" "Yes, Eleanor. I'm carrying on where you left off. I've decided my time is precious so I'm going to hire someone trained. I can't spend my time at this stage in my career training someone." Once, in the Scalamandré fabric showroom, Mrs. D and I were visiting and suddenly she popped up and with a wink said, "Time is money! We must get on with our work."

Lady Anne Gordon, an English potter for over thirty years, has gained a reputation around the world as one of the best ceramic artists alive. Her style of working has developed steadily. When she started selling, she'd take commissions to do specific objects. Now, because she is recognized as an accomplished artist, she no longer creates anything that is commissioned. "When I started out I was eager to sell and get a reputation. I made anything I was asked to; I'd get frightfully nervous and often these custom pieces would break in the kiln and smash everything else to bits at the same time. It was a terrible struggle. But I carried on and I did get better. Now I know that if I make a present for a friend, it will turn out beautifully. So I make everything as a sort of gift. I only make what I want to make and I'm not nervous. Everything I make gets sold and I'm quite pleased." Anne loves nature and, with a reverence for beauty, creates realistic birds, fruits and vegetables.

Ideally, you should approach your work as an artist. Kahlil Gibran said in *The Prophet,* "Work is love made visible." Work is an opportunity to bring something forth—to create something, complete something, invent something authentic and original.

When did you discover your creative gifts and talents? We are all in the process of becoming. All through your life you will discover new challenges and areas of interest. A nun in her sixties moved to Egypt to a desperate place where garbage from all over the country is disposed of. She tries to help the people there improve their quality of life. These people live off the garbage: it is where they get their food and clothing and household wares, and they sell from it for a meager income. She has found a new life there, helping people to read and write and improve their home maintenance and health care. She says this is the most rewarding work she has ever experienced. Because there are so many needs, there are plenty of opportunities to find meaningful work.

I get "high" on work and enjoy challenging myself so I have to stretch beyond what I know and what is comfortable. I embarked on my personal style of working at the age of seven when I had a fruit, vegetable and flower garden—a big undertaking for me then. The happiness that nature brought me radiates throughout everything I've ever done since. My garden gave me confidence and a sense of self. I learned early how satisfying it is to plant seeds, see results and feel the thrill of accomplishment and commitment.

The next work for me was in the form of play—tennis. I began at thirteen, which is considered late, and I played as often as I could to become a ranking junior on the New England team. Then I discovered that design excited me and I threw myself into it with intense devotion. In my twenties I began to write notes, phrases. I wrote an article about my art teacher who died—Phyl Gardner, who had encouraged me to go to art school and pursue a career in design. A professional artist who was a protégé of Phyl's was moved by my article and I discovered that I really love to write. My notes became drafts of chapters and after years of putting words on paper, my books were published.

When I'm not passionate about my work it shows. I can't do something if my heart isn't in it. Recently I was having lunch with a friend who told me she only does what she loves to do because when she does she has boundless energy. Whatever you choose to do, be sure you are excited about it and you will find the energy and endurance to see you through. Thoreau once wrote, "Great God, I ask thee for no meaner pelf than that I may not disappoint

> "THERE IS DIGNITY IN WORK ONLY WHEN IT IS WORK FREELY ACCEPTED."
> —*Albert Camus*

myself." It is a blessing to find work you can fall in love with and then go after with all your heart. And remember, when you do find work you love, you will want to spend a lot of time at it and, as an extra benefit, you are very likely to become successful.

FINDING WORK YOU LOVE

"WHAT WE HAVE TO
LEARN TO DO, WE
LEARN BY DOING."
—*Aristotle*

Once you find the work you want, you will discover that people will go to bat for you. Be certain that what you want is really you and that you are not only being influenced by parents or friends. This must be a personal love affair between you and whatever work you want to pursue. Far better to disappoint a parent or a friend than to let yourself down by not finding your "bliss station."

As a businesswoman I've hired dozens of young summer interns and invariably the best workers are those who really love design and find every aspect of the creative process exciting. When someone loves fabrics, color, designs and textures, the signs are apparent. They play with the materials as they work. No part of the job becomes boring or unimportant because everything goes into improving their own judgment and sense of style and taste. You can't fake enthusiasm.

When you really are suited for a field, all the details involved in it should excite you, not just the so-called glamorous aspects. To an artist, having a show of his work can be interruptive and keep him from working. Our friend the artist Roger Mühl enjoys coming to New York for his exhibitions, but he gets restless in his hotel room because he misses his studio and wants to paint. The glamorous parts of work are often not the "real" work, but a side benefit after you've successfully completed something. I rarely find someone who wants to work for my interior design firm who doesn't come in believing it a glamorous line of work, and they're always disillusioned. The glamour, I find, is dealing in beauty. When I see a project photographed in a glossy magazine and it looks pretty, there is satisfaction, yes—but it is more fun to work than to view completed work.

Magazine editors, photographers, writers, painters, potters, architects and weavers all work long hours and aren't seeking glamour and glory as much as satisfaction from doing a good job. The work process is a combination of many necessary steps, each one as important as the next. When you really find the style of work you love, this is a gift.

Are you willing to begin at the beginning? Start at the bottom? Do anything? I had a dream that the father of one of my assistants called me and got angry with me for making his daughter wash dishes. It was only a dream, but I'd expect anyone who worked for me to wash dishes. If we're at a client's and we're offered a snack, an assistant should rinse out her glass and tidy up.

When you find work you love it humbles you because you want to learn how to make your work better. You'll be useful to someone else if you're willing to do what you're asked. When you do something well and cheerfully, then you're free to do something else until suddenly you are good at many simple, basic skills. You are freeing yourself to take on more. No matter how much work experience you've had, your upbeat attitude and hunger to be helpful are good positive signs. I have been fooled on many an interview, but once someone comes to work for my firm, I know right away whether they have the attitude necessary in order to be useful.

Once you have pinpointed the area of work you want to pursue, use your social contacts, ask for help. Try everything and be persistent. People are busy. When you put your best foot forward and want something very badly, luck seems to follow. Put yourself in a position for good opportunities to happen to you.

Be willing to be useful immediately. Your attitude will help you get a foot in the door. Each company will have its own system of working and you probably aren't trained in the way they want, so you'll have to be spontaneous and willing to do anything. The editor-in-chief of *Bride's Magazine,* Barbara Tober, told me that when she interviews someone she asks the person if they like to file. If she is told "no," the interview ends abruptly. "If someone

"HE IS WELL PAID
THAT IS WELL
SATISFIED."
—*William
Shakespeare*

doesn't like to file they won't file well; what a mess they might cause!"

If you are really willing, there is someone who would love to be your teacher. All people who love their work like to teach. The Roman poet Seneca said, "While we teach, we learn." Nothing is more thrilling and rewarding than teaching a passionate student.

You are blessed to have work you love. Thomas Carlyle recognized, "Blessed is he who has found his work; let him ask no other blessedness."

YOUR STYLE OF SELF-WORTH

You earn money for your livelihood. But you should never sell out and do work that saps your energy and makes you hold back tears. If you're not passionate you'll watch the clock and want time to pass instead of losing yourself in time. If you're not passionate you'll spend time worrying about money because that is all you have. In John Ruskin's *The Stones of Venice,* he observed, "It is not that men are ill fed, but that they have no pleasure in the work by which they make their bread, and therefore look to wealth as the only means of pleasure."

GIVE YOURSELF THE TIME TO PURSUE A SECRET FANTASY.

To the extent possible, remain as independent as your circumstances allow you. If you're put in the position of doing things you don't like, do them knowing that these things done well can help you get closer to the better-quality experiences. For example, Katharine Hepburn didn't act in just *The Philadelphia Story* and *The African Queen.* There were many minor parts she took to keep acting and to keep her name alive. When you find work you love— say, acting—where do you draw the line? You might only want good work but how do you get it? You get good work by working a lot, paying your bills and staying ready for the really good work. An actor takes parts he may not love but he loves to act and he acts as well as he knows how in whatever part he plays. An interior designer might take on a bread-and-butter client to help meet expenses and, while the job will never be seen on the cover of *HG*, it can be a challenge to please the client who has a small budget but loves her home and is very appreciative.

Happiness is priceless. Shakespeare, in *The Merchant of Venice,* reminded us, "He is well paid that is well satisfied."

To be able to live according to your own values—not being forced into doing things you don't believe in—is grounds for contentment. Don't compromise what you know in your heart is right for you.

When Doubleday published my book *Living Beautifully Together,* I went on a book and lecture tour that took me to twenty-eight cities over a three-month period.

In Nashville, a cable television interview was set up in a lovely garden. The camera crew consisted of two women, and the woman who interviewed me had a special combination of poise and commitment. I never enjoyed an interview more and after the show was taped we took a few additional minutes to talk. I learned that she aspires to become an anchorwoman on a network television show. All three women were self-taught. They accidentally fell into producing cable television serials. The woman who interviewed me had acted in high school and college and had studied English and journalism.

I asked lots of questions when I was on tour. Eyes would light up as I'd learn that people were doing work they loved. Bookstore owners love to read. Television interviewers love to act. There is a strong message that we are meant to find work that allows us to do what we are naturally drawn to. And we'll obviously be good at work we find fascinating.

PREPARING FOR YOUR CAREER

"The roots of education are bitter, but the fruit is sweet."
—ARISTOTLE

There are many ways to prepare for work. I don't hire people who are looking for work—I hire people who are looking for a career. Some people, like Louis Auchincloss, have two careers at a time—he practices law and writes. I know artists who also write; cooks who sew.

You may have been given an abundance of talents. Everything you do well will help you to develop them. For example, an interior designer can train his or her eye to become an accomplished photographer. A carpenter can become a cabinetmaker, a house painter an artist, an editorial secretary can become an editor or literary agent. An attractive, lively young woman was extremely successful in a career of banking until she discovered a second career she prefers. Sharon now gives seminars in self-esteem and is working on a book. Are you disenchanted with banking? Do you want to go into teaching? Do you feel a calling to be a marriage counselor? A social worker? If your career is raising a family, you know how essential it is to be a conscientious person because you influence the atmosphere and character of everything around you. It is enormously satisfying to be good at what you do and enjoy the process. If you make the decision to stay home to raise your children, let your children know through your actions how much fun you're having. Do exciting projects with them, have a good time each day, teach through example how exciting life can be. Whatever you decide to do, tackle it with the understanding that your personal vision is unique and you can make a contribution no one else can make. Be true to what you believe is right for you.

"FOR MAN IS MAN AND MASTER OF HIS FATE."

—*Alfred Lord Tennyson*

PROFESSIONALISM

Professionalism is always appreciated. A professional earns money. But you don't have to earn money to act professional. It has to do with doing a good job.

When you have an assignment, do your homework and prepare yourself thoroughly. Peter has taught me a great deal about professionalism because he is a trial lawyer and when he represents his clients in court he is prepared to win the case. Many cases settle out of court at the eleventh hour but he is still prepared.

When I was younger I was disappointed if an appointment was postponed because I'd prepared so thoroughly. Now I'm relaxed about a postponement because it gives me time to gain perspective and digest my material. I have a friend who gives art history lectures and her style is to prepare well in advance so that if there are last-minute distractions in her domestic life, she can think about her talk while she is attending to other tasks. Instead of being nervous, she gains control of her material as her early preparation permits her to absorb the nuances.

Professionals are prepared and on time for their appointments. Dependability allows others to feel confident that you have things under control.

An amateur does something out of love. Often, however, we end up getting paid to do what we love to do the most.

If you can work as an amateur, a lover, and act as a professional, you will enjoy your work and you will approach it with an attitude of privilege, not drudgery.

THE ATMOSPHERE WHERE YOU WORK

The atmosphere in which you create your work reflects your personal style. Olga Vezeris is the director of subsidiary rights at Pocket Books. Olga arrives at the office at 7:30 sharp each morning and has her breakfast of yogurt and fresh fruit on dishes and silverware taken out of a wicker picnic basket. The water glass on her desk is of stemmed crystal. She finds it sets her mood for the whole day when she has her quiet time early before the phones begin to ring. Her picnic gives her pleasure and makes a ritual out of the simple act of eating breakfast at her desk.

When it come to decorating, it seems a good idea to concentrate on the atmosphere where we spend most of our daily life—at work. Beautifying, personalizing and organizing your work spaces so they reflect your personal style will increase your satisfaction

"WHEN AMENITIES ARE LACKING, SO IS CIVILITY."
—*Russell Baker*

and make your work space more productive. Family photographs in interesting frames serve many psychological functions. They subtly remind us we are connected to our families and they make our business relationships more human. They also cheer us up.

Fresh flowers at my office are important for me and I think they are important for all women. Flowers nurture our souls and combat the dullness of high-rise offices or rooms with no view. One-color bunches such as daffodils or all-red tulips are disarmingly simple arrangements and create the greatest impact. Except for irises, flowers should last all week. Get a fresh bunch for your office every Monday and take the survivors home with you on Friday.

A coffee or tea service is vital for your work area and one-of-a-kind china cups and saucers are more interesting than a matched set. Use pretty spoons, coordinating colored paper cocktail napkins and an unusual tray. Beautiful objects turn your coffee break into a pleasurable ritual that can inspire creativity. The more you do to nurture and incorporate the ephemeral and meaningful qualities of beauty into the place where you work, the more you will influence your work in positive and beautiful ways. Beauty is uplifting to your spirit and is possible in all things.

Take a close look at everything that surrounds your work area and choose beautiful "tools." Just as an artist needs objects around for inspiration, try to see that all the functional necessities are as lovely as can be. For example, a letter opener can be a Georgian silver meat skewer or one made of Waterford crystal. Stationery stores have inexpensive pastel letter openers that are attractive and cheerful and come with matching colored scissors. Choose yellow, pink, periwinkle or pistachio. I love paperweights. They're functional and pretty. Choose a crystal prism or a lovely round stone you found on a walk, or a small slab of malachite or phosphorescent blue granite. Use a treasured object as a paperweight such as a carved marble frog or bird so you can play with it while you're on the telephone.

Cover reference books with lovely print wrapping paper or use solid paper as a background and glue on a special art postcard or picture you clipped out of a magazine. This will turn consulting a reference book into a pleasurable moment.

DO YOU LIKE TO DELEGATE?

Organize different projects in boxes covered with marbleized or printed paper. They're available in all shapes and sizes.

Use a beautiful fountain pen. Think of the hours of pleasure the right pen will bring you. For fountain pens with cartridges, a choice of colored inks is offered and it is easy to switch from one color to another.

Consider how many hours you spend at work, and make every effort to have the atmosphere inspire you to be productive and creative. Clean your windows. Even if you are in a skyscraper where window cleanings are regulated, you can clean your own from inside. If you are issued a metal desk, use Krazy Glue to attach Velcro to the front and sides so you can sheer a colorful fabric to hide the cold utilitarian office-supplied desk. Have plenty of good light. Bring in a pretty lamp from home. Select In boxes and Out boxes of a beautiful Pierre Deux fabric, or use baskets or leather. Let your eye feast on everything and be delighted. If you have your own office, light a scented candle, have a basket of your favorite potpourri, wax your wood surfaces to a shine, and enjoy getting down to work!

SETTING UP YOUR SYSTEM

No matter how attractive the atmosphere where you work, you'll want to create a system that is custom-tailored for you and the work you want to accomplish. Someone said that luck increases with efficiency. If you love to work, you'll loathe wasting time. If I can organize myself well and have the things I need close at hand, I can get right down to work without delay.

Whatever your work—whether you are managing your household, running a small business, whether you work for a large firm or do volunteer work—you will want to have a personal system that keeps all your affairs in order and accessible.

I've discovered I prefer attractive portable files to cold metal files that can't be moved. I have a series of portable files covered in marbleized color-coded paper, and each one contains a different project. This allows me the flexibility to take one to the kitchen table so I can catch the morning light as I work, or take it to bed with me to organize my papers in the evening. In this way, my office is where I am. I can even take one of these pretty file boxes to the beach. Whether your papers can all fit into one or will require a dozen, portable file boxes can keep a project in good order. If you love to save newspaper clippings you can set up a box for your clips and have colored file folders separating them into subjects. Once you've clipped something, put it into your system; otherwise it adds to your confusion and sense of disorder. Efficiency experts suggest that you never touch a paper twice. If you open a letter, have a "mail" folder. If you receive a bill, have a "bills" file. The most dangerous thing is to stack one piece of paper on top of another on your desk, possibly burying an important document, a bill, a contract or invitation. The busier you become, the more you'll have to keep current, and file folders free you from confusion. A labeled folder with one piece of paper in it can be a lifesaver. Never have general folders; rather, be specific. You can buy reusable labels for your file folders.

Use brightly colored file folders and color-code for different subjects and projects. Leave these on your desk to add color and to remind you to act. Once you put the folders out of sight they can too easily be forgotten. The commercially available colors are lively and stimulating as well as effective. Folders come in red, pink, orange, yellow, green, blue and lavender. To add more colors to your system, turn the red folder inside out and use it on the pink side. Do this also with the deep blue and green.

The reason getting organized is so difficult for many people may be that they don't have the aid of a really good system. Have fresh colored file folders ready for new material. When you have a system that works, you are ready to take on more work. Today will add to your clutter, so plan ahead and have space to breathe in your system.

Design your system so you can do everything yourself. You will gain uncrushable self-confidence by knowing where everything is at all times. If you have a helper, you can delegate and it won't cause confusion. Write out a manual of how to use your system. Even if you don't anticipate anyone coming to help out, if you list what is filed where and how you like things arranged, it forces you to focus on your unique style of order. Doing this clarifies your own thinking and helps you to streamline things so that they work as smoothly as possible. If you wanted to take on a helper for a special project, it wouldn't disrupt your sense of calm because the manual would tell all. The busier you are the more you can lower stress and anxiety by having your work properly arranged, ready for you to keep going without the interference of lapses in your system.

Be strict with yourself, and with anyone who helps you, in following your manual meticulously. Just as it isn't a good idea to move a man's chair, removing documents from the file is a violation. Insist that a helper use the duplicating machine. Helpers get sick or are out to lunch, are on vacation or work part-time. You shouldn't need to ask someone else where something is, because your manual will have the answer. Don't waste time looking for anything. Your system saves you from frustration and worry. The more thorough you are in setting up an excellent system, the more respect you will give to the smallest details of your work, understanding that everything is an intrinsic part of the whole.

If your Rolodex cards are color-coded so that, say, white is for employees and services, yellow is for clients, pink for public relations people and orange for family and friends, while blue is for artists you represent, would you allow a helper to work for you who was blind to your color-coding system? My personal style is that everything that leaves my office must be visually beautiful—colored mailing envelopes, beautiful stamps—and I won't accept less. Your system becomes the law of excellence for you and anyone else who comes to "help." When the fundamentals of your style are in place, you are ready to take on those special projects that can bring lasting satisfaction. Having your affairs in order is itself exhilarating. Have a copy of every disk on your word processor. Keep all your appointments in an office engagement book as well as in your Filofax. This way your office is aware of meetings and won't schedule you in two places at once. Reconfirm appointments. Weed out your files once every three months. Who has the time? Who has the time *not* to have a beautiful, personally styled system so as to accomplish the best work?

WORKING WITH OTHERS

Very few of us work in isolation. Designers have draftsmen, lawyers have secretaries, bank tellers have assistant tellers. A mother raising a child has to rely on extra help. Many different types of people are involved with whatever work you do, and I believe we work best in teams. It is vitally important not only to get along, but to have respect for their contributions.

For many years, I worked with a designer who did all the architectural drawings for the interior design projects and he was never given credit in the magazine write-ups. John told me once, "I enjoy seeing that I have helped to create something. When I see a pretty cornice molding or a splendid marble floor, I realize I had a part in the creation. That's all one really has in the long run."

We all have our individual roles to play and if we work in harmony we can help each other. If it weren't for my literary agent, publisher, editor, copy editor, book designer, art director and secretary, this book would remain on pads of paper. A book is never a single effort. We're all interdependent.

Confucius said something that we would be wise to keep in mind: "The superior man is distressed by the limitations of his ability; he is not distressed by the fact that men do not recognize the ability that he has." Try to do your very best and don't expect recognition. For over forty years McMillen, Inc. never let an individual name be attached to a job. The credit line always read: Interior by McMillen, Inc. Yet some of the most successful interior designers in America got their experience at that fine firm. As long as you are always learning and growing, no work you do is ever unrecognized. Have a wide vision and think about your body of work as a whole. The pieces will eventually come together; they are all part of your personal puzzle.

"GRATITUDE IS A FRUIT OF GREAT CULTIVATION; YOU DO NOT FIND IT AMONG GROSS PEOPLE."
—*Samuel Johnson*

It takes all kinds of players to make a team. Many of the people you work with have different values, goals and lifestyles. Be cheerful and go about your work. Don't allow others to drag you down when they are feeling put upon or sorry for themselves. An American writer, Agnes Repplier, once said, "It is not easy to find happiness in ourselves, and it is impossible to find it elsewhere." If someone else really bothers you, try not to be a victim. Take action.

If someone is always grumpy and won't talk, don't try to reform him or her. And try not to bring your emotional baggage to the workplace. Everyone has work to do, and being supersensitive is counterproductive. If I ask my assistant to go to the bank, it is understood that this office errand should be done on office time, not their lunch time. No situation is ever perfect. It is wise not to take anything personally. Work hard and help others to create a productive, superior working relationship in which everyone benefits.

HOW IS THE CHEMISTRY BETWEEN YOU AND YOUR CO-WORKERS?

SWITCHING GEARS

Work smarter, not harder. Tackle the most difficult tasks during the part of the day when you feel most refreshed. Use the time when you don't have that creative edge to putter, file or prepare new projects to face at a better time. Quit while you are ahead, and come back refreshed.

Reward yourself when you have accomplished your goal. After working hard under the pressure of a deadline, treat yourself to dinner at a favorite restaurant. Or make an appointment for a massage. You are most likely to face a challenge with equanimity when you plan a reward to follow. Have a haircut, walk to do a personal errand. Call a friend just to chat. Putter around your work space. Catch up on some chores that you've had to put on the back burner.

Switch gears to allow your body and mind to get back in balance. We all have to stretch ourselves at different periods and if you're at all like me you thrive under the pressure of deadlines even if they're self-made.

Pat yourself on the back. You've accomplished something satisfying and now you can change your pace. You're in the driver's seat; never allow yourself to be driven after you've reached your destination. You'll be far more creative and you'll regain your vitality faster if you allow yourself to counterbalance the pace and productivity of your work once the pressure has eased.

YOU'RE THE BOSS

Ultimately, you are in charge and must be accountable. I worked for several firms before starting my own business and even when working for others I always felt responsible for the quality and production of my work. Never make the mistake of blaming a boss for the outcome of your work. Keep a clear vision of your goals. You and only you can control your work quality.

Check your work meticulously. Don't wait for someone else to make corrections. Edit your own work and if you are employed by someone else, don't put your employer in the position of a policeman. Do your best for your own self-respect and satisfaction.

Try to remain objective about your job. Try to keep the big picture in mind. Judge what the priorities are so you'll do first things first. Often the less important things have a way of settling themselves in place and you actually save time if you wait a while so you don't have to do something twice. Trust your intuition and spend your energy on the things that matter most.

Learn from your mistakes. Like guilt, mistakes are warning signals. They're not the end of the world. Failure isn't death, rather a signal to stop and reevaluate. Confucius told us, "Do not be ashamed of mistakes—and so make them crimes." We're all learning on the job. The only fault is when we don't learn from what we've done wrong or what we've neglected to do. Our work is an excellent teacher and we should be attentive students. The best

"TO BE WHAT WE ARE, AND TO BECOME WHAT WE ARE CAPABLE OF BECOMING, IS THE ONLY END OF LIFE."
—*Robert Louis Stevenson*

model of behavior is to act the way you would want someone who works for you to behave.

You have an individual view of what is most important for a fulfilling life. How can you enrich your life through what you do? Alfred Tennyson said, "The world which credits what is done/Is cold to all that might have been." Be as self-sufficient as you can be. Do a commendable job that others can admire. If you take charge of your work, you will find you will be of use to many different bosses and all you'll really need to consider is where you'll be given freedom to do your best work. The American stateswoman and humanitarian Eleanor Roosevelt reflected, "One thing life taught me—if you are interested, you never have to look for new interests. They come to you."

HOW TO AVOID BURNOUT

When something is not quite right, get in touch with the source of your anxiety and ask yourself what you can do to resolve it now. This could mean quieting down, going somewhere so you can close the door and be alone. Do you need privacy? Can you be alone during a break or on your lunch hour? If you feel you need an immediate lift and you can't get up from your work, stop and close your eyes. Ask what it is that is bothering you. The first thing that comes to mind will usually be the answer. Ask, what can I do now for myself to feel better? Again, your answer will be there—sometimes in a picture. The mind is there for you to draw upon, like a computer. You just have to know how to plug in.

I close my eyes several times a day and usually discover the source of my anxiety is something I haven't done that I've blocked and pushed aside. Something often quite simple can be at the root of the confusion. When you remove a straw or two from the camel's back you seem to remove the burden.

Are you eating healthful food? Do you skip meals? Watch your sugar and caffeine intake on the job. Sometimes you become jittery and don't realize it is because you've sipped coffee through a series of meetings. Fruit juice can be a good pick-me-up and you'll feel more balanced.

Keep a running list of projects and alternate working on them from light to heavy. Don't bore yourself and at the same time don't overwhelm yourself with unrealistic expectations. Remind yourself you are human and there is a reason Rome wasn't built in a day. After you've completed a task, check it off your list and tackle something quite different next.

Keep a joke book handy. When you need a good laugh you'll be glad you've thought ahead. You can buy a desk calendar that has a joke each day. We have to remember to take our work seriously, but not always ourselves.

Look out the window and remember there's a world out there. If you don't have a view, visualize a beach or a river, someplace where you'd like to be, and feel yourself calming down. Don't allow yourself to slip into inertia. Get your passport renewed. Often when you're upset about something it immediately makes you feel better to do some necessary task you've dreaded doing. It's never worse than you anticipate and it gives you something concrete to think about.

When you are not working, do you feed your spirit? At work you're usually answering to someone else. I've heard it said that 50 percent of the people we meet won't like us. We've been brought up to believe that everyone should like us and we are responsible if they don't. Matthew Arnold advises, "Resolve to be thyself; and know that he who finds himself, loses his misery!" At night, in the mornings, on weekends, the important thing is to like and understand yourself.

LET ALL YOUR MOTIVATION COME FROM INSIDE YOU.

HOW TO MOVE ON

When Mrs. Brown suddenly stepped down from the presidency of the firm she had founded fifty-five years earlier, Peter and I had flown to New Orleans where I had agreed to lecture. Hearing the news, we thought we'd take advantage of being away and have a few carefree days together. It was autumn and the weather was ideal—Indian summer with clear skies, warm sun and no humidity. We walked everywhere, window-shopped, did some antiquing, and of course ate adventurously in the town's famous restaurants. Peter bought me a little enamel box and gave it to me one evening at dinner. The words on the box read: "All things are sweetened by risk." I looked into his eyes and smiled. I knew what this symbol meant. The boss I had loved was retiring and it was time for me to move on. I would start my own design business. I understood, amidst my excitement and anticipation, what Eric Hoffer suggested in *The Ordeal of Change:* "Every new adjustment is a crisis in self-esteem."

Because we dread uncertainty, we fear change. Possibly you have benefits where you work that act as deterrents, making it hard or impossible for you to consider a change.

Before you lose all your enthusiasm for your work keep a good pace, stay friendly and professional and start taking steps toward some kind of change. Whether someone comes to you or you have to go out and find a firm to work for, don't be afraid. In most cases, change is healthy and can improve your situation. Ask yourself, are you happy at work 90 percent of the time? If you are not, maybe you should think of a move. Don't consider it a failure if you don't work out at a particular job—stay confident. You need to match up your skills to a job and it doesn't always work. Conditions change. However, if you are always switching jobs, this, like eating too much, can be overdone. Figure out why you aren't right for the job, and don't avoid the hard issues. If you aren't happy you are probably not doing a good job, so your honesty will benefit both you and your employer.

When you study the situation you may discover you have outgrown the job and you must move on in order to continue to grow. Or you may admit you don't work well under coercion and you're better suited to a less pressured pace. Maybe you've discovered you want to go back to school. If you are tired of your work and don't know why, possibly you should take an aptitude test.

"OUR LIFE IS FRITTERED AWAY BY DETAIL . . . SIMPLIFY, SIMPLIFY."
—Henry David Thoreau

If you find yourself fighting your work, dreading going to the office every day and resenting the people you work with, consider moving on. Often you discover "this isn't me": you went into a certain line of work at the urging of your mother or father or spouse and now you want to get out.

One woman helped her husband when he left a large corporation and started his own business. She became an equal partner, traveling around the world and working eighteen-hour days. After a series of events including an automobile accident she came to the conclusion that she really wanted to go back to writing and she left the company. Figure out what's been frustrating you and then ask yourself what you'd really rather be doing. Obviously you're not retiring, you're merely making some changes. When you can see clearly what you want to do, go for it.

Don't confide in too many people about your efforts to change work. The others in the office still like the security of their jobs or at least are planning to stay. No one likes being ditched.

After you know a job is impossible for you, don't stay too long or try to stick it out if you know you'll continue to be unhappy. Apply yourself to finding something else that will satisfy you. Face your fear about switching jobs and deal with it. I know a young woman who stuck with a job she dreaded just because she didn't want her boyfriend to think she'd made a mistake in taking the job in the first place. Trust your instincts.

SELF-CONFIDENCE—
AN IMPORTANT STYLE FACTOR

You gain self-confidence by believing in life and in yourself. Make your own positive list of all the reasons to be self-confident. You might write down the following:

"ENTHUSIASM IS ALWAYS INSPIRATIONAL."
—*Sister Parish*

- I believe in good over evil.
- I believe in the dignity of man.
- I believe in love, truth and justice.

- I believe I have the ability and guts to bounce back after I fall.
- I believe in my intuition.
- I believe in my strength of character.
- I believe in certain guiding principles that help me through all difficulties, like taking good care of myself and figuring out what the problem is before jumping to a decision.
- I believe I have the courage and strength to face reality when a serious problem arises.
- I believe I have the imagination to find solutions to problems and I accept that I will have to give up something in order to gain something.
- I believe I am willing to work as hard as is necessary to work through difficulty.
- I believe I will continue to be uncomplaining about the cards I've been dealt and will accept my fate and put it to the best possible use.
- I believe I wouldn't change places with anyone else in the world. I am responsible for my life and can control a large portion of it by the wise choices I make.
- I believe in myself.

As we mature we realize that no one gets it all. Someone may be brilliant but temperamental and moody. Someone else may be beautiful or handsome but also lazy, blaming others for mistakes and relying on good looks. If someone is rich he may be tempted to use money as power. If you're poor or things don't work out for you, you may revert to self-pity and despair. Have faith in a higher being.

Accept and respond to joy as a gift. Each of us has a great deal to be self-confident about. We're all struggling to be more whole, more healthy, more balanced. Each of us has had an illness, a sickness. We are all working on our lives, and when we do a good enough job taking care of ourselves we are free to be useful to others. As we go through life, if we give back whatever we possess in abundance we will be playing a worthwhile part in society.

BECOMING AN ENTREPRENEUR

WHO IS THE MOST
COURAGEOUS PERSON
YOU KNOW?

Is it your style to be an entrepreneur? When you know what kind of work you love and if you have the skills to do it well, you can work for yourself and start your own company. The secret is to start out very small. When I started my business in 1977 I had $9,000 and divided it equally among a law firm which incorporated me, an accounting firm and Tiffany & Co., where I designed my logo and ordered my stationery and calling cards. I began my business out of two maids' rooms off our kitchen hall and used the profit from my first client to have the company telephones installed.

The first Friday after I was officially incorporated, I sat on our sofa and wept to Peter because I was accustomed to Friday being payday, and instead Friday became payroll day! I don't cry on Fridays anymore and the company has done very well. We celebrated our twelve-year anniversary having never taken a bank loan.

I'd worked for four interior design firms before starting my own and it seemed like a good idea to work from home because the children were young and in school a block away. Being my own boss and working from home was a big change from working in a large firm. I immediately discovered I was on my own to sink or swim. If I succeeded it would be my success, and if I failed I had no one else to blame. The firm is my name and reputation.

The word "entrepreneur" comes from the French meaning to undertake, and if you look up "undertake" you'll discover that it means to put oneself under obligation to perform. When you become an entrepreneur, that is exactly what happens—you must perform.

Two immediate discoveries: First, you get right down to work. You have to turn time into making your dreams come true. Second, you are fully responsible. When you get all the credit or blame, you'll work harder than you ever have because there is a high incentive to prove yourself.

Entrepreneurs are efficiency experts, knowing how to achieve results in the most direct way. There are no employees to blame, no bureaucratic delays—it's hands-on work. Motivation is not a problem because you are doing what you want to do.

One of the first decisions is where to set up shop. Women with small children who want to stay home to tend to their children's needs and still have a hand in some business outlet find working at home a temporary solution. I loved it when being home was important, but was later thrilled to go to an office where I could separate home and work once the girls were in school all day. Nothing is ideal. If you decide to stay home, give yourself a room with a door and have a helper sitting with the children while you're working. Even superwoman can't be in two different gears at once without stripping the gears. Once you're set up for work, you can walk into a room and be productive immediately. Children nap and go to school. They play at friends' houses. Even if you only put in two to three hours a day at work, if you do it every day the time will translate into tangible goals met.

GO AHEAD, TRY.

Because there is no financial security in being an entrepreneur, you have to be able to afford your present lifestyle. It's a challenge to see your efforts add up. Keep your fixed expenses low. Beware of how difficult distribution is: If you have to spend enormous amounts of money on advertising, you will delay your profits, so weigh your options and plan accordingly. If you aren't paying a big rent, your image is conveyed through mailings and advertising. I splurged on beautiful stationery, business cards, colored envelopes, labels and bright geranium-red-colored shopping bags advertising Alexandra Stoddard Incorporated.

YOUR BUSINESS STYLE

What can we do to improve our personal style in a business setting? Try at the outset to put other people at ease. This is a gift and some people are better at it than others. You can become more skillful, however, with experience and also by making an effort. Business relationships are especially fragile because money is involved. Many of the people you see and know in business would not be your "friends" without the business connection. This doesn't mean you don't like them, but there are only so many hours in a day and you spend a great deal of time with people in business—understandably so! In addition, a large portion of your out-of-the-office time involves business-connected relationships. If you enjoy your work and are enriched by your business associates this can be time well spent. These relationships often fuel you creatively and provide outlets for your work as well as income and vice versa. So, in a healthy sense, you need each other.

Whenever possible, work with people you like, because you are always influenced by your colleagues. Certain people have special talents and you will work with a wide range of people in your career. How can you make someone else feel comfortable if you don't feel comfortable yourself? This is why you need to nurture yourself—so you can be free of self-consciousness when trying to reach out to others.

In order to be your best self in the various roles you will carry out professionally, don't compromise. Business doesn't have to be a dirty business. Through your healthy professional relationships you allow others to expand in the best sense. If you like your work and you like the character of the people with whom you work, you will probably enjoy healthy, stimulating, lasting relationships. Never stretch yourself to have a business relationship with someone you really don't like or deep down don't trust.

When you like another person it is natural that you will want to break bread with him or her. I don't have many friends or business associates with whom I haven't eaten or had a drink because I find this ritual gracious and relaxing for both sides. If someone has food in his mouth he can't always be the one talking! It's a balanced form of equal time and a subtle and pleasant climate for business decisions, in the way that music can make exercise less of an effort. Food and drink actually set an atmosphere of generosity.

Breaking bread is entertainment. A lot of business is done in a social setting. It softens and eases the atmosphere and decision-making doesn't suffer from grace. A social setting can be a business platform. A close friend teased me that my midtown office was Harry Cipriani's, the New York restaurant that used to be located at Fifty-ninth Street and Fifth Avenue. I met associates there for breakfast, lunch or dinner to discuss a project, an event, a new direction. The word restaurant comes from the French word *restaurer,* which means to restore. If I was out all day with a client we'd rest our tired feet and restore ourselves.

Is it appropriate for you to invite a client to your home? It all depends. We all need our sanctuaries and there are many excellent public places to go to have a good meeting and meal. However, so many of my clients are really my friends and I never feel I have made my life a fishbowl by including them in my private world of retreat. If I ever begin to feel uncomfortable, I hold back. Home is, after all, sacred.

When the chemistry is right it is really a warm gesture to entertain business associates at home. Do what is comfortable for you.

The question of expense is important. How much money is appropriate to spend on a given party, a single event? I believe we should always try to put our best foot forward with those we entertain but I do not approve of overspending. There are times to splurge and have some extra flowers or an expensive dish, but it should be tempered according to your pocketbook and should never be out of line with what feels right and what is affordable. We all tidy up our homes for guests, and when we are entertaining a business acquaintance we tend to want to project a perfect picture of our life. However, if we have to bend so far that is becomes disruptive, I think we should consider alternative choices. Home should not be as pressure-filled as the world outside our sacred four walls.

Your ultimate decision might be for you to expose your humanness and let your business associates experience a touch of your real life, not just what you project for their view. After several years of being entertained by clients in their homes at elegant parties, Peter and I were invited for Sunday lunch with one family. There were no helpers in the kitchen. Everyone pitched in and helped. This informal family gathering drew us into their real life and made us feel we were friends. When this kind of social gathering is comfortable for everyone, it is appropriate and can be very meaningful. Make sure your choice is right and that it is fun for you.

Business acquaintances, like friends, enjoy receiving little thoughtful gifts. If you give a terribly expensive present to a potential client or to someone who could advance your career it appears an unseemly inducement. Give business acquaintances gifts that convey that you are thinking of them, not power presents that may be misunderstood. Flowers are always appropriate with a personal note. If you go to someone's home, a house present is appropriate. A flower container is nice because it's useful and isn't too personal. Guest soaps, a gift package of a variety of marmalades, a smoked turkey, Godiva chocolates, a tin of homemade cookies, some embroidered cocktail napkins or a bottle of really special wine or a book—give what you'd like to receive.

A simple thought can mean so much. If you know that a client loves watermelon and you find a watermelon-design potholder, it will be appreciated when you drop it in the mail with a little note. Any time you genuinely think of someone and find a little memento it is a kindness to pass it on. I am always touched when business friends think of me when they are traveling and I save the postcards I receive. Looking back over the twenty-five years' accumulation gives me a glimpse of faraway places and evokes memories that are very pleasing.

Always, without exception, write a thank-you letter. Use your

"HONESTY'S THE BEST POLICY."
—*Cervantes*

social stationery. I never use business paper except for serious business letters and financial matters. Use oversized correspondence cards bordered with different colors. Have a variety of different kinds of notepaper so you are inspired to match up the paper or card with the person. I like blank art cards, and because Claude Monet is my favorite Impressionist I have purchased hundreds of his paintings on these cards. Old rules about engraving and color don't apply today. What is important is that you write a sincere, prompt thank-you on paper you love. I use art cards designed by my favorite watercolor artist and friend, Joan Brady. I have a variety of these—in fact, one is a painting of a breakfast tray with a coffee cup and saucer, flowers, a croissant and the newspaper, and I love to send it to someone with whom I've just had breakfast.

Don't worry about who pays. Time is more valuable than a free meal. Thank someone anyway. You shared time together. You met to talk and be together, and you should show your admiration. Often when I invite someone to lunch I send a note afterward. After two special hours, a few minutes to show my appreciation later is an effortless gesture and I'm sure is received with gratitude.

When you plan gatherings in your own home you should not create a more formal atmosphere than is natural. I'm always amused at how I run around and tidy up for guests. We tend to clutter our surroundings if we really live in our homes, and having some business friends to the house causes us to put their interests first and neaten up the accumulations of clutter. We see to it that our glasses are sparkling and our silver is polished. But nothing chills the atmosphere more than a nervous host who has overdone the formality: the entire occasion can become a burden to be gotten over with.

Keep everything simple and within your capability. Never lose touch with your personal style of hospitality. If you have too many guests to manage without outside help, have your helpers be as inconspicuous as possible. There is nothing more pretentious than expensive caterers taking charge. It costs just as much to have business people in your home as to take them to a top restaurant.

"ALL GOOD THINGS ARE CHEAP: ALL BAD ARE VERY DEAR."
—*Henry David Thoreau*

Serve the food in your style so there is some of your personality in the presentation. Caterers, like baby nurses, are there to assist you, not to take over your house, your baby or your style.

If you decide to meet business associates at a restaurant, go to a restaurant where you are known and where they will take good care of you. Call to make a reservation well in advance. Never specify what table you want; that is pushy and besides, if you are known at a favorite restaurant they will take good care of you. Call to reconfirm on the day of the meeting. Call your client or prospective clients to reconfirm and give the restaurant name, spelling and exact address. Don't work through secretaries, speak directly. The unnecessary anxiety caused by miscommunication is frustrating and makes one look and feel stupid.

Many find an early breakfast meeting a great way to start the day. It's comparatively inexpensive and often elegant, tends to be quieter so you can hear and converse easily, no wine or spirits are involved and we can still get to the office at the usual time. Afternoon tea is another good meeting time. While tea requires leaving the office early, I can sense, as can the client, the mood of civilization, concentration and calm.

If you have a boss, take your lead from him or her. Do you feel it appropriate to invite your boss to dinner at your apartment? Probably it would be better for you to go first to his or her house when invited. But if you feel intuitively that your boss would enjoy being included in a gathering, send an invitation but not out of a sense of duty. Don't push too hard. In the end, you can't give more than yourself. Whether someone is above you or below you in the power structure, nothing is more gracious than a person who is sensitive to the feelings of others.

COMMUNICATING WITH CONFIDENCE

Surely the key to successful working relationships is communication. Communication is the linchpin to living a full, balanced life. It's important to uplift your communication skills because, once honed, they can bring great personal satisfaction. In the *International Herald Tribune*, I read an article by Ellen Goodman about a survey in Pittsburgh: "The average married couple spends only four minutes a day in meaningful conversation." What kind of relationships have we created if our minds can't flow together in mutual understanding?

When people don't communicate well, they can be misunderstood and can appear arrogant or bored. Others judge us whether we like it or not, and it is always best when we express ourselves by communicating well. In this manner we have less chance of being misunderstood.

When you have an idea and strongly believe what you have to say is important, it is necessary for you to reach out and make the first move. The saddest phrase in any language is "what might have been." Never miss an opportunity to try to express your feelings. However, William Safire, the *New York Times* columnist, reminds us that "the right to do something does not mean that doing it is right." Having the freedom and confidence to express your views is not necessarily always appropriate. Question your motives. If you have a strong conviction that your message is useful, you will find the right way to convey your feelings.

It takes two to communicate. There is a rhythm and a mutuality so one dancer bends and the other flows. Good communication requires a dance partner of equal caliber. If one person is inexperienced or nervous, the other has to limit the steps he can take. If you feel insecure or lack confidence, it is far better to relax, loosen up and follow someone who is willing to take the lead.

A few personal stories of how you've made your way and some of the funny anecdotes telling of your struggles relieve the anxiety for others. None of us feels completely secure. No matter who we are or where we are, we are all vulnerable because of our human condition. I've found that people with a great deal of power and influence are often the most willing to share stories that remind us we are all in the same boat together. Great people are usually encouragers because they want to help others find their own innate greatness.

Speak directly with others. Make your own calls, write your

EXPRESS YOUR
OPINIONS.

"YOU CAN DO
ANYTHING IN THIS
WORLD IF YOU ARE
PREPARED TO TAKE
THE
CONSEQUENCES."
—*W. Somerset
Maugham*

own notes. In an age when manners have almost been forgotten, this personal style of communication is a rare treat and opens people up to being receptive. You are your own best agent.

ONE ON ONE

Having someone else's full attention is ideal. Respect the time and privacy of others. If you want to have a meaningful exchange, give your whole self. If you're with someone who is very funny, this does not require you to be funny too, nor do you need to feel insecure because you are different. You can laugh at jokes and never need tell them. Humor requires an audience.

Ask questions and give lots of time for thoughtful responses. Let others think and dream out loud. Just by giving someone else time with you alone, you may be able to open up something in them that is at the heart of their being. Let the conversation wander naturally. When you are comfortable, often a more intelligent level of communication is evoked.

Show your attention through body language. If you are relaxed and facing the other person, you will appear poised. Fold your hands in your lap. It's calming. Once when I was in a conversation with a younger woman she started doing neck rolls as though she were in a private room doing yoga and I found this terribly rude. Be sure you don't have a foot that wiggles up and down or taps, or bracelets that jangle constantly. Remember we all have our own personal tolerance to body contact, touching and slapping. When people point their finger to make a point and act aggressive, it is not persuasive, it is obnoxious.

Your facial expression is telling. Eyes hold your secret passions. Open up your eyes gently. Look the other person directly in the eye. Eye contact should be soft. Let your eyes light up and dance to your inner music. Smile. When you smile your eyes soften. Respect the moment you two are sharing.

If you have something serious or critical to communicate, be certain you are in a private place. No one enjoys being put down, but to humiliate someone in front of other people is unforgivable. Any insensitivity on your part will reflect badly on you and you will always regret your lack of tact. When you gain people's respect even under difficulty, you will enjoy life more. Learn to be persuasive and always be kind. A wise person once said that our neighbor is really us. If you are unkind even in words you are hurting yourself.

"... WE ACQUIRE A KEENER SENSE OF THE VALUE OF TIME. NOTHING ELSE, INDEED, SEEMS OF ANY CONSEQUENCE ..."
—*William Hazlitt*

GROUPS

How many times have we been in a group and one person dominates the conversation? We can learn from this. Intelligence isn't evaluated by constant noise. Silence often shows grace and wisdom. So many times when I'm in a group, I get the urge to chime in and speak and suddenly, like a gift, the opportunity vanishes and I am spared the embarrassment of sounding ignorant. You may have a question and, by being patient, learn the answer to your question in the course of time, which spares you and others a thoughtless interruption.

First, listen. Then when you speak, begin with a compliment. In all exchanges this is a good way to behave. If you feel you can ask questions and gain information after you have finished listening, do. This saves time for everyone else.

Try to bring out others. Ask questions and listen to what they express. We usually learn the most when our mouths are closed.

SPEECH

Are you pleased with your speaking style? Most of us speak too fast, especially when we're nervous. We should try to be clearly understood. It may be useful for you to have a conversation with a friend and record yourself. No one ever has to listen to the tape but you. Yet you will catch your weaknesses. If you often begin a thought with "uh" or "ah," you can make an effort to pause until you are ready to speak.

When you are in a foreign country and don't speak the language, remember, they might speak yours! You are an ambassador from your country and when you act in a polite, courteous manner you will be greeted with nods, smiles and usually with assistance. Rather than getting frustrated because you don't know how to converse, it is far better to be yourself and gently speak your own language. People say the French are arrogant because they tend to make you feel stupid if you don't speak French, but I disagree. I've felt far more awkward in New York City with a pushy, rude saleswoman.

If you can, it is good to try to learn enough vocabulary wherever you travel so that you show respect. You don't have to feel inferior if you travel from one culture to the next and don't speak the local tongue. Speak beautifully in your own language and you may be surprised how well you are understood and how well you can get along.

PUBLIC SPEAKING

Many of us have to give talks in public. Whether we give a report at work or at a school, at the organization or a club, addressing a group of people successfully can be learned. Even if you can't envision yourself ever needing to speak in public, learning basic, useful tools builds self-confidence and serenity. Anyone who wants to learn and perfect the skill of successful public speaking can benefit from practical advice. If you are enthusiastic about what you have to say and are willing to prepare your material so it is easy for the audience to understand your point of view, you are well on your way.

One of the first times I spoke in public was when I said my marriage vows in 1961 and even though I was told, "Repeat after me," I was a nervous wreck and managed to bungle the meaningful words I knew by heart. Before my wedding day I'd spoken at

"THE LANGUAGE OF TRUTH IS SIMPLE."
—Seneca

"THE MOST MANIFEST SIGN OF WISDOM IS A CONTINUAL CHEERFULNESS . . ."
—Michel de Montaigne

school events, but I never took a course in public speaking. I began to want to give toasts at bridal dinners and receptions, but I had no experience and was shy.

In order to give a good toast or a lecture, you have to want to do it very much. If you can live without doing it, don't do it, because your soul won't be there. There is nothing more patronizing than having a speaker stand up before you and wing it, unprepared and uninspired. If you find that you want to express your point of view and you have something to say, don't be afraid. You can learn how to get your message across effectively when your intentions are sincere. We all begin as amateurs and the more opportunities we have, the more we should welcome each chance to express ourselves. Young people should take every chance they get to speak in front of their peers and make an announcement or give a brief talk. While we may encounter a tough audience, it is good to remember that most groups are willing audiences and are on our side. When we feel people rooting for us we can be a bit calmer.

Develop your own style of speaking. A woman whose job depends on her giving reports and making presentations tried to be humorous when she started out; she quickly discovered that was not her style. The better you are prepared, the more natural your message will appear. As with acting or entertaining, when you care a great deal you will be nervous and you will have an adrenaline rush. Your heart pounds and your knees knock. This is a good sign. If this doesn't happen, watch out. When you get up to begin, look at the audience and take a deep breath. Pause, and start.

You have weeks, possibly months, to prepare for your talk. First take notes about the topics you want to cover. Jot down your thoughts and let your mind experience free association. Doodle. Dream. Pay no attention to organization now; just put down words and images. Next make an outline that best organizes your material. Paper is cheap, so leave lots of space between your points. Number your ideas into a structure with a beginning, middle and conclusion. Draw a circle. Put the ideas clockwise until you see your beginning and ending touching. All speakers are told how

"NEVER COMPLAIN
AND NEVER
EXPLAIN."
—*Benjamin Disraeli*

much time they are allowed. A thoughtful speaker never takes advantage of the time frame. What a seasoned speaker recognizes early on is how difficult it is to edit his material so he can contain his remarks in the allotted time. Once I was at a seminar and a speaker went so far into the time allotted for the next speaker that when he finally finished he had used up the next speaker's hour and it was time for the lunch break. No matter how scholarly a speaker is, everyone is on a schedule and it is an essential discipline that things move according to plan.

The shorter your speaking time, the longer you must prepare. Try to distill each idea until you can reduce it to a brief paragraph. Many people find that writing out the speech is essential after formulating a basic outline. The next step is to emphasize the key ideas with a colored marker. The vital points can be underlined in red. Then take filing cards and write the main ideas down in outline form. Our daughter Brooke studied public speaking her freshman year at college and she learned that the speaker as well as the audience has to go through a transformation. When you believe in something deeply, then a power takes hold. But this happens only if you are committed to your ideas and passionately want to communicate them to the audience.

When you have something to say and you have outlined and shaped the material, the best way to make your point is to look at the audience, take a deep breath, and begin. We've all gone to hear a lecture where the speaker takes out a typed speech (which may have been written by someone else) and reads it. Why wouldn't the audience prefer to be home where they can be comfortable and listen to, or watch, a tape? The reason for giving a speech is to make the subject alive and vital and to tell a story you are enthusiastic about.

Do you want to overcome speech shyness in order to do a good job? Keep reminding yourself that you want to spread your message and you are being given an excellent opportunity with a good listening audience. Is it your style to record your speech several times and play it back? How do you sound? My friend who felt it was necessary to lace some humor into her remarks learned how flat it was when she heard her tapes. It became apparent after she listened to her delivery that she is not a comedian. She wasn't herself and the audience felt uncomfortable for her. We don't have to be Lily Tomlin or Bette Midler to give a talk. People come to lectures to learn about a subject and also to get to know more about the speaker. When you speak, think that you are having a conversation with a friend. It may seem obvious, but we need to be ourselves. We are only electrifying when we are talking about a subject of personal passion.

How many drafts of your talk do you need to do until you cover your topic in an order that is logical and that makes sense to you? The more you work on what you're going to say, the more natural and effortless you will appear. By reducing your lecture to notes covering your main ideas you will stay on course. Your mind will be triggered by the written material even if you don't actually have to refer to it. Have your written speech available on the podium. It will give you confidence. Review your note cards and memorize your lead sentence and opening paragraph. Once you begin, you will find your adrenaline helps you and before you realize it your memory is triggering you to your conclusion. No matter how much ad-libbing you do, have a tight conclusion. It need be only a sentence or two, but it will wrap things up in an orderly way and complete your story. Make your personal style of speaking as natural as if you were talking to a friend. If you happen to say something funny and the audience laughs, pause and enjoy a laugh yourself. You are talking with your audience, not speaking at them.

TELEPHONE MANNER

The telephone saves you time and money and can be as effective as a meeting face-to-face. You don't have to see someone to be able to spot their mood, and a cheerful telephone manner can make a big difference. I especially enjoy having a good brief conversation

"KNOWLEDGE IS THE ANTIDOTE TO FEAR."
—*Ralph Waldo Emerson*

"DEAR FRIEND, ALL THEORY IS GRAY, AND GREEN THE GOLDEN TREE OF LIFE."
—*Goethe*

on the telephone with someone who is extremely busy because I feel I'm not wasting their time.

Unlike a scheduled visit or a letter you can read at your leisure, a telephone call is always an interruption. Even if you're doing nothing, a telephone call catches you by surprise. Think about your personal style of telephoning. Calls should be made at a reasonable hour so no one in a household will be awakened too early in the morning or too late in the evening. When you call a friend and a parent or child answers the phone, it is polite to identify yourself right away rather than just asking for your party. If you answer the phone and the call is for someone else who's not home, write down the message with the date and the time.

There is always a purpose when someone calls you. When you call someone else let that person know right away why you're calling. You don't know how much time the other person has, so plan to make it brief. If there's good news, tell it and if there's bad news, get to the point. If you're calling just to chat, say so. Someone may be dashing out the door and if you don't immediately get to the reason you called, you can hold up someone who doesn't want to be rude.

If your call is business-related, make the call to the office instead of the home. Family time and private time are so precious and there is so little of it; if most of our business conversations took place at the office, we could enjoy more quality relaxation. If someone specifically asks you to call them at home, that is the signal that it would be appropriate. If someone works from home they probably have another phone number that is different from their private line. Unless you are close friends, weekends should be reserved for family and social life.

Your voice tone is your key form of communicating over the phone. Check to be sure your voice is pleasant, because one tends to raise voice levels when under stress. Before you answer the phone, pause, take a deep breath and smile. It might be a loved one who is thinking of you.

COMMUNICATING ON PAPER

Recently Peter and I came back from a strenuous trip to China where he was on business. Immediately after opening the front door we saw that our large hall table was stacked high with mail. The ten-day accumulation appalled us; most of our mail is delivered to the office. Much to our delight there were half a dozen handwritten letters, including one that was hand-delivered. The bills and junk mail got dumped into shopping bags to be dealt with after we got settled in, but we immediately sat in the kitchen and read our personal letters. What a welcome home! These letters eased the reality that both our daughters had now left for college. What struck us was how expressive and revealing a letter can be.

Each envelope had a different shape, size and color. The handwriting ranged from bold to refined: The letters were written with fountain pen, felt tips and ballpoint, all guided by the personality of the writer. One of the nicest ways to express yourself is in writing and sending a personal letter, postcard or note. Letters have great power and influence. Because many are saved and reread, the beauty of the paper combined with the handwriting and the choice of words can bring lasting pleasure. In the hype of our materialistic age, when people have lost sight of the most fundamental values, taking a few minutes to write a personal note is a nicety that is always appreciated.

In my book *Gift of a Letter,* I discuss how little time it takes to write a letter once you are set up with all your necessary paraphernalia. While some people spend money on gadgets, those who enjoy sending and receiving letters enjoy the equipment that goes with the territory. I get more thrills from a good fountain pen than I would from having my own yacht. After the Book-of-the-Month Club selected one of my books, Peter bought me a Waterman Centennial pen with enough refills to write another book. The salesperson inquired, "How many is that?" Peter replied, "A lot." A new box of stationery is more delicious than a two-pound box of Godiva chocolates. When someone enjoys writing a letter, it shows. There is a burst of enthusiasm and spirit that shines through.

Business letter writing can become your personal style. It is a good habit and once you're in the swing, the anticipation of having a relaxing time to visit with several business friends through the pen is a special time. We always feel satisfaction once we pop a letter into the post. If you don't enjoy letter writing, analyze why. Handwritten business letters are a powerful tool to communicate your image. Possibly you don't have good handwriting. Don't be too critical. If it's vaguely legible, it's good enough for a personal letter. If I love the person who writes me, I can always interpret the words, even if it takes an effort. If you really feel your handwriting is unmanageable, use a typewriter. I have lots of friends who do. It is a substitute, but far better than a letter sent through a secretary. Maybe your fountain pen has dried up or you've run out of stationery and haven't had time to reorder. Gather your supplies and put them together in one place. If your desk is too messy or crowded with work, put your letter-writing equipment in a basket or wooden box. This way you can go sit in a serene place and write some notes.

Get in the habit of sending postcards. Keep stacks around, prestamped, and as you think of someone, send them a pretty postcard. We all send postcards when we travel and we can send them from our kitchen table or desk, too. Personally I have more free time at home than I do when I'm away in some exotic place soaking up the beauty and culture.

Even the lists and notes you make for yourself can be beautiful. If you sit down in the morning and make notes and write a "To Do" list, you will see it and be influenced by it all day. If you enjoy organizing your thoughts on paper, it becomes a constructive game that will benefit you and your work. I have a friend who refers to this kind of behavior as "constructively compulsive." When you know you must do certain things anyway, make them more attractive. The aesthetic details of your daily life deserve the same style and attention as you give your friends. Take time to enjoy writing yourself neat notes and lists. Dream of things you really want to accomplish. What's more rewarding than com-

"VIRTUE IS A KIND OF HEALTH, BEAUTY AND GOOD HABIT OF THE SOUL."
—*Plato*

"ALL GOOD THINGS WHICH EXIST ARE THE FRUITS OF ORIGINALITY."
—*John Stuart Mill*

municating well with yourself? Make editorial comments in your engagement book where it has a space headed "Notes." Maybe you are inspired to keep a journal. Once you get into the habit, facing a blank sheet of paper is as refreshing as awakening to a crisp, sparkling day after a good night's sleep. Communicating your feelings—to yourself and others—is rewarding and exciting and you have this opportunity every time you pick up a pen and paper.

Begin now to make your morning list a creative, meditative act. Write down everything that comes to your mind that you'd like to do today. There are many things you have to do and by making good lists, you increase your choices and fuel your imagination. Get into the habit of writing things down. You will see how much better you'll feel when you see something in writing. When you communicate on paper you instantly can see what's important. You can increase your capacity for pleasure simply by making wonderful lists. After you make your list you then prioritize it in order of importance. A dream is only a dream until you act. A list forces you to see and make your dream a reality.

Concentrate on civilizing your office. Have more than one briefcase or tote bag so you can bring selected projects home. Use flowered tote bags or museum art shopping bags to hold work you need to bring back and forth. Examine these items to be sure they are attractive.

"THE GREAT INSTRUMENT OF MORAL GOOD IS THE IMAGINATION."
—*Percy Bysse Shelley*

OPENING UP YOUR SENSES

Marcel Proust illustrates how we remember "things past" through sense associations. An unforgettable flavor, the smell of lilac, the sound of the church bells, the touch of a gentle hand, the sight of a garden full of sunlight and dew in the early morning—these are the associations that last your lifetime and you can retrieve happy memories by tapping into your senses.

Learn how to communicate more positively through your senses. You can become more aware of what your senses are telling you once you realize they speak a language and have a vocabulary. Make your personal style sensuous. I have an elderly friend who sleeps all the time and it is impossible to get her to wake up. I've found, however, that I am able to communicate with her through touch. My voice helps her to sense my presence and when I rub her forehead and her cheek she responds. Somehow I feel she knows I'm there and as I rub her and talk to her, I sense that she's responding. Learn to trust your ability to connect with nature, others and yourself through your senses.

Receiving messages from others is such an important element in a relationship and often the clues you receive are subtle. Sense the signals. Experience different feelings of touch and imagine how they feel to the other person. Everyone experiences touch, taste and smell differently because of their own sensibilities. You can increase your awareness of your senses. Concentrate on what you smell and try to describe it. For example, a carnation smells of cloves.

Communicate with the world in minute detail. Let a walk on a beach or in a garden or up a snow-capped mountain open you up to the pure majesty of everything you see. Notice the smallest detail of a seashell, a snowflake, a flower petal and a shadow. In the hectic race of life it is wise to take time to be quiet and available to what your senses are communicating to you. Be open to see, hear, touch, taste and smell what they communicate.

What is your sixth sense? Is it intuition, which brings everything into personal focus and makes what you feel and experience have special meaning for you? Once you find your personal style of communicating, you will trust your instincts in all circumstances. Peter's sixth sense is appreciation. A friend's is love. Another friend believes his is curiosity. What is yours?

You find your essence by tapping into your senses and listening to the song that your heart is quietly singing. Try not to let this personal voice get drowned out in schedules, agendas and the programs of life. Your senses are your greatest communicators. Become one with your six senses. They live deep inside you. All your communications with yourself, the world and others can be sweetened by your intimacy with your senses.

"OPPORTUNITIES ARE USUALLY DISGUISED AS HARD WORK, SO MOST PEOPLE DON'T RECOGNIZE THEM."
—*Ann Landers*

GRACE NOTES

❧ Keep a birthday calendar of coworkers' birthdays and have a card on their desk to greet them.

❧ Check your own work so no one else has to correct it.

❧ Bring a box of cookies to the office to sweeten the afternoon tea ritual.

❧ Never make excuses. Work to create good results.

❧ Look at a problem as an opportunity, not a disaster. Creatively search for solutions and have a constructive plan of action. You may discover a superior plan of attack.

❧ Make your own potpourri and bring it to the office. One possibility—bay leaves, peach pits and balsam wood soaked in pear juice.

❧ Be yourself with *all* the people you work with.

❧ Ninety-five percent of our work is necessary; make it as pleasant for yourself as possible. Don't fight work.

❧ Respond promptly to invitations and announcements. Decide yes or no and then accept or send regrets. You're going to have to act eventually and it's thoughtful not to delay.

❧ Dive into a new project—beginning is half of finishing.

❧ Prepare your desk for the next day's work. I remember seeing a picture of a desk in a formal living room that was so ordered—with carriage clock, writing paper, glasses and pen—that I felt the person's presence. When you greet a well-arranged desk in the morning, you flow into your work with greater ease and pleasure.

❧ Have one great hand-blown drinking glass near your desk so you can enjoy sipping water in style.

❧ After an important business meeting, have a messenger deliver a handwritten thank-you letter. The impact will leave a lasting impression.

❧ Make a punch list of the things you want to accomplish today. Add a few embellishments that are aesthetic rather than functional. For example, stopping off to buy some colorful storage boxes so you can enjoy organizing your clippings.

❧ When someone tries to help you by showing you a better way to do a task, don't take offense; delight in help so long as it is an improvement.

❧ Clutter and messy work areas cause confusion and irritability. Give your mind a spa and take some time out to rearrange your office. Block off a few hours on your calendar and use the time to putter. Edit out the unnecessary and enjoy putting your own imprint on all the surfaces. By sorting through everything in a block of time you will remember where you want to put things and you will be more efficient. Your time will be well spent.

❧ Remember you don't have to be at a desk in order to be working; your office is where you are. Make it your style always to carry a small memo pad with you. You never know when you'll have a brilliant idea.

❧ Take classes, attend lectures to improve your effectiveness on the job and to expand the range of knowledge of your work.

❧ Keep your personal telephone calls to a minimum.

❧ Respect your coworkers' need for silence. Most work requires freedom from idle chatter.

❧ Work smarter, not harder. When you overdo, you spin your wheels and lose necessary judgment.

❧ Know how to say "no" when your heart's not in something. Maybe it's time for a change.

❧ Light up your life. All light-reflecting objects will perk you up and give you energy. Colorful flowers reflecting in glass and mirrors will fill your surroundings with light and energy.

❧ Make dates with yourself. Plan ahead and mark your calendar, blocking out time to be alone so you can have free time for yourself in your busy schedule.

❧ Plan to work late at the office Monday nights when you are rested after the weekend. You can set a good pace for the entire week.

❧ "Fortune is infatuated with the efficient."—Persian proverb.

❧ Try. Effort is its own reward.

❧ Focus on self-worth, not net worth. Others will also respect your sense of self when you do.

❧ Put all papers into colorful, labeled file folders immediately. Never lose time and energy looking for one paper in the cyclone of unmarked papers on your desk. Better a stack of color-coded file folders.

❧ To the extent it's possible, answer business letters by hand and make a carbon copy for your file if you don't have a Xerox machine. Make this your personal style.

❧ Have good lighting for winter evenings when you work late and need a boost. Light gives you energy, so light the lights.

❧ Try to eliminate every ugly necessity. A stapler can be well designed and functional, and a clipboard can be beautiful. Beauty restores us, so be sure your work space feeds your soul.

❧ Carry more than one pen with you at all times! You needn't concern yourself with a pen that keeps conking out.

❧ Never say "I'm going to be honest with you," "frankly," or "truthfully."

❧ If you are unclear about instructions or scheduling, inquire right away. Tomorrow may be too late.

❧ Be willing to let your staff grow. Delegate responsibility as your work load increases. Often workers do live up to your expectations. At the same time, it is wise to know who you are, what size you want your firm to be and who your product is for.

❧ Sometimes it's hard to leave personal difficulties at home. If at all possible, find a way to let your staff know you are under outside stress. You may find your troubles don't bother you as much and your coworkers won't take unintended slights personally.

❦ Order a piece of ¼-inch-thick glass cut 20 × 13 inches and beveled. Put a sheet of hand-marbleized paper beneath it. This is your new writing table.

❦ Get caught up and stay on top of the routine realities so you're free to tackle a new project.

YOUR GRACE NOTES

FIVE

Your PERSONAL STYLE OF LEISURE AND TRAVEL

RELAXATION AND YOUR HEALTH—PRIVACY

 our personal style is like a chain. Every-thing interconnects. How you choose to spend your evenings, your weekends, de-fines you. Think of taking leisurely walks to work by different routes. This coming and going time is your own. Make it meaningful. Plan to have breakfast at a fancy hotel or inn as if you were in another city. When you do this, whether alone or with a friend, you renew your appreciation for where you live and you add luxury to the routines. Make it your style not to dribble away your weekends catching up on office work. Read, go for walks, do some decorating improve-ments around the house, organize your wardrobe and spend time alone and together with your loved one, free from the reminders of your work week.

Leisure time allows you the opportunity to balance your life. The more hectic your schedule, the more you tend to want to

"MAKE HASTE SLOWLY."
—*Caesar Augustus*

spend leisure time alone. Leisure is to life what water is to fish. We can go along for a while flitting around but unless we have privacy and unscheduled time on a regular, predictable basis, we can't keep going. Leisure is a treasure, a luxury beyond all material goods; leisure is time off to experience freedom from demands made on you by others.

Free time when you are relaxed and unhurried is good for your health. You need to have unrestricted time when you do the things you most enjoy doing. Because so much of your time is scheduled when you are answering to others, you need freedom so you can decide what you feel like doing. Leisure time, unlike travel (when you have to plan a schedule well in advance), should be spontaneous and flexible. Use it wisely. What's wonderful about leisure is that you can be in seclusion and even secrecy—especially if you don't have to go anywhere to obtain it. Leisure time should be spent doing whatever you like, at your convenience. How do you define your style of leisure?

How often can you answer only to yourself? These moments can be some of the richest, most memorable times because you can be completely honest with your feelings. You can putter, organize, rest, read or arrange flowers. You can garden, write a poem, take photographs, love, paint or begin writing a story. You can organize your kitchen cupboards and take stock or you can lie on your bed and look through the new issue of *McCall's*. The magic of leisure is that what you do is entirely up to you. Time off is rare. Most of your time is spent doing things in relationship with others, on a set schedule. Each time you relax you discover what you need to do to center yourself.

Keep this precious leisure time unscheduled. Free yourself so you can slip into activity or inactivity according to the rhythm of your body and spirit. One time you will need a nap—take it. Another time you may feel the creative urge to sit at the piano. A federal judge unwinds from his demanding work load by becoming absorbed in his music in his leisure time. An investment banker spends all his time off painting and has a gallery show once a year.

"THE GOOD AND THE WISE LEAD QUIET LIVES."
—*Euripides*

Half of your leisure time should be spent in privacy or privacy for two. The most intimate couples can share leisure time together because neither one makes any demands on the other. Save spaces in your schedule each day. One busy friend with a demanding job needs a break in the morning when she can collect her thoughts, read several newspapers, write letters, prepare her work for the day and sip her coffee in peace before her fourteen-hour work day begins. She feels she never has enough time to see her friends and she has to squeeze in exercise also. Her solution is going to a dance class, meeting two busy friends there every Wednesday night. They move about enjoying themselves and the companionship. To have the same friends share Judy's quiet time in the morning would be inappropriate. Leisure is not a luxury reserved for the lazy rich. It is what busy, hardworking people need to keep an even keel and accomplish their goals. Leisure time restores our balance and provides spaces for us to open up our creativity.

When you crowd your days and go from family events and obligations to work responsibilities to social commitments, you appear to be juggling it all. But wait. You've kept your engine running but haven't taken time to communicate with yourself. Free time must be programmed just the same way you plan a trip, a business meeting or an appointment with your dentist. You are responsible for the way you manage your time.

Even if you are retired, everything you do can become more imaginative once you deliberately try to avoid anything routine or passive. Every action requires some degree of personal choice. Teresa Amabile, a psychologist at Brandeis University, believes "creativity is a fragile phenomenon, easily crushed . . . You have to take risks to be creative." Let it be your personal style to have plenty of time alone so you can enjoy being innovative, so you can take time to add finishing touches to things. When you do a simple task and totally focus on it, other ideas will come to you and you can act on them. Creativity requires time and is enhanced when you are enjoying yourself. Each time you do something beautifully, you are delighting yourself. By making a conscientious effort to tap into your imagination and do everything with

"THE ESSENTIAL ELEMENTS . . . OF THE ROMANTIC SPIRIT ARE CURIOSITY AND THE LOVE OF BEAUTY."
—*Walter Pater*

your own twist (Emily Dickinson believed we should tell the truth but tell it at a "slant"), you raise each moment into an opportunity to do something original.

But the busier you are, the more demands there are on you, the greater your need to have time off. We should take Joseph Campbell's suggestion that we have a specific room or a space where we go each day where we can find our "bliss station." If you create the physical space but your schedule doesn't allow you time to go there, you will never find your "bliss station."

Take time to be quiet and alone. If you are becoming fragmented because of everyone else's demands, plan even more private time during your most stressful periods. A powerful publisher got caught in a trap where he felt awful and kept pushing himself until one day he called the office and said he was taking a personal day. It takes guts to admit enough is enough. All his appointments were easily rescheduled. There are times to back off, be quiet, rest, unwind. The tensions and pressures that make you anxious exhaust you so you are no longer effective. One day off can be more valuable than a week-long vacation with no real quality time to be free to be yourself. When you listen to your body and are sensitive to your feelings, you avoid illness, the worst time waster imaginable. Leisure is a stitch in time saving nine.

SPORTS

Playing tennis or golf, swimming, body surfing, scuba diving, skiing, sailing, biking, hiking, running, playing croquet—evaluate which of these outdoor activities brings you the most serenity, invigoration and pleasure.

Your life has radically changed since you were a teenager and learned a variety of sports. I remember with delight having the luxury of playing tennis every day, the summer I was sixteen and playing on the junior tennis circuit. Tennis was my project and I completely focused on what I most enjoyed doing. I played with pros and with friends. I dated boys who loved tennis, and because

"MANY THINGS DIFFICULT TO DESIGN PROVE EASY TO PERFORMANCE."
—*Samuel Johnson*

I played all the time my game improved and so playing became my most enjoyable, all-consuming passion.

Twenty years later, working in New York as a designer, raising two daughters and writing a book left me little time for serious tennis. Playing top tennis was the thing I had to let go because my life had opened new, exciting chapters. My tennis suffered badly as I encountered new doors I wanted to open. We live our lives in stages.

I was at a cocktail party and a friend told a contemporary, "There is a woman in this room (she was referring to me) who can beat you in tennis." Liz was furious because she'd kept up her tennis and played every day. She inquired, "Who can beat me? I'd like to play her." What began as an innocent challenge ended as dangerously as a duel. Early one hot, sultry July morning we played our blood match on a hard court on the West Side of Manhattan. Liz was out to win and her fierce competitive spirit inspired me to fight harder. I was out of shape and out of breath, but I kept trying to hold my own. After two hours, we split sets. I had to get to my office. I felt faint. I was about to throw up. Liz agreed to stop and we agreed to meet the next week, which we did, and she polished me off the court in two straight easy sets. I learned a lesson from Liz. She has played regularly for twenty years while I was doing other things. She deserved to win because she takes her tennis seriously and has kept it up religiously.

What activities really make you feel good? How competitive are you? Do you enjoy playing or winning? When you lose, do you sulk? List all the sports activities you most enjoy participating in and why they please you. Then list the ones you least enjoy. Maybe you are a thrill seeker and enjoy rafting, soaring or gliding. Look over your list and add up how many activities you enjoy that are competitive, how many sports where you are a spectator and how many sports you enjoy doing alone. My daughter Alexandra enjoys horseback riding where she and her horse are together and alone. I enjoy swimming. My literary agent, Carl Brandt, likes to climb mountains and has been alone hiking for up to fourteen days. Bill Blass enjoys walking his dogs in the woods near his Connecticut house. What do you most like to do?

You will discover by this simple exercise that you are quite opinionated about your preferences. You might enjoy watching a sports event on television but wouldn't necessarily want to be there as a spectator. Perhaps your primary interest is to get some exercise, or you may enjoy the social aspects of making regular dates with good friends and playing golf, tennis or croquet. Do you engage in sports to see others or to get regular exercise and feel fit? Do you enjoy contemplating nature and being alone?

If you discover you are going through the motions of bowling, playing croquet or fishing to please a spouse or friend, stop. The prime reason people don't have enough time is because they aren't protective of the time they do have. It seems a bizarre reality to do things you don't enjoy in your leisure time! My friend Mary Anne Dolan, a writer, played many competitive sports when she was younger but she prefers to sit them out now. Wherever she goes she has her electric typewriter with her and is happy to go along on ski trips and not have to ski. She knows what she wants to do and she is content. This is now her style of sports—she enjoys the company and the scenery but not the activity.

INTERESTS

Whether you are an avid gardener, a bird-watcher, collector, amateur painter or bookbinder, your thoughts and energies lead you to make time to enjoy your interests. I have a friend who is fascinated by eighteenth-century costumes and spends all her free time learning more about old textiles. Another friend inherited some fine old silver and decided she would learn about the markings and the makers. What began as a practical idea developed into a fierce interest and now Kathleen is quite an expert on old silver.

The activities you do for your personal pleasure and not for money or to please others are never fatiguing. Most of us pursue our interests when we are alone. I know someone who collects butterflies, associating her collection with hundreds of lovely hours alone. I have a client who collects seashells from beaches wherever she travels. She makes them into intricate decorations that she frames behind glass and gives to friends as presents. The art and her generosity combine to make magic.

A lawyer enjoys collecting American antiques and has met wonderful dealers and like-minded people in his search around the country. Another lawyer is an avid scuba diver and underwater photographer. An executive search recruiter is an amateur photographer and carries his camera with him whenever he will be in touch with nature.

One of my keen interests is collecting art postcards and I've been doing this all over the world for thirty years. I've filled many shoe boxes with postcards and I enjoy cataloguing them. I have collected cards of Claude Monet's paintings that I'd never known existed. I lose all track of time when I sit at my desk surrounded by these cards and I study each one as though it were the original painting. I'm sure I have the largest Impressionist art collection in the world in handy, uniform cards.

Whether you collect postcards, stamps, coins, miniature furniture, seashells or quilts, you become knowledgeable. The more excited you are about your interests the more interesting they become to others in addition to yourself.

What do you most enjoy doing with your free time? My friend Jeannette Ching loves to grow herbs and cook with fresh herbs, and she also enjoys arranging flowers grown in her English garden and her garden room. Patsy Corbin likes to dig in her garden, creating rose arbors and a rainbow of fragile, fragrant blossoms. She studies seed catalogues whenever she's not gardening, and her husband enjoys making trellises for her garden.

Let your interests guide your leisure time. If you enjoy baking or canning, set yourself up so that when you have a free hour or two you can get going. Gather your yarn and designs so you can knit a one-of-a-kind sweater. Create your own needlepoint patterns for your dining room chairs. Have your sewing machine ready for an evening when you can make a dress with the silk fabric you brought back from Thailand. Create a place where you can sort through your photographs and put them in order. Content people do what they like to do as often as possible.

"MAN [WOMAN] MUST CHOOSE WHETHER TO BE RICH IN THINGS OR IN THE FREEDOM TO USE THEM."
—*Ivan Illich*

A two-career couple with no children has an interest in eating out at a different restaurant every Friday night. They live in San Francisco and love learning about restaurants from friends and colleagues.

Maybe you enjoy meditating and doing yoga. My friend Katherine and her friend Connie are going on a yoga retreat this spring. Or perhaps you really love to dance so you go to a dance instructor two nights a week. An artist friend who has a tricky back has grown to love to take early morning four-mile walks. Her back is fine now, and her solitary walks which began as therapy are enjoyed as regular time for meditation.

Don't wait for others to encourage you to pursue your interests. I know a man who enjoyed restoring an old dollhouse and spent all his free time working on this project. His wife got frustrated that he never mowed the lawn or raked leaves so he got a student to come and do the yard work because he wanted to free his time to do the project he found exciting.

A husband who enjoys hooking rugs receives no encouragement from his wife who wishes she could have her library back in order. The boxes of yarn and the rug take up half the room. But your interests animate a room. Sharon knows how much Eric loves to work on his rugs and still be with the family, so they rearranged a closet in the library to incorporate his yarn collection, freeing up a great deal of space. Neil Simon has an antique pool table in his living room, believing it makes a room come to life when it is put to use. Hobbies needn't be relegated to the basement or the attic. Many rooms are too impersonal and stiff, and a loom or a harp or a telescope tells something personal about your style.

What are your most passionate interests? What plans are you making for rearranging your schedule to gain more time for your interests? Some of these require planning ahead and others can be pursued on a whim. Have lots of different options ready so that you can act when you have time. Carefully plan the projects that you can do at home so there is a place to work and safely store your project.

WHAT ARE YOUR
FAVORITE BOOKS?

HIGH ARTS

Take time out from your hectic life to appreciate music, theater, the opera and dance. Artists will inspire you and give you fresh insight. Whenever you are deeply moved by a performance, it confirms your own beliefs. Years ago I had season tickets for the New York City Ballet and went with a friend from my office who also loved dance. During intermission after we had just experienced Nureyev leaping into the air in suspension as if he defied gravity, my friend smiled and said, "I'm so glad he's dancing for me and I don't actually have to do it myself. I don't enjoy dancing, but I'm thrilled to experience dance."

I remember being touched beyond measure by Julie Harris's performance in *The Belle of Amherst* in which she portrayed Emily Dickinson's life. I went back several times and was transformed each time. A friend describes these rare moments of transformation as times when she is out of her body. Mary told me that she becomes so in tune with a superb performer that she is not aware of her body at all until the experience is over.

Remember these jewels of experience in your life. Think freshly what it was like for you to see the costumes and the color of a particular ballet or opera and how you felt. When was the last time your whole body tingled and you cried in sheer joy listening to a concert or a soloist or watching an actor perform? What theater have you experienced recently that you really enjoyed? An actress passionately goes to the movies and is freshly inspired by her peers. When was the last time you were at a lecture when you couldn't stop applauding because the speaker spoke to you in such a powerful way? When has a performer, an educator or an entertainer moved you deeply?

What kinds of entertainment do you most enjoy? Never force yourself to see a violent movie or a cheap, vulgar play. I remember going to a movie that was playing in Nantucket in August, 1974, that had a rape scene that still frightens me. We all have different tolerances and have to be selective about what we take in. There will never be enough time to see every play that opens or go to every cultural event. If you want to be uplifted, inspired, entertained and informed, you have to be selective.

Define your personal taste in entertainment by editing out the things you know are not you. Whenever you make a mistake and go to a performance that is tacky or cheap, walk out. Once you pay the price of a ticket, feel free to cut your losses. This careful screening process has nothing to do with your intellectual curiosity. Rather, it reflects your discernment. When you subject yourself to experiences that will dampen your spirits, you show lack of judgment and self-regard.

Guard your precious time. If you skip a trashy television show you've saved over two hours. Think of it: two free hours to spend doing something positive. If you go to a play to laugh and you find all the humor sick, what's so funny about that? Frankly, it's more fun to laugh among friends.

Your personal style will dictate to you what makes you feel comfortable and what makes you squirm. Be honest with your feelings. If someone you really adore continues to invite you to the opera and you'd prefer to go to the ballet with the same investment of time, politely say you have another engagement and arrange to go to the ballet instead or have a cozy evening at home reading.

SING A SONG.

Use your free time to the depths of your vision, to enrich you and allow you to see how vast your opportunities are. Tap into all the affirmative things that give you pleasure and that help you to use your energy constructively.

HEALTH SPA

I read recently in *W* that interior designer Mario Buatta was too busy for a vacation but he headed up to the Norwich Inn in Connecticut "to be pampered." Bill Blass goes there too. William Buckley stayed in a villa there to work on a book. If you work so hard and such crazy hours that you exhaust yourself and are too tired to enjoy your leisure time, the benefits of a health spa might be ideal. You can feel you're doing something therapeutic for your tired body, mind and soul.

Health spas are expensive but so are doctors and therapists. Believe in prevention. If you can have a massage, a soak in a whirlpool, a few minutes in the steam room or do some laps in a big clean swimming pool, you will instantly feel physically and psychologically better about your life. Pressures melt away.

Recently I hurt my back and was not allowed to travel. After seven weeks my doctor told me I could take a short trip outside the city on the theory that this would be good for my spirits. Peter and I headed to the Norwich Inn and spent a glorious day and night there in a beautiful, peaceful setting. I had my first seaweed wrap where I perspired and was cleansed of all the toxins in my body. Sitting on a terrace under an umbrella, I ate a light lunch—swordfish and a spa salad. It was a twenty-four-hour quick fix. I returned to New York refreshed and content.

Add up all your medical-related bills and the money you spend on medication each year. Consider putting a certain amount of money aside for a few spa experiences. You don't have to go away to an expensive place for a week if you can't spare the time and money. Go for a short visit when you are on a business trip nearby. Or have a massage at Elizabeth Arden or Georgette Klinger as a therapeutic treat.

Psychologically you feel good about yourself when you do something good for yourself. And you always feel refreshed afterward.

WORKING IN YOUR LEISURE TIME

When you love your work and have lots of interesting projects, your leisure time becomes sacred and you can look forward to it as some of your happiest time. You are not meant to totally vegetate when you have time away from the pressures and stress of your job. When you have precious little time to yourself, be sure you use it intelligently. This is your most creative, valuable time because you are filling your own well and doing things in your own time in your own way. No one is judging you. Your time off is not the moment to do repetitious household chores. Take a break. Train yourself to tune in, not tune out, when you have a short block of time. Learn to use your escape time when you're waiting at a dentist's office or riding on a bus. When you have real leisure time you can do something creative, but minutes add up and you should be feeding your personal style. When you have a block of real time, use it—because when else can you write poetry or paint?

Let the chores wait. This is your time, not time for office, household or family. Interesting people need time to pursue their interests. Give up worrying about dust. Give up worrying! Delve into projects you are passionate about and keep busy. Play dumb to petty interruptions and attempted interferences. If someone thinks you should be doing something useful when they see you sitting peacefully reading, writing, or listening to music, possibly you need to spend your leisure time alone.

"IMAGINATION IS MORE IMPORTANT THAN KNOWLEDGE."
—*Einstein*

LEISURE ALONE

One of this country's top editors is also a wife and mother of a young child and she passionately pursues her interest in her work. While her leisure time is spent working, she sits on a bed alone, not at a desk at her office. She fuels her right brain and no one disturbs her because this is a clear priority in her life—it is her life's work. She has a secret place where she works. She told me recently that she has a phone there but has never received a phone call. No one has the number where she works. The phone was installed so that she could make calls but not be interrupted by them. People like her take their leisure time extremely seriously. This is her private time and she knows she can't have the same-quality experience if her family makes demands on her at the same time.

Be tough. Close a door. If you have to, leave the house and

go to a public library or a park. You need to feel you have safe, peaceful hours when you are free and undisturbed. When you do carefully schedule and plan your leisure time, you are doubling your joy.

Most creative people need some solitude in order to create. If you have a problem with others feeling excluded, have a talk and explain your needs. Have set times when you want to work during leisure time, and let your spouse or children know when those times are. Have your time-alone schedule on a sheet of paper attached to the refrigerator door with a magnet. I know that some women with fulfilling careers feel guilty wanting to pursue their own interests when they are away from the demands of their job. This has to change. Leisure time alone fuels you, gives you vitality and makes you more excited about everything. Meet your own needs regularly. Perhaps you can arrange to have every other Saturday morning to yourself. If you want to meet your spouse or child for lunch or to go to a movie, invite them. In this way they are free to make their independent plans.

Books are written in leisure time alone. Poems are written. Plays. Paintings are painted. Music is created. Open up to the knowledge of how much you need to express yourself for your own pleasure and fulfillment.

"IN SOLITUDE ALONE CAN HE [SHE] KNOW TRUE FREEDOM."
—*Michel de Montaigne*

LEISURE SHARED

Leisure time can be shared when two people complement each other. If you are a close-knit couple and there is an understanding that neither of you is allowed to put pressure on the other, but rather extend an invitation, you have a good basis for success. If a partner wants to go for a walk or a swim and invites you, you must feel free to say "no, thank you." If your partner wants to go to a movie when you need time alone, you must learn how to say no politely and not feel guilty. Guard your leisure time so you can share it well. Anyone who really loves you wants you to have

DO YOU EVER HAVE BREAKFAST IN BED?

sacred times when you do exactly what you want to do, free of domestic chores and worry of interruption.

If you don't want to swim at ten, possibly you can make a date to swim at four, when it is more convenient for you. In this way you have each other's companionship and you don't break the rhythm of what you're doing. What many of us long for and fantasize about is blocks of uninterrupted, unscheduled time when we can begin a project and know we will have enough time to see some results.

Talk things over. Set specific dates and times when you will be free to share yourself. This frees everyone to do what they individually want to do without feeling guilty.

Often we don't have to be completely isolated in order to enjoy productive, meaningful leisure. If you find you can sit in the same space with a spouse, a partner a friend or family member, do. We get energy from each other and we can enjoy each other's company while being absorbed in our own world if we trust the other person to respect our need not to be interrupted.

What is your style of sharing leisure? If your temperament is easygoing, you will have more success at this than if you need total quiet and concentration and find that minor distractions create huge setbacks. The truest test of a relationship is how satisfying you find your shared leisure time. When you both know the rules it can create a pleasant haven from which you both emerge feeling fulfilled and refreshed.

FOR VACATION, WOULD YOU GO TO A CITY OR THE COUNTRY?

PERSONAL AWARENESS

There are times when you really need to expose yourself to experiences that are out of the mainstream of your everyday life. Without upsetting anyone, you might decide to go to a weekend seminar or spiritual retreat where you have time and space to focus and grow. Often problems seem overwhelming. If, however, your life is running smoothly at a fast pace and you want to take time out to reflect, you need this freedom. Sometimes it seems scary to do this kind of thing alone, yet you probably will benefit from the experience if it is your initiative.

FITTING LEISURE INTO A BUSY DAY

Ideally you should take minor retreats during the hectic schedule of your work life. There was an article in the *New York Times* recently called "The Healing Power of a Bit of Solitude" in which Dr. Pierre Mornell, a psychiatrist in Mill Valley, California, said, "The pendulum has swung . . . In the 1960s and 1970s, the emphasis was on togetherness, but now Americans are realizing that time alone is important, too, because people cannot do a good job or relate to others unless they are meeting their own needs."

There is a tendency among conscientious achievers to think that they are indispensable. While they may be of vital importance, everyone can escape for brief periods.

Define your style of enjoying short periods of leisure alone. Have lunch by yourself. Go to a museum exhibition alone. Have a facial or a massage instead of a regular lunch and have a light lunch at your desk with the door shut. Listen to soothing music for a few minutes and write a chatty letter to a friend or call a friend and enjoy an unhurried conversation.

WHAT ARE YOU AWARE OF AT THIS MOMENT?

Walk home from work so you can window-shop and involve your senses. Go to an art lecture or movie alone. Have a cappuccino at a coffee shop so you can look through a magazine you bought at the supermarket. Twenty minutes of privacy will make you more eager to face a difficult afternoon at the office before returning home to an energetic three-year-old child.

Is it your style to get up early and begin the day doing something unrelated to your work? Remember the Wall Street broker who has an exhibition of his paintings every year and does all his painting between 5 A.M. and 8 A.M. A lawyer and mother of two active young sons has a fast walk every morning at 6 A.M. before practicing the piano. A lawyer rides his bike around one of the bike paths in Connecticut before bathing, having breakfast and commuting. He savors his train ride, during which he is working on a first novel.

Going to the office early and putting in several productive hours before breaking for a leisurely lunch can be a most satisfying way to keep yourself in balance. If you work where you have only an hour for lunch and long lunch isn't feasible, make a date to meet a friend for after-work tea or a glass of wine at a local hotel or inn. It is such a pleasure to have a friendly, unhurried time when you don't have any more business obligations.

If you are going out in the evening, always try to go home first and putter, read the mail, bathe and change. If this isn't possible because your home isn't nearby, you might arrange to have your hair done or go someplace for tea alone so you can collect your thoughts before going from one event to another.

You may not be able to paint at the moment but you can keep up with the latest tools of the trade and stock up on vermilion red, cobalt blue and a two-inch sable brush at a supply store. An amateur photographer enjoys spending his leisure time when he comes home from the office looking at his photographs and making scrapbooks of them.

Make it a habit to do something that puts a smile on your face before you begin your workday. Twenty well-spent minutes will make a big difference. Try to sprinkle little moments of fun throughout the day that change the pace and bring you a sense of grace and pleasure.

EXERCISING YOUR MIND

Chances are your boss won't assign Chaucer for you to read. Make it your daily habit to study something. Education prepares us for living by continuously stretching our minds. When Joseph Campbell and Bill Moyers had a dialogue on the television show and in the book *The Power of Myth,* Campbell said, "The spirit is really the bouquet of life. It is not something breathed into life." Moyers asked Campbell, "Who interprets the divinity inherent in nature for us today?" Campbell replied, "It is the function of the artist to do this. The artist is the one who communicates myth for today. But he has to be an artist who understands mythology and humanity and isn't simply a sociologist with a program for you." Moyers inquired, "What about those others who are ordinary, those who are not poets or artists, or who have not had a transcendent ecstasy? How do we know of these things?"

"I'll tell you a way," answered Campbell, "a very nice way. Sit in a room and read—and read and read. And read the right books by the right people. Your mind is brought onto that level, and you have a nice, mild, slow-burning rapture all the time. This realization of life can be a constant realization in your living. When you find an author who really grabs you, read everything he has done."

It is when you are free from stress and deadlines that you can explore greatness in others and tap into what is noble, authentic and fine within yourself. Nourish your mind whenever you can with the best literature that's available. Have a rich menu of books to read. Read several different authors at the same time. It's like having a party with these great minds attending. Do you keep a reading journal? A spiral pad is good for this. I've enjoyed filling up these notebooks since I was a teenager and didn't want to forget certain passages from F. Scott Fitzgerald's novels. List each book and jot down some quotes or passages that are especially moving to you. Make regular reading your personal style of living. Why read to escape when you can read to become enlightened? So many busy people feel they only want light reading, but great literature is far more stimulating and rewarding.

BALANCING LEISURE THROUGHOUT YOUR LIFE

Intelligently used leisure time provides regular periods of refreshment and lends balance to life. Leisure keeps you looking forward and gives opportunities to take risks, learn about new interests, and reflect on all that is beautiful and good in your life and in the world. It gives a nice rhythm to your days, balancing between intensity and letting go. When you are personally content and enjoying your family, you feel the satisfaction of your efforts and hard work. Reap the rewards of a balanced life by recognizing discipline in your leisure time.

This time is not automatic. Wise use of it should be your personal commitment. If you leave leisure to chance, it will never happen. One third of all waking time should be well spent in your personal style of leisure. Do you achieve this? One of the reasons leisure gets short shrift is the attitude that every project you begin has to be finished before you do something else. This is really the procrastination syndrome. All the pretty, fussy, small tasks will never be finished. Life is a multi-flowing process, not a linear caravan. Seize your free moments. Once you are in the habit, you will depend on this pattern as your way to live.

Leisure time can't depend entirely on voids. You schedule work hours and you plan your leisure. A top executive writes her business appointments in her engagement book in red and her leisure time in blue. Sheila can quickly see whether she has maintained the right balance between the two. "When I only see red, I go on red alert and concentrate more on my 'blue time.' " If you crowd your schedule down to the last quarter hour, how can you daydream or look up a word in the dictionary or enjoy making a rhyme for a birthday card? Leisure time can't be just squeezed in if it is to be effective.

ONE OF THE HAPPY REWARDS OF GIVING IS THE CONTENTMENT IT GIVES YOU.

Effective leisure requires concentration and focus. You are the guardian of more time than you may realize. Set limits on the time you spend doing chores. Simplify. Give yourself equal time for leisure. You will find that when you have given yourself an hour or two you are less tired, less troubled, and you manage the maintenance side of your life with more grace.

Take a fresh look at your calendar. Look at the blank spaces as gifts of time. Begin today to take charge of your leisure. Get a yellow outliner and set aside blocks of time—early mornings, a lunch date during the week and three evenings plus all weekends. Weekends are yours. Don't worry now specifically what you will do with this bonus, free time. This simple step helps you to avoid doing things that become chores, that fill up your calendar and fill you with frustration. Be extremely guarded of anything that invades your bright yellow spaces. They are your sunshine.

Next, keep a running list of all the interests you want to pursue, from books you want to read to a new shop you want to go to. This can be tucked into your wallet or put in your Filofax. Make a tab label: LEISURE. Fill lots of pages. Face your free time with your list in hand. Don't get distracted doing spring cleaning if that's not on your list. However, if you are anxious to get your house in order and you've set some time aside to do this, make it a pleasant experience. Listen to some jazz and dance around. Take breaks. Enjoy the beauty of where you live. If you want to electrify the barn and you have set aside time to do this, you will enjoy the pleasure of having accomplished a task that will directly benefit you and you will have concentrated so totally on those wires that you shed your job concerns.

Recently I spent an entire rainy Saturday reading the Pulitzer Prize-winning biography of Edith Wharton by R. W. B. Lewis, along with her letters. It was a feast to my spirits and I filled my sunny yellow space in my engagement book to the brim in a most pleasant way. The next day I looked around the apartment and saw some areas that were not expressing my personal style of home and I decided to attack some of the detritus. I enjoyed the contrast of my two very different days. Both satisfied my senses and my mind. I found my mind wandering to Wharton as I tidied up the living room. She and her architect, Ogden Codman, wrote the important book *The Decoration of Houses* in 1897 which we decorators study as our bible.

On Monday morning I felt refreshed. My mind alert, our apartment looking attractive, I began a busy week. Peter and I had simply taken the weekend off. Off to others. We spent it alone together, enjoying the richness of the rare gift of free time. Statistics indicate that the average American household has less leisure now than it did six years ago. We need more. Leisure time is our "bliss time." One of my favorite things to do in my leisure is to dream, and plan about traveling.

"THE FUTURE IS PURCHASED BY THE PRESENT."
—*Samuel Johnson*

MAKE A TRAVEL LIST

One of the great rewards of travel is the excitement of anticipation. Thinking about a place you'd like to explore someday awakens you to mysteries and colorful images you wouldn't experience any other way. Right now, jot down on a piece of paper some countries to which you would like to travel and some specific sights you want to see. By looking at your list you will be able to see some personal style clues that are extremely revealing. This is your dream travel list.

WHAT DO YOU TAKE
WITH YOU WHEN
YOU TRAVEL?

A few years ago in Charlotte, North Carolina, I gave an il-lustrated slide lecture called "How to Put Magic in Your Life Every Day." My fantasy person had a magical day, traveling from home in Charlotte to Paris for lunch. Magically, she was in New York for an Impressionist exhibition at the Metropolitan Museum and was in Washington for a dinner at the White House. The lecture was such fun to put together because I was able to draw on slides of favorite paintings, statues, architecture and gardens, illustrating a magical day that in reality would be a magical lifetime of travel.

Dreams do come true. You make yourself more aware of what your hidden desires are when you see them written before you. Then you can point toward turning them into reality.

Date your travel list and tuck it into your Filofax or notebook. Make a tab label: TRAVEL. Add to your list as you have new yearn-ings.

Are the places you most want to explore exotic, far away and hard to get to? Are they sophisticated? Primitive? In the wilderness? What do you want to do in those places? If you have Africa on your list; is it your dream to go on a safari? If Colorado is on your list, do you intend to ski or climb mountains? Switzerland? Do you want to stay at beautifully run country inns and eat well? Or are you anxious to ski? To go to a spa?

Refine your list so you have a country, a region and also note about what you would like to do with your time there. If you have Turkey on your list and you are an archaeologist you will probably indicate that you want to go on a dig. Each country and city has its own magic, depending on your interests. You may have friends or family in these places so a large part of your desire to travel could be to have a reunion.

Study your list. Are you a risk taker? Do you want to go to colorful places you've never been to before, where you don't know anyone? Do you want to be in European cities where there are shopping and luxury hotels? Do you want to go to Hong Kong? Or do you prefer modest country inns in the quiet of a far-off place in the Swiss Alps? Are you seeking escape or culture? Both?

Your travel list, as you will see, tells you everything about your interests and curiosity. You may look at your list and find that every country and city is a place you've already been to, but you long to go back. Or you may find that your list includes mostly places where you've never been. Some places you will want to travel to because of the natural beauty. Perhaps you'll want to ride a bike through the wine country of France. Or you may want to see museums, cathedrals and works of art. Your dream list won't deceive you. Traveling is time-consuming, expensive and tiring. Your list is the key to some ideal trips which you will take! You probably have a mixture of places that are colorful, exotic, primitive, deserted, crowded, sophisticated, cultural and beautiful. A mixture of all you need to be satisfied.

> "IN ORDER TO CARRY OUT GREAT ENTERPRISES, ONE MUST LIVE AS IF ONE WILL NEVER HAVE TO DIE."
> —*Marquis de Vauvenargues*

YOUR OPTIONS—KEEP A TRAVEL FOLDER

The next step is to turn your imaginary trips into reality. Keep an attractive accordion travel file handy and fill it with information about the places you are interested in. Such files can be found at the Mediterranean Shop in New York, Il Papiro and Pierre Deux in a variety of patterns and colors to accompany your color scheme in your bedroom. Or buy one from an office supply store and cover the front and back with wallpaper or fabric and sew on some colorful grosgrain ribbons to tie the top together. I read magazine and newspaper articles in bed and have my file handy for articles from interesting places. *Gourmet* magazine has wonderful suggestions of where to go as well as where to eat. If you gather information from a friend, put it in your folder. Keep your folder up-to-date. When you read an article in the travel section of a newspaper that interests you, clip it and put it right into your folder. Clip enticing ads and editorials. When you're in an airplane, browse through the in-flight magazine and clip out travel articles that interest you. If you don't have time to read an article right away, it will be safe and in your travel file when you have more time.

Clearly mark each individual place and file alphabetically by country. If you intend to go to the Loire Valley to see châteaus, you will probably also want to spend some time in Paris. File everything under France. Date each article you put into your file so you will know how current the information is when you plan a trip. If you have a real passion for a particular part of the world, say, the Far East, have general categories and then labels that are more specific. The better your travel file the better your trip. Enjoy reading about these places that interest you and take pleasure in putting the information away in a safe, organized manner.

Just like having your passport up-to-date and handy, you will discover that your personal travel folder will help bring you magical moments in romantic, exotic places. Be prepared for a dream trip. It may happen sooner than you think.

A friend of ours met a man at a party and within three weeks they decided to get married. "When it's right, it's right." Both these lovely people had lost their spouses years before, and they were so busy working on their careers they hadn't thought of remarrying. Bang! They both knew right away. One evening at dinner they discussed their honeymoon and later Connie showed her fiancé her dream travel folder which had articles about Paris, the Orient Express, Venice and the Villa d'Este in Lake Como. He smiled. "I've always wanted to go to those places too but early on I was too busy with my work and then I didn't want to go alone. We'll fly to Paris and take the Orient Express to Venice and then end up at the Villa d'Este." Travel dreams come true. You may change jobs and spend some time traveling before you begin your new job. If an aunt dies and leaves you a little windfall, you can put it toward a dream trip.

TRAVEL BOOKS

Some of my favorite reading is travel books, my special favorite being *The Spirit of Place,* by Lawrence Durrell. Writers feel so enthusiastic about the places they write about that often my senses are awakened to a pitch. I feel I can smell the spices, taste the local food and savor the local wines, experience the majesty of the local monuments and feel the pulse of the people, their culture and their rituals. Travel books help to keep your dreams vital. Picture books of beautiful spots remind you how many places you have still to explore. Some things never change about a city or a town—the architecture, the character and the ambiance—yet other things change depending on the weather and season. Think of Nantucket, Bermuda, Paris, London and Rome. Each visit we make will be different. Crowds of anxious people and foul weather can change the kind of memory you have; yet when you are in Paris in the sunshine of April before the arrival of the tourists, you see through rose-tinted, romantic glasses.

"THE WISDOM OF A LEARNED MAN [OR WOMAN] COMETH BY OPPORTUNITY OF LEISURE . . ."
—*Ecclesiasticus 38: 24–25.*

PLANNING YOUR TRIP

The more thinking in advance you do about your trip, the more fun you'll have and the more you'll learn. A good travel agent is a must for sophisticated travelers. You should have a trusted, reliable person who conscientiously works on your reservations so things have every opportunity to go smoothly. The travel agent doesn't take the trip. He or she helps you plan it. You are ultimately responsible. You have to check your tickets and be sure all your documents are in place. If you prefer to make your own travel plans you still need some assistance. When you can talk over the phone about what your needs are and have someone help you to realize them, it makes traveling less of a burden.

A travel agent doesn't need to have an art history background to help you with your trip to Rome. You need to get there and have the hotel greet you with a confirmed reservation. If you establish good rapport with a trusted travel agent you will find that you have fewer disappointments. An agent is given a discount on the airline tickets and hotel reservations so it doesn't cost you any money to use one.

Busy people have to make plans way in advance and often plans change. Travel agents all receive the same fees so you should find one who is cheerful and glad to help you. Avoid the social ones who act as agents in order to get discounted rates for their own personal travel. They're never around when you need them. When you find the right person, the relationship will thrive and will develop over years of travel. Never feel guilty asking for the least expensive fare to Chicago for an overnight stay or for the best deal on a trip to London. Everything adds up and repeat business provides a steady profit for an agent with long-range vision.

YOUR BUDGET

When Peter and I came back from our honeymoon in Paris, a business acquaintance asked, "Didn't you find Paris expensive?" Peter smiled and answered, "No more than New York or Tokyo." There is no question about it, when you pay for transportation, a place to stay and meals in restaurants, expenses add up quickly, no matter where you travel.

It is important to select a trip that fits your temperament. If your style is to be frugal, flying to Paris on the Concorde wouldn't be appropriate. However, if you enjoy making financial sacrifices in order to save for an exciting, luxurious, extravagant trip when you can indulge your senses in some carefree fun, then you will not look at the price of things and make comparisons. Certain experiences come once in a lifetime and you are fortunate to be in a position to splurge.

Know yourself and be realistic. If you are a romantic and enjoy elegance at home, you will enjoy it even more in Marrakesh, Hong Kong, Tokyo or Florence.

Is it your style not to take a trip unless you can do it properly, having enough money to see the sights and taste the local food without concern about the cost? Or perhaps you can be in a foreign place with limited funds but are willing to move around inexpensively, sightseeing and eating modestly.

How you spend your money is a personal matter. The fact that you travel at all indicates that you are curious, like variety, a change of scenery, adventure and want to learn more about the world.

Set a budget that makes you feel comfortable. Allocate money for transportation, lodging, food, sightseeing and shopping. Decide on a budget ahead of time. Your style might be to spend most of your money on living expenses once you arrive, keeping your transportation costs as low as possible. Do you fly coach or first class? Do you enjoy a luxurious first-class train trip? You might decide to stay in modestly priced hotels and inns until the end of your trip when you might go to a well-known luxurious hotel for a few nights. You might decide to spend all your shopping budget on one perfect suit.

Your trip is one of a kind. It can be a revelation in terms of your appreciation of life and the excitement of discovering new scenery, new cultures and fresh insights. Draw from everywhere you go to widen your understanding and vision. These moments when you isolate yourself from your daily-ness and pack your bags to go on a great adventure will be treasured times filled with memories that will last a lifetime.

Have a travel savings account so you can watch it grow as you gain enthusiasm for your adventure. Planning a dream trip gives you incentives to save. When I was young and poor, I began a travel savings account by dropping my change into a quart-size mayonnaise jar. After a year, I'd saved enough to go to Italy.

Somehow you always remember the romantic, delicious meals you've had on a trip and you can relive the harmony and *joie de vivre* in your mind. Far away from any practical demands, you appreciate everything so much more because your usual life is temporarily on hold and you are on a real "trip." Saving ahead of time specifically for each trip intensifies your expectations of the fun you'll have and gives you confidence that you are spending your money wisely.

How often you travel, how you travel, how much you spend, where you go, who with and even whether you travel have to do with your style. No one but you can tell you if you're getting your money's worth. Value the intangibles of travel—they are treasures that are more beautiful than gold or diamonds.

ANTICIPATION

Once you call your travel agent and settle on your itinerary and book flights, you can activate your magical powers to see that your dreams come true. If you've seen the movie *A Room with a View* you might think all hotel rooms have good views. A wealthy widow from Texas went to the Gritti Palace in Venice and was placed in a room where the ceiling was taller than the width and depth of the room. It was a maid's room on the alley, and the Grand Canal would have seemed closer had she stayed home and used her VCR. An interior designer and his wife went to St. Barts and stayed at "the" place on the beach only to discover that it was under renovation. At 5:30 A.M. the noise of hammering and sawing drove them crazy.

Be sure your high expectations are realistic. Just know that you are going to have a wonderful time, no matter what. Often people expect perfection, which is unobtainable at home or anywhere on earth. Strive for refreshment. A darling woman who is manic about cleanliness loves Morocco and goes there every other year. One year she arrived exhausted, and when she was taken to

"THE GRAND PERHAPS!"
—*Robert Browning*

her room Emily was discouraged by the dirt and dust. She complained to the maid who politely went to the window, threw open the shutters and exclaimed, "Isn't our country beautiful?" Emily smiled and settled into the joyful spirit of colorful Marrakesh.

If your travel agent gets you a "garden view" and you are on an island, the room may be down a dark alley a long distance from any sight or sense of the water. Realistic expectations make you always appreciative, not complaining.

Before you commit yourself to a specific resort, hotel or accommodation, go to the library and look up the places where you will be traveling and read up on the different places to stay. Many of us love to spend time in our room—reading and relaxing, savoring our time away and being refreshed by a change of scenery. In a foreign land your room becomes your anchor and your home. If it ever rained for an entire trip, you know how important your room could be.

Whenever you know of a friend who has recently returned from a place where you intend to go, arrange to hear an honest evaluation of their experience. Hindsight will benefit you and you can avoid unnecessary pitfalls.

The room where you live when you are away from home is of differing importance to individual personalities. Be aware of your personal needs. If you tend toward claustrophobia and need lots of space, you might have to sacrifice the best view. A couple asked for a suite in romantic Hotel Splendido, high on the hills along the lovely coast of Italy at Portofino, and when they arrived they discovered they were put in two average-size connecting rooms! Splendido is for lovers and there are no suites there. This couple was miserable and fled to a large suite in a Milan hotel.

No matter how much homework you've done, there's no substitute for being in a location to sense firsthand the spirit of a place. Pick up a local map and some brochures and enjoy the adventure of living for a suspended time away from home. You will put your personal imprimatur on your experience.

WHAT'S THE CLIMATE?

Most places where you travel have an ideal season. The more flexibility in your schedule, the greater your chances of having beautiful weather. Constant rain is discouraging at home and depressing when you are in a strange place. You can't see the usual colors and it restricts your mobility. Even a cheerful room becomes dreary in gloomy, wet weather.

If you can, avoid the August crowds. We always travel in August because Peter is a trial lawyer and judges take the month of August off. But you may not have to.

Determine what your favorite weather is and match it to a certain month in a place. May in Holland. December in Utah. If you enjoy September weather in New England, inquire when Florence has the same humidity and temperature range. Know your limitations. If humidity wipes you out, you will not have the same energy to explore the local sights as you would in cooler weather with lower humidity. The weather should be ideal for you to walk around among the people and experience the smells and spirit of the place. Every town and countryside has its own smell and you want to be in its midst. Being in a car is like watching television. It is passive.

If light is vitally important to you, find out the sunniest times of year. If you have a choice, go in May, June or early July in the Northern Hemisphere, when you will have light until almost nine—or later—in the evening so you can extend each day. When you have researched the ideal weather pattern and the hours of available daylight, find out when there are local events planned for the coming year, like an international art exhibition in Venice or the fashion collections in Paris. It would be a pity to miss a major Rembrandt exhibition in Paris by two days because of some arbitrary planning. However, such events draw vast crowds so you have to weigh whether you want to be there in the thrust of these events or go when it won't be so crowded.

WHAT IS YOUR
FAVORITE SEASON?

ITINERARY

Carefully planning the proposed route of your journey allows for greater ease and flexibility once you arrive at your destination. People who demonstrate the greatest personal style of travel work out the details specifically so they'll have enough time in each place to see and do what they want to without being rushed.

A well-planned itinerary is like an accurate map; it guides you. Being lost in a strange place is dangerous and causes unnecessary anxiety. Too many things can go wrong to move around without a real plan. Have an ace in the hole at every port, and then if you feel like making a few minor adjustments you can do some local fine-tuning.

Make copies of your itinerary and give them to family and close friends and to a trusted colleague at the office. Arriving at a new city and discovering a letter waiting for you can give you a real lift. The telephone and fax can connect you within seconds to people anywhere in the world. Just knowing you can be reached in an emergency eases people's minds. It's a thoughtful act of kindness for those who love you.

"LIVE DANGEROUSLY AND YOU LIVE RIGHT!"
—*Goethe*

TRANSPORTATION

How we get around is so much a part of the experience of traveling. At home we consider our transportation time rather routine, but when we travel our mode of transportation leaves a major impact. One of the most memorable and exciting adventures I've had was in Peru, taking a steep bus ride in the Andes to Machu Picchu to see the ancient ruins of the City of the Sun.

Choose the kind of transportation that will bring you the greatest pleasure and the least frustration. Coming and going adds up to a considerable amount of travel time. Compare the expense of taking a first-class train ride versus a coach seat on an airline. Do you enjoy driving or being driven? Do you need a guide? Do you

"LEISURE WITH DIGNITY."
—*Cicero*

want to rent a car or take local transportation? How time-conscious are you? The side trips you take become your "trip," so think through your priorities.

Bill and Jessie Sibert determined that walking through Britain would be the most satisfying for them. Kate and David Montgomery decided they wanted to take a bicycle trip through the wine region of France. Some people enjoy going on a beautiful sailing ship, stopping at places of interest and living on board. One of my most memorable sailing trips was down the Dalmatian coast to Greece. Often what you crave the most in travel is to experience the sights and activities that are entirely different from what you do at home. To be able to perceive the gradual changes in the landscape and intimately sense the local influences is preferable to flying great distances from one place to another and not being able to connect the human links.

You spend time considering when you want to go and where you want to make hotel and restaurant reservations; consider spending as much time thinking about your transportation. About one third of your travel budget is spent on transportation. Consider your options. Think of the total amount of time you spend actually getting to the places you want to go. Consider the fun factor and the time commitment of your choices.

TRAVELING ALONE OR WITH ANOTHER?

When you have no one else to answer to you are free to move about on your own, according to your own agenda. Some people really enjoy traveling alone. You may, however, feel you want to share the sunset and dinner with someone and you'd feel lonely traveling alone. Many women who enjoy living alone feel uncomfortable traveling alone and they plan a trip with a friend. This might be a sensible idea but it could be a risky business.

Two women went to South America together and one ditched the other every night to pick up men in bars. Another pair of women traveled through the South of France together and one discovered that her companion was a complainer and it ruined the trip.

Traveling isn't for prima donnas. If you don't know your travel mate well it is more prudent to take a trip alone. Women traveling alone in the evening are still suspect, however. A woman alone at night is vulnerable and might send out the wrong signals. If you are a female alone, take certain precautions. Stay in a hotel or inn that has attractive dining facilities with a local flavor. The Hilton in Athens is a good example. During the day you can explore the sights by yourself, but at night you can eat in the place you stay, where you will be protected. Obviously you are blessed if you have local friends who can join you for dinner, but this is not necessary if you stay at an appropriate place. For example, I was in Massachusetts for some meetings alone and stayed at the Deerfield Inn. Dining alone was pleasant. My waiter was a local teenager and sensitive. I felt safe and the food was delicious. Had I stayed at another type of inn possibly I would have felt more comfortable remaining in my room and ordering room service. To me, staying in my room for dinner, which I've done several times, including in Paris, is a mild punishment and an utter waste of travel time. When I travel I enjoy people-watching too much to be in isolation and I want to learn something. It's a lot less expensive to stay at home for an evening when you are literally at home.

There are times when you need to be alone. One way you can accomplish this is to take a trip by yourself. I enjoy occasional trips alone when I'm free to be silent, to have the luxury of room service at whim and to have time to think. I always end up feeling more appreciative of others and more connected after I've had some solitude.

TRAVELING WITH OTHERS

Everyone travels differently. You can think you know someone well but when you take a trip together it exposes a side you never saw before. Often people act differently when they are away from their comforting habits and under stress.

Be prepared to make necessary sacrifices for those with whom you are traveling but don't make concessions you will regret. If there is a museum you really want to see, persuade your traveling companion how important it is for you to do this. Don't go all the way to Taiwan and miss the treasures at the National Museum. Make it clear that you are willing to give up other things to have the time to see the things you believe are personally important. It is better to take a side trip by yourself than to sit and pine over the fact that your traveling mate was uninterested or too tired.

Assume that every trip to a particular spot will be the last time you'll be there. If you really love a certain part of the world—say, the hill country between Rome and Florence—and are blessed with repeat visits, you are living under a lucky star. Don't take anything for granted. Consider each moment as the opportunity of a lifetime. Treasure every architectural detail, every breathtaking bit of scenery. Offer options to your traveling mate, but don't be a twosome at the expense of failing to live out your dreams. You've come too far to feel cheated.

If your companion wants to explore and take photographs, you may wish to stay where you are and do a watercolor painting or write in your journal. If one person wants to shop, the other may be content walking around the square and absorbing the flavor of the place. Togetherness needs moments of space. Allow for it and encourage someone who wants to do something you don't want to do, to do it. No matter how close two people are, you have different styles of travel. Don't limit the freedom and pleasure of one by insisting you be in sync twenty-four hours a day. At home you probably have large blocks of time when you are separated. When you travel it is astute to realize that this can be a mild strain for both people. By encouraging some independence you will be allowing someone you love to pursue their personal interests in their own style without feeling guilty. You can even consider booking separate rooms.

If you want to make some purchases, you may prefer to go alone. Only go shopping with enthusiastic companions. One of

WHEN YOU TAKE PICTURES DO YOU TEND TO TAKE THEM OF PEOPLE OR OF LANDSCAPES?

the greatest pleasures of traveling is to discover local crafts and objects of beauty and to be able to bring them home for yourself, your family and friends. Be uninhibited in your delight.

If your traveling companion wants to have an evening off, it shouldn't keep you from having a nice dinner.

TRAVELING ON BUSINESS

My clients from Buffalo, New York, invited me to come work on their house. A secretary sent me my plane ticket. It was December and I was working under a deadline to finish an article. I'd always enjoyed writing on airplanes. My coach seat, however, was in the middle—I was sandwiched between a woman so large she needed an extra extension for her seat belt and a mother holding a sick, crying baby. I had to use the airplane time to work despite the awkwardness; I forced myself to concentrate but discovered I couldn't think—the noise and the lack of elbow space overwhelmed my fierce ambition to carry on. I became so frustrated I held back tears.

On the day of my return flight, there was a heavy snowstorm in Buffalo and by three in the afternoon, when I had completed my work, I was driven to the airport, where I spent the night— the flights had been canceled due to the storm. But there at the airport coffee shop I spread out my writing pad and worked on the article. So one's determination to use travel time in one's own way can prevail!

An even more difficult trip was when I had to fly from Bermuda to Paris. It was June and Peter and I had been enjoying an annual vacation in Bermuda with the children. But my client needed answers to some questions or the renovation of her home would be delayed. I agreed to leave Bermuda a few days early to help out with the schedule in Paris. My flight was at 7:30 in the evening and my tickets said "BED." I was thrilled. I envisioned a sleeping flight. Wrong. BED was a code abbreviation for Bermuda. I was in a seat at the back of a crowded flight. The seat

WHEN YOU TRAVEL DO YOU RETURN TO THE SAME PLACES OR DO YOU EXPLORE NEW ONES?

didn't recline at all because it was up against the wall of the lavatory. I'd imagined an elegant, relaxing evening so I had decided to wear a white cotton dress and feel comfortable on board. I would arrive in Paris in the early morning and could change into fresh clothes. In the cramped, dreary plane I fidgeted all night in hopes of a moment's comfort, thinking about my family and the al fresco moonlit dinner of grilled fish they were having on the terrace overlooking the dazzling sea below.

The flight was a "direct" flight, not a nonstop flight, and it stopped in London. I deplaned at the request of the crew and my dress looked like a crumpled white cotton sheet the morning after. On to Paris. My suitcase and sample bag didn't arrive until late that evening. That fiasco made me learn a great deal about traveling on business the hard way.

The first thing I learned from my miserable experience was to purchase my own airline tickets and bill my client later. If you have a miserable experience you won't be as quick to resent your client because you made all the arrangements yourself. If you are on a crowded plane and your air time is particularly precious to you, upgrade to first class and pay the difference personally. Arriving for an important business meeting wrinkled, exhausted, or frustrated can be avoided. Your travel time can be useful to you for last-minute review of your client's project or for some work you are doing on your own. Plan to utilize your travel time by making the best arrangements that are appropriate.

Second, don't squeeze your trip schedule too tightly. Leave some room for serendipity. A widow on limited funds did a lot of traveling for her clothing company. She always researched where she was going and usually left time to go to a local museum and botanical garden. She actually stayed over the weekend in cities of special interest, feeling grateful the transportation costs were paid for by her company.

If your job is extremely hectic you will find refreshment in business travel, when you use it as an opportunity to recharge yourself. One executive woman told me recently that her schedule was worse than any doctor's office. She condenses some meetings into fifteen minutes and when they go twenty-five minutes she gets behind schedule and has people lined up in the hall outside her office. For people like Madeleine, an airplane ride away from the office is refreshing, and she loves the luxury of room service and quiet time alone in her hotel. You can still make a lot of phone calls, but somehow when you're in a bathrobe and barefoot it seems like fun rather than a burden. Change refreshes.

Make a breakfast meeting with yourself. Indulge in the gift of time. Wake up early and enjoy several unrushed hours. Savor your coffee and the local newspapers. Order something for breakfast you don't have time to make or appreciate at home. Crisp bacon you don't have to make is a treat. If you are on a diet, order something sinful, like eggs Benedict and eat only half. Or, better yet, order "egg" Benedict.

Do some yoga stretches. Draw a warm bath. Take time to appreciate the change of scenery and tempo. Remind yourself that you are on a business trip. You are working! You don't have to have gray circles under your eyes in order to be conscientious. On business travel you will discover a double pleasure. First, you have time to pamper yourself and open up your senses to new experiences. Second, your clients will pamper you.

A business trip takes you away from your own normal world; it thrusts you into another element. How blessed you are when you enjoy your work and are thrown into a local setting where you have a purpose and focus. Seek the moment and enjoy the pleasure of being on a trip you might never have taken on your own.

One of the most exhausting aspects of traveling on business is having someone else in charge of planning your schedule. Whenever possible stay at a nearby inn, hotel or country club rather than with your client. If you do stay in a private house, request breakfast in your room. At night, retire to your room rather than staying up until 2 A.M. talking. Pace yourself and request some time alone in order to prepare your work, collect your thoughts and catch up on some sleep.

Even if your host or hostess doesn't intend to change clothes for the evening, you will feel better if you do. You are on display, you'll be introduced to everyone and the impression you make is

> "PUNCTUALITY IS THE POLITENESS OF KINGS."
> —Louis XVIII

important. You always feel better after washing, freshening up and putting on clean clothes.

Bring a well-equipped beauty bag that has all your necessities plus some niceties. The Gold Clip Company sells gold metal safety pins. Tuck some into your beauty bag; you may have to pin your curtains closed to block out light. Select an attractive beauty bag so it is a touch of your own personality in a strange place. You can buy a colorful flowered zippered beauty bag at Porthault linens that has hand towels to match. Tuck in an enamel pillbox and a framed picture of a loved one. Imagine how cozy you can feel in a strange bathroom when you bring pretty touches from home.

What is your personal style of making the room where you stay yours? I bring a baby pillow with a pretty flowered pillowcase, a framed picture of Peter and another one of Alexandra and Brooke, a reliable alarm clock, a marbleized letter portfolio, a journal and several of my favorite pens, and a bundle of my own stationery.

Carry one small bag on board the plane to guarantee you can function well in an emergency. If you have your beauty bag and one fresh change of clothes you don't have to panic when your suitcase doesn't arrive right away. Or on a long train or plane ride when you may want to change your shirt or blouse but can't, your beauty bag can help you to freshen up before you arrive.

> "LITTLE MINDS ARE INTERESTED IN THE EXTRAORDINARY; GREAT MINDS IN THE COMMONPLACE."
> —*Elbert Hubbard*

KEEP A TRAVEL JOURNAL

Even if you don't keep a daily journal when you're home, like most of us you are probably willing to record your trips. One well-traveled couple buys hardcover guidebooks; they mark these up, indicating the places they visit, and make comments in the margin. Then they date the book with a label on the spine and give a name to each trip before putting it on the shelf next to the last trip book. Whether you buy a little leather travel book you can toss into your pocket or purse or a blank book, it is fun to record each trip. Each of us, wherever we live, has to find our own blank book that will inspire travel entries. Before you leave home, clip some pretty square paper clips in your book so you can safely keep cards from stores and restaurants as sources for the future.

Travel notes in some form are enormously helpful when you love a place and want to go back. You can instantly look up what room you liked when you keep a detailed journal. Record what restaurants you enjoyed and what you ate that was delicious. The pleasure can be relived. Before I die, I must return to the spot where I had grilled truffles in Siena twenty-five years ago. Fortunately, I kept a travel journal then. You reap many happy rewards when you make this discipline part of your personal style of travel.

It is a waste of time to remember a shop's address in a foreign city. If you have a book it relieves you of cluttering your mind with trivia. I usually write on the right-hand side of a travel journal and keep the left-hand side free to insert notes and addresses, with paper clips for calling cards, a brochure or souvenir. Save ticket stubs and wine labels as nostalgic memorabilia.

Mention the weather in your journal under the date. This is helpful when you return to a place so you can remember what kinds of clothes to bring. You may go to the Chelsea Flower Show in London every few years and it is useful to remember how rainy and damp it was the last time you were there.

If you keep a Filofax you can add a travel tab and make a page for each city. After you've returned from your trip, flip through your journal and list the best of the best and insert these listings in your Filofax. Jot down names of hotel managers, waiters and the name of your favorite bistro.

Traveling is an intensely personal experience, and it is always worthy of recording. "Around the corner of every minute is the fascination of the unknown," Peter's friend Donald Twining used to say. Keeping a travel journal gives you an opportunity to absorb the atmosphere and flavor and also to express your reactions to your experiences. This can be a rewarding experience and once you return home you may find you want to keep a journal because you found it so satisfying.

"A MISSION TO EXPLAIN."
—*Peter Jay*

TRAVEL LIGHT

One of the best ways to travel with ease is to travel light. The better you plan your trip, the more discerning you will be about what you'll really need. You may want to have a few items on your trip to comfort you, like a favorite baby pillow or some inspirational reading material. Carefully think through the logistics of your trip and bring the basics. Analyze where you are going. Are you going to a place known for shopping, say Hong Kong or Paris? Or to Leningrad or Beijing, where you have to remember to pack toilet paper and a flashlight so you can read in your bedroom that has only a 20-watt bulb?

Think of clothes and supplies differently. Keep two running lists of basic things to remember in both categories and Xerox dozens of copies so each trip can have a list that can be personalized. Put the name of the trip and the dates. I write my travel list on color-coded Filofax paper so I can add and subtract to the list until it seems ideal.

By making your travel organization fun you can fine-tune a trip ahead of time on a train or bus or at a coffee shop. What you discover by being specific and personalizing each trip is how easy it is to take only the essentials. What a delightful feeling it is to have the right things instead of lugging excess baggage.

No place on earth is completely safe. It makes sense to bring only costume jewelry with you when you travel. Good, fun costume jewelry allows you to be more carefree. Have one suitcase that you can lock. One of the reasons to travel is to escape the burdens of routine life and to be free to explore new territories and customs. Treat yourself to being truly free by taking with you only the things that will allow you to feel comfortable.

If you're going to a place where the shopping is terrific, you can buy additional things to wear when you're traveling. Same with makeup and bathroom supplies. You can usually have your laundry done on the trip plus pressing and dry cleaning. You can rinse out stockings, bras and panties, so you really should bring only a few items in each category. Campers on a trip learn to be

"THE INCOGNITO OF AN INN IS ONE OF ITS STRIKING PRIVILEGES."
—*William Hazlitt*

intelligent about packing. Every item has to count because you carry your belongings on your back. The same principle should apply to all travelers. In this hectic world, some packing experts can raise carry-on luggage to an art form.

Recently when Peter and I went from Hong Kong to Beijing we packed all our belongings in one small soft leather carry-on tote bag. We were there for two days and nights of sightseeing and we brought toiletries and underwear plus fresh shirts and blouses. Our weekend in Beijing was not the trip in which to dress in high style. I wrapped a colorful silk scarf around my neck for dinner and my white blouse took on an entirely different character. Peter's blazer remained the same but a fresh striped shirt and change of colorful necktie and silk pocket square created a different mood.

WHAT TO BRING WITH YOU

Determine what style of trip you are taking. Focus on the place, your mood, the climate, who you'll be seeing, where you'll be going, and in what kind of accommodations you're staying. If you feel like indulging yourself by dressing up for dinner each evening, start there. Your daytime clothes can be simpler. If you have meetings during the day and will be on your own in the evenings, simplify your evening clothes.

Some of your favorite clothes won't travel well. Crushing good clothes in a crowded suitcase seems a shame. Judge which clothes are the most comfortable for traveling and which are best left at home. If you are going to the Caribbean, for example, simple silk and cotton dresses are better than dresses that have lots of construction and need to be professionally pressed. On the other hand, you will need dressy evening clothes if you are going to Rome or Paris and will be eating in restaurants.

Color-coordinate each trip. If you do this well, you can travel light and with great style. Establish what your color scheme will be for your next trip, based on where you're going and the

DO YOU ENJOY
WINDOW SHOPPING?

NOW! HERE IS THE
SECRET! NOW!

weather, how dressy the trip will be and what fits you well and is appropriate. Limit yourself to blue, black or brown for your basic neutral.

Bring one pair of shoes for evening and alternate between two pairs that are suitable for daytime. They can be polished every day. Your shoes are your lifeline to your ease in traveling. Wear the most comfortable shoes you own. If you wear the same shoes every other day it won't be great for your shoes, but it will be ideal for your poor tired feet. When you're comfortable you look more radiant.

Go down your basic clothes list and fill in the colors. One trip may be a navy-blue-and-red trip, another will be black-and-white with colorful accents.

The fun of this is that everything can mix and match. Scarves and ties and striped and patterned shirts and blouses all can be reworn and look and feel different because of the subtle ways you've isolated your colors. Your strict editing will inspire you and by seeing a trip in a particular color palette you are putting an artistic twist of flair and personal style to your looks.

Examine everything you have in the color range you select and lay everything out on the bed that you think you want to bring with you. Separate the things into categories. If this is your pastel island trip, keep editing until you feel you have the ideal sarong for your bathing suit or the best colors for your polo shirts that go with your bathing trunks.

This advance planning makes everything so easy that you hardly have to think about your clothes once you're away. Have one great jacket for evening. One daytime purse, one evening purse.

Distill your selection until you have your favorite things. Remove approximately half of what you originally laid out. If a blouse doesn't fit you well at home it won't fit you when you are in Texas, either. Getting ready to take off on an exciting trip is no time to shop or tailor your wardrobe. Everything in your closet should be ready to wear at all times. While we have to select the simplest items for each category, never bring clothes you don't truly love to wear. Years later, you'll remember what you wore because you're often photographed while on a trip.

When you look at your bed strewn with attractive clothes in a harmonious color range, take a close look. Pretend you are going on your honeymoon. Don't take anything that is less than the best of what it is. If you are sensitive to the aesthetics of what you bring, you will have a better time. You are representing your country, your family and yourself wherever you go.

There is a great decline in the way people dress when they travel. Airports now look like gymnasiums and locker rooms. I remember seeing an exhibition of travel at the Victoria and Albert Museum in London where there was a display of Louis Vuitton luggage. The exhibition showed the costumes and paraphernalia that went inside these well-made, well-stocked travel bags. Travel once was an elegant, genteel exercise elevated to an art. I certainly regret having arrived in Paris in a wrinkled white cotton dress. What was wildly appropriate for Bermuda was dumb for Paris. Crisp cotton and linen don't do well on overnight, overseas coach airplane flights.

There are clothes that are chic as well as comfortable. If traveling is to regain its lost charm, each of us has to make a greater effort to travel with style. I see mothers looking awful with small children who are all dressed up attractively. When we travel we leave the ho-humness of our daily-ness and slip into a fantasy world. Be part of a dream and make it come true by dressing up to travel. Lewis Carroll's unforgettable character Alice said, "There's no use trying . . . one can't believe impossible things." "I daresay you haven't had much practice," said the Queen.

Bring simple, classic, tailored, lovely clothes. Make your trip more pleasant for yourself and for your fellow travelers by dignifying the process.

Keep your personalized list so that after your trip, as you unpack, you can make a few comments about your selection. Were there any things you didn't need? Did you have enough? How well did your clothes travel?

Review your supply list also. There is nothing more infuriating

"WHAT IS NATURAL IS NEVER DISGRACEFUL."
—*Euripides*

than spending vital travel time trying to find an adapter for your hair dryer or having to see a foreign doctor in order to get a prescription filled.

File your lists in your travel folder so you can help yourself if you ever return to the same place. Also, your information will be invaluable to a friend, family member or colleague.

PACKING

There is an art to packing. Once you learn the technique, you will find it a challenging game. Begin with the suitcase. One small tote bag goes with you and you never give it to a porter and it never gets checked. This bag has a book, a journal, a beauty bag and one change of clothes (or underwear) plus medication or any original material you can't check because it is irreplaceable.

List your clothing categories by day and evening. Suits, shirts and blouses, dresses, skirts, coats, shoes, underwear, jewelry, swimsuit accessories. Next, list the supplies you need: passport, tickets, visas, foreign currency, traveler's checks, credit cards, itinerary, your travel folder, guidebooks, hotel confirmations, address book or Filofax, your beauty bag or dopp kit, prescription medication, costume jewelry, sunglasses, umbrella, tennis racquet, scuba gear, golf clubs, books, magazines, notebooks, files, pens, refills, scissors, baby pillow, framed picture of family, camera, flash and batteries, hair dryer, electric curlers, portable iron.

Determine the number of bags you will need and the size you feel is appropriate, based on where you're going and for how long. You have selected appropriate things for your trip but if they don't fit into the bags, you will have to do further editing. Some airlines have strict limits and won't allow more than two suitcases and one carry-on bag. If you are taking a trip that has two distinctly different personalities—beginning in Frankfurt on business and ending in Switzerland at a spa—try to pack each "trip within a trip" in a separate suitcase. If you are going to a city to be wined

"THE ABILITY TO SIMPLIFY MEANS TO ELIMINATE THE UNNECESSARY SO THAT THE NECESSARY MAY SPEAK."
—*Hans Hofmann*

and dined and will end your trip climbing Kilimanjaro, your mountain-climbing boots don't have to be unpacked in your London hotel. This is especially helpful when you are going to two extremes in climate or in activity.

Tuck in a folded-up Le Sportsac nylon bag for day trips or to bring home dirty clothes and some of your purchases. Be sure you can manage your suitcases if you arrive someplace where there are literally no porters. This happened to us at the train station in Avignon and it took all our strength to carry our bags from the train platform to where we could signal for a taxi.

Kenny Wagner, a friend full of style and personality, is a seasoned traveler. He has tried every kind of luggage and he now swears by soft Sportsacs. He has a Sportsac garment bag that hangs up for his suits—the kind you carry with handles. These are so lightweight he only carries the weight of his clothes, not the weight of his suitcases too.

The secret to successful packing is not to be too conscientious. If you stand over your clothes ironing out every wrinkle before folding and placing them in the suitcase, you will find a mess when you unpack. Don't wash, dry and iron clothes at the last minute. The dampness will have a field day if you do. Try not to do anything at the last minute other than pack, because your good intentions can cause you problems. A bachelor took his friend on a trip and he waxed his leather suitcases before he left home. Unfortunately they rubbed against his white pants as he rushed to catch his plane, leaving orange-tinted grease stains. The time to wax your leather suitcases is after you return from your trip.

Pack in layers, as with a club sandwich. If you will be traveling to a place where you only spend one night, you shouldn't have to rifle through your entire suitcase to find socks and a shirt. Pack based on your itinerary. You wouldn't unpack an entire suitcase for one night. Have a clear plastic bag with a fresh change of clothes inside on the top of the suitcase to make your life away from home easy. Buy large Snap-off clear plastic bags at the hardware store. They are an ideal, versatile size, compact yet large enough to hold folded dress, trousers, skirts and blouses. When

STYLE EMERGES IN TIME AND SHOULD NOT BE FORCED.

packed in these plastic bags, clothes resist wrinkling. You can pack in a series of these bags so you can keep whole outfits together including a suit, blouse, scarf and colored stockings.

Use smaller clear plastic bags for shoes and put them as well as books in the bottom of your suitcase. You can pack more clothes when you layer your suitcase with these flat plastic bags. Remember, too, the center of a suitcase tends to bulge, so avoid putting too much in the center.

When you pack to come home you can put your clothes back in the plastic bags systemized to how they relate to where you'll put these items once you get home. You can separate clothes that need to be dry-cleaned, washed by hand, washed by machine, ironed or sewn. After a trip I love to unpack immediately and put these bagsful of clothes in the laundry room out of sight. Clean, folded clothes return to the drawer along with clean underwear.

WHAT TO BRING HOME

One of the best ways to keep a trip alive in your memory is to bring back pictures, postcards, local crafts and books. Your well-trained eye will help you to find inexpensive local objects to buy that are authentic examples of the local crafts. Unfortunately, greed has spoiled most places and most of the "local" crafts were probably made in Taiwan and shipped in. A good place to buy attractive mementos from a trip is from a museum shop.

Trust your instinct. Once you get home and unpack, you'll be glad you bought lots of little items. I bought some red lacquer chopsticks from a street vendor in Singapore years ago and whenever we use them at home I remember my trip.

Buying inexpensive local items wherever you travel is fun. I spend my professional life helping clients buy more serious objects for their homes, so I enjoy hunting around dusty places in dark corners for a colorful find. We tend to get carried away in a new culture. If you buy, out of sheer enthusiasm, some items that are out of character for your own style, once you get home you can give these little gifts away. These little presents brought home from your trip show thoughtfulness and don't have to be taken seriously.

It is always fun to make a luxurious purchase while traveling. I bought a new red Chanel tote bag while in Hong Kong. It holds my Filofax and file folders and I remember my trip every day I use it.

COMING HOME

There should be no place as nourishing or as comfortable as home. No matter how beautiful your trip was, you can't get home without some awkward discomforts. After putting up with the cruel delays, the inconveniences and impersonal atmosphere of so much travel today, you can open your front door and freshly rediscover your home. No matter how strenuous your trip, your spirits will quicken once you rediscover your private world. You see everything with amazing clarity as though your trip had been at a spa where your senses were rejuvenated.

Savor your return. Don't rush to open all the mail or try to read the stack of newspapers and magazines right away. Enjoy the tranquillity of being away from the madding crowds, at home.

The key to keeping your trip alive is not to rush. Relax. Take a hot bath, wash your travel weariness away. Have a few peaceful moments to reflect on your trip. Unlike a shower, which is quicker, a bath can be a meditative time. No matter what time of day or night you arrive home, create a meaningful reentry ritual. Put on a lovely nightgown or freshly ironed pajamas and a colorful bathrobe. Feel the privilege of being at ease, alone or together, at home. Make some favorite tea and use your prettiest cup and saucer. Enjoy unpacking. Pretend you're in a personalized luxury hotel suite and have a good time. You're home and safe and your trip will last in your memory all your life. The first hour you are home after traveling should be one of the sweetest moments of your trip.

Ideally, plan your trip so you can have at least half a day at home to relax and get settled in before rushing out again. You know your own style best. Many people come home from a long trip on Saturday so they have Saturday night and all day Sunday to be cozy at home before they go back to work or off on a business trip Monday. The more experience you have traveling, the better you can plan your reentry. You may want to return Thursday or Friday so you have the full weekend. Think of the joy of returning home after a wonderful trip and how much better you'll feel if you have time to appreciate it, and give yourself time. Home requires your nesting there or it becomes just another way station. Have a fresh, bright-eyed reunion with your own spirit of place, and schedule unhurried time to settle in at home.

For years I suffered from post-travel blues. I would come into our apartment late at night, exhausted. I'd go right to sleep and the next thing I knew, the alarm clock would ring and I'd have to go to the office. Where was my joy of returning? Now, ideally we arrive home in daylight. Our apartment smiles more brightly in the sunlight and I have more time to putter and appreciate everything.

What is your style of reentry after a trip? Do you like to walk around absorbing the beauty and rearranging your objects? No place in the world should be as beautiful as your own home, because it is yours. Everything is nourished, loved and lived with by you. A favorite upholstered reading chair can conjure up memories of reading Mark Twain or Charles Dickens. Play your favorite music and be sure there's lots of light. A personal room is alive and is breathing your vitality and sensibility. You are welcomed by your own character and essence. Take time to sit and absorb the clarity of your fresh vision.

After having tea, a cup of fresh-ground coffee or a glass of mineral water, relax. You live intensely in time, feel rejuvenated and even transformed by your reentry home. Get two pretty shopping bags before shuffling through your mail. Throw away your junk mail and put all your bills into one bag, and magazines and catalogues in another. Look for a handwritten letter from a friend. Warm letters always make home more welcome. Sit down and

"PLEASE, SIR, I WANT SOME MORE."
—*Charles Dickens*

280

slowly read your personal mail. The shopping bag of bills goes to the office in a day or two and the magazines and catalogues can be sorted out later. Now, isolate yourself from all harshness. Appreciate your trip from this comfortable, private retreat.

Getting a change of environment and escaping the responsibilities and frustrations of normal life is therapeutic. Feel your own personal powers and see all you've done to carve out your specific style. Rediscover everything with clear eyes. Hunger for adventure and diversity, go to different parts of the world to experience the vastness of beauty, and always delight in returning home. I have an elderly friend who sometimes leaves trips early because she's homesick. No matter how wondrous your experiences may be, is there any greater joy than to come home, put your feet up and feel your personality smiling all around you? Welcome home!

WHEN YOU DO WHAT YOU WANT TO DO, NOT WHAT YOU SHOULD DO, THIS *IS* YOU.

GRACE NOTES

❦ Buy a yellow highlighter and block out leisure spaces in your calendar for months ahead till the end of the year.

❦ Begin your leisure-time list.

❦ Buy and read Joseph Campbell's *Power of Myth* (Doubleday, paperback and hardcover) so you can find your "bliss station."

❦ Never say you don't have time. It appears that you are either disorganized or not in control.

❦ Leave all social engagements by eleven on weeknights so you can stick to your leisure schedule.

❦ Go to Greenfield Hill in Fairfield, Connecticut, in May to experience the peak dogwood. Drive around the harbor in nearby Southport. Or, go to see your local flowering trees at their peak.

❦ Go to Santa Fe, New Mexico, and ride horses and go on long hikes, and in the evenings go to quaint restaurants in town. Shop in the local craft stores for inexpensive silver jewelry and enjoy the local artisans' work.

❧ Go to New Orleans for a long weekend. Listen to jazz, eat in great restaurants, browse in the antique shops along Royal Street in the French Quarter.

❧ Buy postcards of everything you like and all the different sights and scenery you've enjoyed. Keep a master set together to save as a permanent visual record.

❧ Wear comfortable, low-heeled shoes. We don't travel well in new shoes.

❧ Leave your house or apartment neat as a pin so it will be there to greet you with a big smile upon your return. You will have a fresh eye after you've been away.

❧ Take a few small, inexpensive gifts with you wherever you go. You never know when you'll want to give one away.

❧ Take your personal stationery with you so you can correspond and communicate in your own style wherever you are.

❧ Use a colorful marking pen to write on the back of a photograph. I have a friend who always brings me back a little gift from wherever she's traveled and her note card is a photograph from her trip. I love this close glimpse from her travels.

❧ Just as with shoes, your camera should be an old friend also. You can't risk experimentation when you need to catch the moment as it flies by.

❧ Keep some cash and traveler's checks in a locked box or drawer at home with your passport so you can fly away on the spur of the moment. Once we were unexpectedly invited on a trip on a Sunday and were glad we had these necessities on hand so we could grab them and go.

❧ I love buying flowers wherever I am and bringing them back to the hotel room. A few simple water glasses make fine containers for short-stemmed flowers if the style of the hotel vases does not please you.

❧ If you have to be separated from your love, bring a travel-size bottle of his aftershave or cologne and spray some on your bed pillow.

❧ Always take a couple of safety pins with you, inside your toiletry bag. They can save the day in an emergency.

❧ What a luxury to sleep later than usual and wake up naturally instead of to the harsh sound of an alarm clock! When you know you're going to have a restful weekend, prepare an elegant brunch so your day starts off beautifully.

❧ When you take a long car trip, pack a cooler of drinks and have some fresh fruit to make the trip more special. Prepare a picnic so you can stop at a pretty scenic area and have lunch. Planning the menu and preparing the food is fun— watercress, cucumber and tomato sandwiches, avocados stuffed with egg salad or tuna, a thermos of refreshing gazpacho, and cantaloupe wedges for dessert.

❧ When passing through cities where you have friends, call or write ahead of time, giving as much notice as possible. Even if you only meet for tea it is an easy, fun way to stay in touch.

YOUR GRACE NOTES

SIX

Your PERSONAL STYLE OF GIFTS AND GIVING

WHAT SPECIAL GIFTS DO YOU HAVE
TO OFFER OTHERS?

hen you have defined your own style you are automatically contributing to others. Giving becomes a natural extension of your essence. Your own enthusiasms and passions may be unique but they will inspire others.

Everything is linked. By finding your personal style in every part of your life, you become aware of the art of simplicity and the grace of cohesion.

Simplify your thinking. Everyone has a personal choice to be a generous giver and a thankful receiver. Think of the people you admire—are they both givers and also able to let others give back to them? Do you think about others naturally, in giving ways? Giving people know how to relinquish. There is an ease and grace about this reaching out and connecting with others. Don't you find that contented people give effortlessly and have a beauty about

"GIVING REQUIRES GOOD SENSE."
—*Ovid*

287

their manner that is authentic? People who go through life genuinely finding it a positive journey tend to be givers and they also appreciate affectionate gestures from others. Can't you usually tell if someone is reaching out to you from the heart? Those who live their personal adventure deeply are the best givers because they have more to give!

Giving feels good. When your spirit—your gut feeling—calls you to act generously, do. Giving is action. It is a spontaneous action, not calculating and self-serving. Giving results from feelings of self-worth, contentment and fulfillment. If you give what you have, it comes from inside you.

There is a difference between those who graciously receive and those who only take. Do you know some takers who tend to deplete your inner resources? Avoid them!

Recently I went to the hospital for a minor operation and was there only one night, not long enough to get the telephone connected. Early the next morning I looked up from my book and there was my older daughter, Alexandra, who was concerned about me. When she couldn't reach me by phone, she came down to New York from her school in Connecticut to surprise me in the hospital. Nothing could have made me happier. She gave the greatest gift of all—herself. She had papers to write and it was a big weekend at college, but she wanted to come. It wasn't out of a sense of duty but out of an inner need to visit me. Alexandra enjoys surprising those she loves—so she surprises us by joy. If I'd asked her to come I would have been putting pressure on her and her sacrifice wouldn't have been her personal style but a duty.

Think about what you have to give. Giving should never be a burden. People may try to force you to give and put pressure on you, hoping you will feel guilty. Your gift is never as genuine or as meaningful as when it is your own idea. You can give a large sum of money. You can give to someone by gracing an occasion with your presence. Who's to say which is more useful? Never underestimate how much you might mean to others.

Grace allows you to let go, relinquish bonds, ease up. When you really give, you don't control or manipulate. You want to touch but not hold on.

I recently received a phone call from Sharon Newman, a space ambassador for NASA who was a finalist to go to space on the *Challenger*. She wasn't picked for the mission and was heartbroken, but soon afterward became an admirer of the late Christa McAuliffe, who took her place. Her need to make space education and the whole notion of space important in all of our lives has grown increasingly deeper since the tragedy. Sharon became aware of the temporariness of life. She had read about me and she and her husband want me to help them build a dream house on farmland in Michigan. I am the fortunate one Sharon has turned to for help in making her dreams come true. Sharon sees her role in life as "a cheerleader and an encourager."

When Sharon was in India on a Fulbright scholarship she met Mother Teresa. She inquired, "How do you do this? All these millions of people every day?" Mother Teresa told her, "I do it one by one."

You give and make a difference one by one. Each act of generosity springs from a well of gratefulness for what you have received and want to pass on. Genuine giving springs from an appreciative heart. We give what we receive.

> " . . . PUT YOUR ARMS AROUND EACH OTHER."
> —*Barbara Bush*

PRESENTS

The art of giving presents requires diplomacy and a sense of style. You may want to give tangible things to others to let them know you care. You don't want to overdo it and make someone feel embarrassed or awkward. This is a delicate line to cross. If you give a present and really expect something in return, some favor, it is inappropriate. When you give joyfully from your heart you usually don't overdo. You are guided by instinct.

Sometimes you give someone something you would like to receive. Usually if you think of a friend when you read a book or see something pretty, chances are it will be warmly appreciated. Other times you give someone exactly what they want and ask for. Two friends have wish lists and they enjoy giving each other a specific present that hits the mark—one year beautiful stationery, another year some lovely sheets. I have a friend I go shopping with and we give each other a silk scarf every year. We can then remember each other when we wear our colorful scarves. It is fun to give something you share in common. Yesterday I received an overnight air package containing a bouquet of Fantan-Latour roses in shades of pinks and yellows because Junie thinks of me every time she works in her rose garden. Now, that's a surprise package of joy. I remember when the interior designer Mario Buatta came to lunch at the apartment of Mary Jane Pool—a former editor-in-chief of *House & Garden* (now *HG*)—and gave her a moss-and-ivy topiary bear for a house present, catching her completely by surprise. It tickled something inside her and she responded with sheer delight. Mario had gone to his favorite flower shop to select Mary Jane a bouquet of the freshest cut flowers available. "When I saw him I couldn't resist," Mario mused. Purely and simply, he wanted one himself. Topiary is made by shaping wire to a desired form and then covering it with moss and ivy. Whenever they are shaped to resemble an animal they can be whimsical or fierce.

Your personal style rubs off on your friends. When you give presents that have meaning, you are giving something that will be a reflection of yourself. If you want something badly enough you will find a way of getting it sooner or later. Yet only you can give something that you find lovely, special and meaningful to someone else. When you are attracted to something personally and connect it to someone you care about, you are giving far more than a present. You can be connecting two sympatico souls.

In this age of mass production, any present that has hand work on it is special. When something has been hand sewn, planted, baked, potted or painted, it has spirit and soul. One-of-a-kind presents may not necessarily have more style than commercially produced objects, but they have energy and life.

When hunting for the unusual gift, search for something you like that connects your style to the receiver. What do you share that can be made tangible? A book after a discussion, some flowers, a trinket, or a joke present.

"FRIENDSHIP MAKES PROSPERITY BRIGHTER . . ."
—*Cicero*

NONMATERIAL GIFTS

Some of the rarest of all gifts are the least obvious. Think of your past. You probably had one or two teachers who stimulated you and sparked you to learn more about certain subjects which opened doors for you. A Mr. Keating who excites you and shares knowledge can be a present that continues to expand over a lifetime. Your gift can be a seed. You can give soil and seeds that will continue to grow and blossom.

You can give the gift of listening. Pause and hear the silent cries of family and friends. Listen well without judging; this is a gift that will long be remembered. When asked your opinion, give healthy, sound advice. Tell the truth. Few people do. If the person asks, tell him what you feel he should do, under the circumstances. It may not be what is expected but you can help open up a new perspective. When everyone else tells your friend what doctor to see about his sour stomach, you might tell him to go on a week's vacation. Some new, unbiased view might help him put the pieces together.

Give confidence through encouragement. When a friend is struggling, it takes so little effort to give a compliment. Sometimes you can share some of your own struggles which illustrate how many defeats you had before you found your own way. As an encourager, you give the greatest gift through your example.

When you're enthusiastic about your own private world, you are radiant. Like a candle, you have the power to spread light farther than you dare dream. There are many people whom you have not known personally, yet whose lives have enriched you. The great individuals before us give us hope to go on. There are many powerful ways you can give precious gifts to others. Think of the most meaningful gifts in your life and you will understand how simply and naturally they are given and received.

DESCRIBE A FAVORITE CHILDHOOD MEMORY.

WHAT'S APPROPRIATE?

Giving should be without strings. Once you give a present, let go. Give freely. If you give a house present to friends, there's no need to look around the house for it the next time you visit. Be certain you aren't keeping score. Presents from friends can be tucked away and rediscovered on occasion for a surprise delight. Often friends give us silly gifts as jokes and while they're funny and endearing they don't belong permanently on our coffee table or mantel.

If you love to cook and entertain, it is appropriate for you to invite a friend repeatedly to your house, whereas your friend may bring you thoughtful handmade presents and rarely, if ever, entertain you. Have your own style and do things for others in a way that is satisfying. There is no place for tit-for-tat in giving. If two people meet for lunch and one decides to bring a book or a small present, the receiver should never feel embarrassed. The more delight you take, the more pleasure you will give.

DOING FAVORS

I had a boss when I first started out in interior design who told me, "If you ever do a client a favor, never let her know. Once you do, she'll grow to expect it." Never tell. When someone asks you to do them a favor, decide whether it is appropriate or correct to do it under the circumstances. When you see an opportunity to seize the moment and do someone a favor spontaneously, often you don't want to take credit. Taking credit is taking; doing a favor is giving.

Put in a good word for someone to the appropriate person. This is a gracious act, costs you nothing and could make a huge difference. This kindness is far more meaningful than telling someone how great he or she is. You do a favor by mentioning someone

"WHAT'S MINE IS
YOURS, AND WHAT
IS YOURS IS MINE."
—*William
Shakespeare*

where it will make a difference. When you hear from an acquaintance that a friend said wonderful things about you, that is a real gift.

The best favors are unsolicited. Try to avoid asking someone to do you a favor. There are times when you will feel it is necessary, but think through each situation carefully. If you a going to Paris for a few days at the end of your business trip in London and you see a friend, you might inquire, "May I bring you back something from Paris?"

Try to be the one who offers a favor. "Would you like to spend the night?" "Would you like to use our country house for the weekend?" "Would you like to borrow my car?" These are questions you ask when it is convenient for you. When you want to do someone a favor it is a delightful feeling. When someone invites you to do them a favor, it is pressure.

GIVING A PRESENT WITHOUT AN OCCASION

Never wait for a special occasion to give a present. In fact, an unexpected, out-of-the-blue gift adds joy to any moment. In my book *Living a Beautiful Life* I talked about celebrating the 95 percent of our lives that is lived every day. We can't afford to put our lives on hold and only live for the special occasions which make up 5 percent of the time. Today is as important as any other day in your life. I believe in celebrating the moment. How can we look forward to tomorrow with hope and the fun of anticipation if we have wasted today in boredom?

"Tomorrow" never comes. The future is illusory, a mirage. All you will ever have is now. If you are generous now and give as you go along, you are giving in harmony with your style of living. Giving is a healthy habit. When you are in the giving spirit, give. You shouldn't be restricted to birthdays, anniversaries or holidays. Some people stay in touch with distant friends only at Christmas time. Others send cards and notes throughout the year.

A small present, like some Chanel bath powder, with a note—"I'm thinking of you"—can mean more on a bleak rainy Tuesday in November than an expensive belt opened at holiday time along with dozens of other packages.

Don't wait for an excuse to give a present. Just the other night I chose for my coffee after dinner a mug a friend had given me from the Chelsea Craft Show in London several years ago. The design is colorful polka dots and flowers and it reminds me of Matisse's color cutouts. But, more important, it reminds me of Henrietta Howard and the fun we had at the craft fair together. I received a surprise phone call the next week from Henrietta, who told me she's coming to New York on a business trip. "I used the mug you gave me from the Chelsea Craft Show and I thought of you." She seemed pleased. Gifts have this magic. We do make these associations. Henrietta probably doesn't know my birthday and I don't know hers. We give to each other as we meet so we can let the moment live in our memories.

What is your style of present giving? Maybe you prefer to give a good time rather than an object you buy and wrap up in a box. You might invite a friend to have a leisurely lunch with you at a special restaurant.

There is no need to have a birthday or anniversary in order to celebrate. It is easier to get into the mood to write a letter if you have attractive stationery supplies at hand. The same is true of gift giving. If you have pretty boxes, colorful tissue, gift cards, tape, ribbons, attractive shopping bags and small gifts on hand, you can enjoy giving presents to loved ones at any time. Why wait for a special occasion to give a small gift? Keep a large box stocked with small presents you acquire when you see things you like. Have another large box stocked with wrappings and supplies. Aside from giving to friends and loved ones, remember to give small gifts to employees, employers, and service people.

Record special days—birthdays, anniversaries, the date you met someone, or a day you know holds a lot of meaning. This list makes it easier to deliver presents on a whim.

"EVERY DAY, I WISH TO MAKE THE WORLD MORE BEAUTIFUL THAN I FOUND IT."
—*Madame de Pompadour*

"THE SUPREME HAPPINESS OF LIFE IS THE CONVICTION THAT WE ARE LOVED; LOVED FOR OURSELVES."
—*Victor Hugo*

THE GIFT OF YOURSELF

When you give your presence, you are giving the most. Ultimately, time is all you have. When you pay attention to someone else, you honor that person and the other person can honor you. You act not out of duty, but because you want to. A doctor lost his wife to cancer and greeted his friends at the back of the church after the service thanking each person for coming. The church was packed with devoted friends. I kept overhearing the same reply: "I wanted to be here. I loved Kay."

There will be times when a quick phone call can make someone's day and there are other times when being on hand can make all the difference. When a spouse in the hospital says, "Oh, you don't have to stay," that might be translated, "Oh, dear, please stay a little longer." Being at the right place at the right time requires sensitivity. Often you have no choice except to wait. A mother whose son was dying of colon cancer retreated from the world and wouldn't let anyone come to see her. "I needed that time and knew I'd return to living after I spent some time grieving over the reality I had to face. No one could rush me." Friends had to stand by and be patient.

There are times when you can give the gift of yourself where your physical presence would be inappropriate. You can give a teenage child money to travel with a friend or to go to a restaurant on a romantic evening out. Give of yourself in a variety of ways. Provide opportunities for others. Have faith in your giving when you won't be part of the laughter and champagne. When it is correct you will feel great warmth of spirit.

When you are in a position of power and are enthusiastic about someone else, you can make a huge difference. I remember when I was in my twenties and a friend's mother was building a Georgian-style house on a beautiful piece of property in Greenwich, Connecticut. Mrs. Sheppard made a date to see my boss and me at the office of McMillen, Inc., and she brought with her a huge roll of blueprints. "Mrs. Brown, I want Sandie to decorate my house. I know you'll oversee the details and I want to give her this opportunity." I brought in a large job which meant the world to me. It gave me an opportunity to learn from a classical architect all the steps to take to turn a drawing into a dream house.

I was involved with every detail, and the architect loved to teach. I asked hundreds of questions and found that he enjoyed pointing out subtleties and telling me how he arrived at his decisions. We pored over those drawings together with Mrs. Brown to be sure the doors hinged gracefully, not blocking light or interfering with the furniture arrangements. All the horror stories I'd heard about arrogant architects not recognizing the value of interior designers were immediately dispelled by this thrilling project.

Over twenty years the whitewashed brick has mellowed beautifully and the trees have grown proudly around my first substantial job. I went to mix some paint last summer when we were repainting the grand hall and I felt quietly proud and extremely grateful.

GIVING TO THE WORLD—SHARING YOUR TALENT

What is your unique talent? How are you communicating that special gift to the rest of the world? What are some of the ways you like to give back? Whatever you do with your life, you want to be able to have your passions shed light on others. You want to help others to understand their own journey better and at the same time you want to feel the continuity that long after you're dead the consequences of your acts will still be remembered.

If you are an enlightened teacher or a dedicated artist, if you are a writer, editor, publisher, a musician or a dancer, think of the lives you can affect. If you are a designer, a decorator, mother, gourmet cook or a collector of letters and manuscripts, think of the lives you can affect. If you are a politician, a photographer, a doctor, scientist, philosopher or historian, think of the lives you can affect. You are doing a part, in your own style, and when you are joined by others, collectively, you can make a powerful impact.

As with every other form of giving, give in your own style when you contribute to the world's causes. One person will raise money for a cause that is of particular interest; someone else will teach. Someone entertains and another counsels.

Define your talents. Exceptional people admired throughout history all had a mission. What is yours? Think of all the different people you know who are givers. One may be a rabbi, another a poet. One may be a fashion designer and another a secretary. An artist, an architect. A jewelry designer, a gardener, a lawyer. A contractor, a social worker, an educator.

Choose your path. That is a gift to yourself and to the world.

PHILANTHROPY

Everything is connected. You have to find the links. When you are privileged to be a financial giver you see a wide range of causes and individuals who have great needs. You have two things to give, time and money. What is important is to decide which areas are of the greatest concern to you and then focus your energies.

Saying no is hard for all of us, yet it is essential. You have a limited amount of time and resources. Give where your greatest concerns are and let others do the same. Everyone you know has their own favorite causes and it is up to you to think things through so you give with a glad heart. Fund-raising is part of how we contribute to our causes and we have to remember that our friends are doing their job when they encourage us to include their cause in our giving plans.

Set up a budget. All givers will enjoy being philanthropists. Whether you are extremely rich or are struggling to make ends meet, give approximately ten percent of what you have to religious institutions and charitable organizations. However you give, a percentage basis is clean, easy, and once you establish your giving budget then you can divide the money into different categories

"THE LOVE OF MONEY AND THE LOVE OF LEARNING RARELY MEET."
—*George Herbert*

and then specific institutions and causes. If you are interested in politics you will earmark a large portion for political candidates of your choice. If you are concerned about AIDS, a large percentage will go to help with AIDS research. My friend Bette-Ann Gwathmey lost her seventeen-year-old son Robert Steel to cancer. She has set up the Robert Steel Foundation for Pediatric Cancer Research at the Memorial Sloan-Kettering Cancer Center. Her friends give gladly to this worthy, necessary foundation. You may pledge a percentage of your income to your church or synagogue. You will give generously to the homeless. You will want to give to educational institutions, especially those where you were educated and where your children went to school.

Once you've budgeted your giving for the year, don't feel guilty if you can't give to each and every worthy cause as you open your mail. If a friend writes a personal note attached to a benefit invitation and it is for a cause you haven't planned to give to this year, write a note back and tell her you're sorry you can't go. If you have some money left in your budget for miscellaneous contributions, send in a check as a donation. It is perfectly possible you'll consider budgeting money for her charity for next year.

Keep a philanthropy file. If you read about an organization that is doing a good job, clip it and put it into your giving file. At the end of each year reevaluate the last year and reestablish your priorities. One thing always leads to another. If you give generously to one group one year, they will want you to increase the amount the next year. But if you don't have the money, don't feel guilty. Feel good that you are giving a portion of what you have to others. Give in your own style. My late aunt Ruth Elizabeth Johns was a well-known international social worker who told me when I was sixteen, "You can tell a great deal about a person by looking at their check stubs." Certainly we want to give more money away than we spend on shoes!

Giving generously is satisfying. But don't get "auction fever" with your promises. Set up your limits before the new year. Giving should not be a competition, but a private matter. The categories that are nearest to your heart come first. If you are put on the board of a school or museum, you are expected to make a sub-

"TRULY THE LIGHT IS SWEET, AND A PLEASANT THING IT IS FOR THE EYES TO BEHOLD THE SUN."
—*Ecclesiastes 11:7*

"GREAT THOUGHTS COME FROM THE HEART."
—*Marquis de Vauvenargues*

stantial contribution during your term. If you are on the vestry of your church or a leader at your synagogue you have to consider that a giving priority. If your interests are in conservation and preservation you will give accordingly. I have a retired friend who is buying a seventeenth-century house in Connecticut and intends to spend the next five years fixing it up before he gives it to the Historical Society. A client in New York is giving her American art collection to the Metropolitan Museum upon her death. If your financial circumstances have improved, readjust your budget.

Giving is a habit. I was moved when I spent some time with a family in Tennessee. On a bulletin board in the kitchen was a list of causes and envelopes with the names of the three children. Each week when they received their allowance they divided up their giving portion by putting money in the envelope and labeling it with the cause they wanted their money to go to. With a family with three young children setting this example, all of us can feel the rewards as we are in a position to give.

LOVING OTHERS

In the foreword of Erich Fromm's *The Art of Loving: An Inquiry into the Nature of Love,* he tells us, "I want to convince the reader that all his attempts for love are bound to fail, unless he tries most actively to develop his total personality, so as to achieve a productive orientation; that satisfaction in individual love cannot be attained without the capacity to love one's neighbor, without true humility, courage, faith and discipline. In a culture in which these qualities are rare, the attainment of the capacity to love must remain a rare achievement."

I remember first reading this book in 1956 when I was fifteen and my curiosity about the theory and practice of love was keen. Fromm writes simply and wisely about the most important element of life.

Rereading this intelligent book recently has helped me to remain true to my principles of simplicity, appropriateness and

"TENDERNESS IS THE REPOSE OF PASSION."
—*Joseph Joubert*

beauty. While love is mysterious, there are some practical truths permitting us to get closer to the core of what love is.

Who supports your journey and tries to help you live deeply and beautifully? Who is patient, generous, spirited and understanding? Who has realistic expectations of your heights and your limitations? Who loves without controlling? Who gives without being possessive? Who finds sheer joy in loving you? When we ask these questions we feel the paucity of love.

Erich Fromm believes we are culturally conditioned to pay more attention to things other than love. "Almost everything else is considered to be more important than love: success, prestige, money, power, security—almost all our energy is used for the learning of how to achieve these aims, and almost none to learn the act of loving."

Loving others has a gentle harmony, requiring (of all things) paying attention and concentrating. Loving—the world, yourself and others—is giving and receiving the mysterious treasures of your human existence. The wider you open up your own heart the more deeply you can understand others. Understanding illuminates the way.

Fromm also discusses how love and giving are joyful. "For the productive character, giving has an entirely different meaning. Giving is the highest expression of potency. In the very act of giving, I experience my strength, my wealth, my power. This expression of heightened vitality and potency fills me with joy. I experience myself overflowing, spending, alive, hence as joyous. Giving is more joyous than receiving, not because it is a deprivation, but because in the act of giving lies the expression of my aliveness."

All we have to give is ourselves. Fromm urges us to be disciplined, to concentrate, be patient and practice fairness in loving others. Be authentic, Fromm suggests, have faith and value harmony. Seek the company of higher-minded people. "People capable of love," Fromm cautions, "are necessarily the exceptions; love is by necessity a marginal phenomenon in present-day Western society."

Point your life to loving others and you will have the ultimate

> "IS IT SO SMALL A THING TO HAVE ENJOYED THE SUN, TO HAVE LIVED LIGHT IN THE SPRING, TO HAVE LOVED, TO HAVE THOUGHT, TO HAVE DONE . . . ?"
> —*Matthew Arnold*

reward. When I asked international designer Andrée Putman what gave her the most pleasure, she said, "Helping unknown artists." Andrée, who is French, told me that we need more love in America. Thinking in part of the awful homelessness of so many, she said, "In France there is always a grandmother who has a cabbage in her backyard. We have no homeless problem in France."

EXPRESSING LOVE

Love can become as natural as breathing. Pick up the phone when someone is on your mind. Send a note, a book or flowers. Send a pertinent clipping from the newspaper or a magazine. Visit an elderly friend or someone who needs cheering up. Plan a party. Give a compliment. Thank a friend. Praise a child. Hug a loved one. Express your appreciation. Say, "I love you."

Find creative ways to express your love of life, yourself and other people. Write a song. Sing. Write a letter or a book. Dance. Skip. Plant trees. Teach. Preach. Care for the homeless. Read to the blind. Surround yourself with harmonious colors, beautiful objects. Inspire through example. Raise a family, be a nurse, do cancer research. Nurture a passionate belief that you can make a significant change. You are individual, yet connected.

You will continue evolving as you close certain chapters in your life and open new ones. Experiment, and look for the surprise links that connect you to all that is beautiful—all that you dare to be.

PEACE!